D1336412

Asia's Giants

Comparing China and India

Edited by
Edward Friedman
and
Bruce Gilley

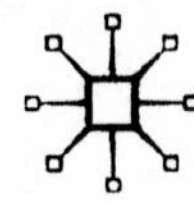

ASIA'S GIANTS

First published in 2005 by
PALGRAVE MACMILLAN™
175 Fifth Avenue, New York, N.Y. 10010 and
Houndmills, Basingstoke, Hampshire, England RG21 6XS
Companies and representatives throughout the world.

PALGRAVE MACMILLAN is the global academic imprint of the Palgrave Macmillan division of St. Martin's Press, LLC and of Palgrave Macmillan Ltd. Macmillan® is a registered trademark in the United States, United Kingdom and other countries. Palgrave is a registered trademark in the European Union and other countries.

ISBN 1–4039–7110–2

Library of Congress Cataloging-in-Publication Data

Asia's giants : comparing China and India / Edward Friedman and Bruce Gilley, editors.
p. cm.
Includes bibliographical references and index.
ISBN 1–4039–7110–2
1. China—Social conditions. 2. India—Social conditions. 3. China—Economic conditions. 4. India—Economic conditions. 5. China—Politics and government. 6. India—Politics and government. I. Friedman, Edward, 1937– II. Gilley, Bruce, 1966–

HN733.5.A77 2005
306'.0951—dc22 2005049188

A catalogue record for this book is available from the British Library.

Design by Newgen Imaging Systems (P) Ltd., Chennai, India.

First edition: December 2005

10 9 8 7 6 5 4 3 2 1

Printed in the United States of America.

Contents

List of Charts and Tables

Charts

Tables

List of Contributors

Edward Friedman is a professor in the Department of Political Science at the University of Wisconsin, Madison. He has most recently published *Revolution, Resistance and Reform in Village China* (2005) and *China's Rise, Taiwan's Dilemmas, and International Peace* (2005). His earlier comparison of China and India, "Development, Revolution, Democracy and Dictatorship" appears in Theda Skocpol, ed., *Democracy, Revolution, and History* (1998).

Bruce Gilley is an Adjunct Professor of International Affairs at the New School University. He is the author of four books on China, most recently *China's Democratic Future: How It Will Happen and Where It Will Lead* (2004). His current research is on cross-national measures of state legitimacy and its determinants.

Huang Jinxin received her Ph.D. in political science from University of Wisconsin, Madison with a dissertation on economic reform and the pension system in China. Her article "Economic Restructuring, Social Safety Net, and Old-age Pension Reform in China" was published in 2003.

Huang Yasheng is an associate professor in the Sloan School of Management, Massachusetts Institute of Technology. He is the author of *Selling China: Foreign Direct Investment during the Reform Era* (2003) and many other works on economic reform in China.

Tarun Khanna is the Jorge Paulo Lemann Professor at the Harvard Business School where he has taught since 1993. His research focuses on the relationship between institutional context and firm strategy in emerging markets worldwide. He is the author of many journal articles on firm strategy and organization, including "Business Groups and Social Welfare in Emerging Markets" (2000).

Roderick MacFarquhar is the Leroy B. Williams Professor of History and Political Science and current Director of the John King Fairbank Center for East Asian Research at Harvard University. He is the author of a trilogy about the origins of the Cultural Revolution—*Contradictions Among the People: 1956–1957* (1974), *The Great Leap Forward: 1958–1960* (1983), and *The Coming of the Cataclysm: 1961–1966* (1997). He has completed a new book about the Cultural Revolution, jointly authored with Michael Schoenhals. He was born and brought up in India and has revisited it often as a journalist and TV commentator.

James Manor is Professor of Political Science and Director of the Civil Society and Governance Programme at the Institute of Development Studies, University of Sussex. He is the author of several books, including *Power, Poverty and Poison: Disaster and Response in an Indian City* (1993), monographs, including *The Political Economy of Democratic Decentralization* (1998), and journal articles, including "Making Federalism Work" (1998). His current research is on civil society and governance, democratic decentralization, and state–society relations in East and Southeast Asia.

Joydeep Mukherji is Director, Sovereign Ratings Group at Standard & Poor's. His work is on credit ratings of sovereigns in Asia and in Latin America. His papers include "India's Long March to Capitalism" (2002), "The Indian Economy: Pushing Ahead and Pulling Apart," in *India Briefing*, ed. Philip Oldenburg and Alyssa Ayres (2002).

Tony Saich is Daewoo Professor of International Affairs at the Kennedy School of Government, Harvard University. His current research focuses on the changing relationship between state and society with a special emphasis on the provision of public goods and services. He is the author of *China: Politics and Governance* (2004), *The Rise to Power of the Chinese Communist Party* (1996), and joint editor of *Financial Sector Reform in China* (2005).

Aseema Sinha is an assistant professor in the Department of Political Science, University of Wisconsin, Madison. She is the author of *The Regional Roots of Developmental Politics in India: A Divided Leviathan* (2005). Her current research is on the impact of World Trade Organization on state capacity and collective action in India.

Subramanian Swamy is Chairman and Honorary Professor at the School of Communication and Management Sciences in Kalmaserry,

Kerala, India and a faculty member of the Harvard University Summer School. He is the author of *Economic Reforms and Performance: China and India in Comparative Appraisal* (2003), and *Economic Growth in China and India: A Comparative Appraisal* (1973).

Kellee S. Tsai is assistant professor of Political Science at Johns Hopkins University. Her publications include *Back-Alley Banking: Private Entrepreneurs in China* (2002), *Japan and China in the World Political Economy* (coedited with Saadia Pekkanen, 2005), and various articles. She is currently completing a book manuscript on the political orientations of private entrepreneurs in China.

I

Overviews

1

Preface

Edward Friedman

This book is about the comparative performance of India and China, an issue that greatly influences government policy all over the developing world. Specialists writing for this book build on new subnational and sectoral literatures and offer informed judgments on future trajectories for China and India. These diverse authors take a host of different approaches to judging how well Asia's giants, China and India are doing today and what ongoing dynamics portend for the future. The reader will be provided with a variety of entrees to a vexing and vital question, comparing India and China. This then is an invitation to enter an important and open dialogue.

Getting the two Asian giants right is important in looking for clues on how to address the pains and paths of less developed countries. Yet too often, the world has got the comparison wrong. Overly positive illusions about China not only lead observers to miscalculate its actual performance but, in addition, provide a false metric for measuring how well others, particularly in Asia, are doing.

From the economically stagnant Mao era to the dynamic age of reform, Chinese statistics remain unreliable. China intentionally hides the value of the U.S. securities it holds. Urban poverty is underreported by omitting migrants. One can politely describe the problems as a "lack of transparency" or "opaqueness," but the heart of the issue is local administrators "lying to Beijing" (Ramo 2005). Rural poverty is understated by the consequences of overwhelming pressures on lower officials whose careers are judged by reports of developmental success.

Yet, virtually everyone still ends up using Chinese numbers. The informed reader is therefore invited to be critical even of the efforts in this volume because even the most hard-nosed analysts, despite heroic attempts at critical independence, get taken-in by exaggerated Chinese claims.

Take one example from Mao's 1966–1976 so-called Great Proletarian Cultural Revolution. It was a brutal and economically irrational campaign that spread terror, torture, and turmoil. Yet major newspapers in Japan touted Mao's policies as morally superior ways to promote equality and solidarity, in contrast to a supposedly amoral Japan said to have lost its soul to Americanization. Nationalists in many countries, similarly worried about the traumas of the market, looked to copy Mao's self-wounding antimarket policies that were presented to the world by the Chinese regime as anticapitalist justice.

Reports from China still inflate Mao-era performance. In 2004, *The Economist*, Britain's prestigious magazine, misleadingly took the cruel and inhuman Mao era as a time when the Chinese "people's basic needs were reasonably well looked after. Health care . . . was provided across the country by the state. Adequate pensions were provided in the same way. . . . schooling was free" (August 21, 11). In fact, not a word of this assessment is true. Actually, as Anthony Saich points out in this book's penultimate chapter, the rural–urban gap in China at the end of the Mao era was the widest in the world.

Schooling was not free. And there was, for the over 80 percent of the Chinese people locked up in the countryside, no state-provided health care or pension coverage, none at all. Mao-era China did miserably. Stagnation and famine were institutionalized. But that is not how governments in developing countries saw it. They did not understand that following Mao meant taking the path that led to Hoxha's Albania or Pol Pot's Cambodia. Getting China right in comparative perspective really matters.

The Chinese government, however, is so good at dramatizing policies as successes that outside observers cannot easily assess accurately how well or poorly China is actually doing. This remains true today. In 2003, contrary to the popular perception of China outperforming India, the World Health Organization, in ranking 191 countries on health delivery, ranked China as 144, that is, near the very bottom, while India was placed 113, surely not great, but substantially higher than China. Popular perceptions about Chinese performance misunderstand much.

Most recently, many analysts have stopped treating India and China as simple, one-dimensional entities weighable on a single scale to judge which was the success and which the failure. Indeed, each, as revealed in the chapter by Huang Jinxin, increasingly sees the other as better in some ways and worse in others. Chinese envied Indian successes in postindustrial sectors such as information technology (IT) software and biotechnology pharmaceuticals. The city government in Beijing, worried that too many Indian software firms were being established in Shanghai, set up a Sino-Indian Cooperative Office to woo Indian IT to Beijing (Aiyar 2005).

Indians, in contrast, envied Chinese growth rates. But which matters more for the future, performance in particular advanced sectors or general growth? And is economics all that counts? These are questions whose answers involve both objective facts and also value judgments. The contributors to this book address both of these vital matters.

Both India and China seemed to be doing so well entering the twenty-first century that a BBC survey of households in 22 nations issued in January 2005 found that Indians and Chinese were far and away the most optimistic about their economic future (Giles 2005). An analyst in "the West" worried about splits between America and Europe because "the West . . . only has about twenty years left before China (and then India) becomes a great power. . . ." (Judt 2005, 40).

Academic and international financial institution researchers increasingly look at China and India in terms of common success, looking, as do the chapters by Kellee Tsai and Aseema Sinha, for similarities in their subnational institutions, exploring successful regions in both or economic lead sectors in each or particular crucial institutions such as finance, which is so central in the post–Bretton Woods era where private international forces can drive financial values. The 2004 survey by A. T. Kearney management consultants, putting America aside, ranked China and then India as the world's two most attractive destinations for foreign direct investment (FDI). India's reforms in finance, however, have advanced faster and further than China's.

Although specialists, aware of complex commonalities and differences, increasingly tend to abjure general judgments on China as a whole versus India as a whole, pundits are not so restrained. Some saw China rapidly rising, inevitably soon to overtake America and become the world's largest economy. Others, such as financier–philanthropist George Soros, an investor in China's Hainan Airlines, in a 2004 conversation with the American Political Science Association, worried that China might be entrenching the vested interests of a pervasively corrupt single party dictatorship such that the political system could grow rigid and inflexible. As a result, Soros speculated, rather than completing its reforms out of Leninist style command economy, a sclerotic political system could even eventually collapse.

If the economic bubble might well burst for China as it did for Indonesia, then surely it made no sense to talk yet of China as a success. India, too, still seemed to "face severe challenges" (Wood 2004, p. 38). Much about the future remained contingent.

A recent book (Halperin, Siegle, and Weinstein 2005) found that, in general, over time, democratic systems outperform authoritarian regimes, not only on growth, stability, and flexibility, but also on measures of human well-being such as health, literacy, and life expectancy. This is surely true in Asia for democratic India versus authoritarian Pakistan, democratic Thailand versus authoritarian Burma, Cambodia, and Vietnam, democratic South Korea versus authoritarian North Korea, and democratic Japan and Taiwan versus authoritarian China. How about India versus China?

The high bets of transnational corporations placed on China's economic future, making authoritarian China far and away the number one recipient of fixed FDI in the world, surely suggest that China can keep on rising rapidly despite its authoritarian system. That matter of the impact of so much FDI is worth clarifying by area specialists and economists. The chapter by Huang and Khanna in this book does just that. They are skeptical about so much FDI being a measure of success for China. There is much to rethink about how China and India are doing.

So much seems wide open and possible. The China–India future could even become more cooperative and less competitive. The two have begun a security dialogue. Surely the world is a better place when China and India cooperate against the big pharmaceutical houses to bring down the price of drugs for the poorest and most vulnerable on the planet. To imagine China and India as other than always and inevitably opposites and competitors opens new horizons.

For this author, the particulars of Indian politics (not the reality of a political democracy) are keeping India from including all of its people in the benefits of reform. Should India, because of particular vested interests and the nature of its nationalist mobilization, continue on such a constrictive political path, one that hinders reform and its benefits, then China, based on an extraordinary investment in integrative infrastructure, greater openness, and a phenomenal growth rate, will continue to increase its economic lead over India.

But the chapters by Swamy and by Manor in this volume disagree with this authorial judgment. They offer contrasting yet deeply informed assessments, seeing India advantaged by everything from political flexibility and stability to financial reforms and IT performance that China lacks. While few analysts doubt that democratic India is more politically stable, as MacFarquhar details in the Introduction, the Chinese people are bombarded by their authoritarian regime with "news" to persuade them that only the Chinese Communist Party dictatorship can provide societal stability. The problem of potential political instability in China festers.

Judgments on India versus China depend on numerous debatable complex variables and projections. Judgments can also differ in part as well as in whole, depending on the sector, institution, dimension, or region one is examining. How complex societies should be assessed is not an easy question with a simple answer.

The Japanese reporters and editors who naively comprehended China's Mao era of cruelty as uniquely moral were, nevertheless, sophisticated and wise not to limit their comparisons to suspect economic growth rates and instead to inquire also into arenas of life that touch basic human matters—values, fairness, family life, religion, dignity, and ultimate commitments. After all, it matters that India is a democracy and China is not. But precisely how it matters or how much it matters is not obvious. Clarifying that mind-boggling matter, the focus of the chapters by Bruce Gilley and by myself, is a major task of this multifaceted volume. By the end of the dialogue in this book, the informed reader should have a more solid basis for comparing Asia's giants, India and China, in all their complexity.

References

Aiyar, Pallavi (2005). "Beijing to India IT." *The Indian Express*, January 26, web edition.

Giles, Chris (2005). "Chinese and Italian Poles Apart in Economic Optimism Survey." *Financial Times*, January 26.

Halperin, Morton H., Joseph T. Siegle, and Michael M. Weinstein (2005). *The Democracy Advantage: How Democracies Promote Prosperity and Peace*. New York: Routledge.

Judt, Tony (2005). "Europe vs. America." *The New York Review*, February 10, pp. 37–41.

Ramo, Joshua Cooper (2005). "China Must Come Clean about Its Energy Needs." *Financial Times*, February 18.

Wood, Alan T. (2004). *Asian Democracy in World History*. New York: Routledge.

2

Introduction

Roderick MacFarquhar

Asia's Giants: Comparing China and India contains many illuminating approaches to the subject of the title, especially focusing on the binary of authoritarianism versus democracy. In comparisons between various aspects of the development of these two mega-nations since the late 1940s, the chapters tend to make the case that, contrary to received wisdom, India's record compares quite well with China's, and in some instances surpasses it. Rather than preview those issues, in this introduction I seek to draw attention to some interesting coincidences and, more significantly, differences in the political development of the two countries, in particular, how their institutions are able to handle potential crises. I conclude that in two key arenas, handling succession and dealing with society, India has built better than China.

I

To run any country is hard. To run a country of hundreds of millions is surely harder. To run a developing country with a population in the hundreds of millions, rapidly growing, with enormous backwardness in agriculture, industry, employment, health, education, housing, welfare—the list is endless—must seem at times as a Sisyphean task. Some outside observers thought that the combination of such problems with religious and linguistic diversity meant that India would be unable to preserve unity (Harrison 1960) Fissiparous tendencies seemed less of a problem to China with its greater ethnic and cultural homogeneity, but during the "civil war"—the phrase was Mao's—of the Cultural Revolution in the mid-1960s, the breaking away of frontier regions like Xinjiang became conceivable.

Both countries weathered those dangerous decades, and each government sees unity as a source of legitimacy, whether it is through quelling desires for autonomy in Kashmir or the northeast in India's case, or in the unceasing campaign to recover Taiwan in China's. The idea that globalization may mean that national governments are no longer necessarily the best repositories of traditional national powers would be rejected in both New Delhi and Beijing.

Even if united along the road to power and subsequently on the issue of national inviolability, it would be hardly surprising, in the light of their enormous problems, if the leaders of a vast developing country soon found themselves falling out over some of the many critical decisions that they had to take. An Indian political scientist once put it this way:

> In most newly independent nations a struggle for ascendancy takes place within the ruling coalition soon after independence as the leadership begins to turn governmental power to policy ends. Only those that have managed to resolve this conflict to a quick and orderly end have succeeded in passing from the phase of consolidation to that of purposive development and orderly change. India under Nehru succeeded in doing just this after 1950.[1] (Kothari 1970, 169)

Interestingly, despite their very different forms of government, both India and China suffered political crises almost simultaneously.

In India, the early struggle was between Nehru and his deputy prime minister, Vallabhbhai Patel. Patel was the down-to-earth organization man of the Congress leadership, and his views were to the right of Nehru's in both domestic and foreign affairs. Patel refused to accept that Nehru's premiership gave him unquestionable dominance over his colleagues, and soon after independence both men appealed to Mahatma Gandhi on the issue but without resolving it. Patel successfully challenged the premier in 1950 to have his right-wing candidates made president of the Congress Party and president of the Indian Union. But with Gandhi's assassination in 1948 and Patel's death at the end of 1950, within four years of independence Nehru's position changed from "first among equals" to "first above equals" (Pandey 1976, 334–335).

Mao was already first above equals when the Chinese Communist Party (CCP) captured power and over the years his position became first without equals. He was never faced down so decisively as Nehru by Patel, though he was challenged by Marshal Peng Dehuai in 1959, but in China too there was a major internal power struggle—the Gao Gang affair—within four years of the CCP coming to power (Teiwes 1990).

Perhaps more striking than the coincidence of early struggles within the leaderships of both countries is the fact that both China and India underwent profound, if significantly different, political crises in the mid-1960s. In the disastrous Cultural Revolution, Mao purged most of the Communist party leadership at the center and in the periphery. In India, Nehru's daughter, Premier Indira Gandhi, split the once dominant Congress Party, and indeed was expelled from it. While the parties were later reconstituted, in neither country did they ever regain the position of unquestioned dominance they had held earlier. In both cases, the origins were diffuse, but principally lay in leaders' concerns over personal power and the direction of the polity.[2] But the coincidence of timing suggests a form of collective exhaustion among the political elite after some two decades of grappling with apparently intractable problems, leading to mutual distrust and a consequent inability to overcome difficulties together.

II

As striking as the similarities are the differences between the development of the two polities. Jawaharlal Nehru died 17 years after taking power as the first prime minister of independent India; there was a smooth succession to Lal Bahadur Shastri, arranged in advance. Seventeen years after Mao took power as chairman of the PRC, he launched the Cultural Revolution; it was the occasion for upsetting the smooth succession arranged in advance. In India, there was a second succession due to death within a year, and the party leadership again agreed on the new successor, though almost immediately there were challenges to the appointed candidate, Indira Gandhi, but she withstood them. In China there was a second succession arrangement due to death within three years; the chairman picked three further successors but none of them lasted. After Mao's death, there was a palace coup against the most radical section of the leadership, and thereafter even his chosen successor and his allies were purged and Deng Xiaoping came to power. Deng, too, chose three successors, but only the final one, Jiang Zemin lasted. Deng even grandfathered in China's leader at the outset of the twenty-first century, Hu Jintao. A stable succession system is the basis of political stability in any state; but to date, the CCP has failed to institute one.

The relative smoothness of the Indian succession system has had a major retrograde ingredient, which the Chinese have eschewed: the dynastic principle. Indira Gandhi was chosen in the crisis caused by the sudden death of Shastri in 1965 because she was Nehru's daughter. Similarly, Mrs. Gandhi groomed her younger son Sanjay to succeed her and when he died in an air crash, she conscripted her reluctant elder son Rajiv, who became premier after his mother's assassination. On Rajiv's assassination, a politician who was seen almost as a family retainer, Narasimha Rao, became premier, but after the Congress party's defeat by the BJP, gradually Sonia Gandhi, the Italian-born wife of Rajiv, took over the leadership of the Congress party. After winning the 2004 general election she chose Manmohan Singh as premier in order to avoid controversy over her foreign origins, but Sonia's son and daughter both carry the aura of potential dynasts.

In the Chinese case, Mao's wife Jiang Qing had hopes of succeeding him, but the deeply ingrained prejudice against ruling "empresses," coupled with her behavior during the Cultural Revolution, ensured her arrest after her husband's death. Perhaps if she had played a backroom role and had kept a low profile, she might conceivably have been a kingmaker too. But then she would not have been Jiang Qing.

III

Another similarity between the two countries was their attempts to run command economies. In communist China, this was only natural since it was assumed that "the Soviet Union's today is China's tomorrow." A first five-year plan was initiated in 1953, and until 1960, Soviet technical specialists helped guide their Chinese comrades.

In democratic India, Nehru was a Fabian socialist by upbringing and, like many leaders of newly independent countries, immensely impressed with the manner in which Stalin had transformed the Soviet Union into the world's second super power. He, too, abetted by his economic adviser P. C. Mahalanobis, and encouraged by Soviet aid, introduced a system of five-year plans.

Both countries had some successes, but even with a single dominant party, the command system was less workable under the democratic conditions of Indian politics than under the disciplined control system of the CCP, although Mao evened up the odds by leading China into the successive disasters of the Great Leap Forward and the Cultural Revolution.

After the end of the Cultural Revolution, it became clear to Mao's successors that the command system had to be changed. All across East Asia, in the area where historically Chinese culture held sway, countries and peoples had become prosperous. Only China had squandered the fruits of the victory of 1949. Slowly at first, but then with increasing speed over the past quarter century, Deng and his successors abandoned the Stalinist command system in favor of what some have called "market Leninism." The successes and downsides of this economic revolution, and the growth of China as an export juggernaut, are almost daily trumpeted by the international media and to a lesser extent in China. There are now more than 10,000 businessmen worth more than $10,000,000, while tens of millions of peasants barely scrape by (Kahn 2004). CCP leaders regularly intone that official corruption could be the party's undoing, but rarely does a party cadre of any seniority get punished. Across the country, from week to week, there are reports of riots or demonstrations by the disadvantaged, the dispossessed, and the disparaged. And since the CCP claims nationwide control, each riot is in principle a blow at its hegemony. The CCP is particularly quick to clamp down on any demonstration of more than local significance, such as the democrats in Tiananmen Square in 1989 and the Falun Gong spiritualists after 1999.

Not having suffered a disaster equivalent to the Cultural Revolution, it took the Indians longer to wake up to the need to abandon the command economy model. Moreover, multiple interests had been built up under the socialist project and it was impossible in a democracy simply to write them off. As a result it took a foreign exchange crisis and the fall of the Soviet Union before the Indian government would grasp the nettle of economic reform. Even so, it proceeded in fits and starts, buffeted by political crosswinds. A leading economic reformer like Chief Minister Chandrababu Naidu of Andhra Pradesh, a state whose capital Hyderabad has become an international symbol of high tech and outsourcing, bit the political dust in the 2004 election because he was seen by poorer voters as having neglected their interests. This result illustrated the greater stability of the Indian system.

India, like China, is bedeviled by glaring inequalities of wealth and official corruption. Riots and demonstrations have been a regular feature of the Indian social scene ever since independence. But even a violent demonstration in the heart of the Indian capital does not threaten the stability of the political system, because both protesters and politicians know that the moment of truth will come as a result of the turn of the political wheel at the next election. By contrast, Deng and his gerontocrat colleagues evidently decided that a peaceful demonstration of students in the heart of their capital in 1989 *did* threaten the whole political system and brutally put it down.

But perhaps the sharpest contrast between China and India is over identity, an issue normally formulated and worried over by intellectuals, but of intrinsic importance to politicians seeking grand themes with which to lead their peoples. In both countries, there are worries about Westernization and the disappearance of traditional culture, but there the similarity ends.

In China, traditionally, intellectuals have identified themselves in terms of, or sometimes in opposition to, the state ideology. For two millennia, it was Confucianism; after 1949, it was Marxism-Leninism. Both were totalistic ideologies designed for both governance and society. With modern techniques of organization and propaganda, communist ideology penetrated far more deeply, into the remotest villages. But with Deng's elevation of "practice" to be the sole criterion of truth, ideology has effectively disappeared as a guiding principle.

The disappearance of orthodoxy has left a gaping hole at the heart of the Chinese polity and society. In the nineteenth century, early reformers reassured themselves with the formula "Western learning for practical use, Chinese learning for the essence." The problem today is that the nature of the Chinese "essence" is no longer clear. And while most Chinese may be satisfied to rely on orthopraxy to define themselves on a day-to-day basis, millions have sought more spiritual answers, espousing Christianity or more traditional type belief systems like Falun Gong.

The contrast with India was pointed up for me in the late 1980s by a Chinese scholar official who had just returned from his first visit to India. He had noted that Indian elite males dressed in Western clothes, their families spoke English and an Indian language interchangeably, they sent their kids to Western-type schools either at home or abroad, there were even a few roads and statues that recalled the former colonial power. "And yet, these people are without any doubt Indians. What have we Chinese been worrying about for the last century?"

Indians have not had an all-encompassing politico-social ideology down the centuries, and though many worked for Moguls and maharajahs, that did not define them. Identity was wrapped up rather in religion and caste. This has not been an unmixed blessing. Terrible loss of life has occurred as a result of violence between Hindus and Moslems, a type of communal conflict far less common in China, and between upper and lower castes (Varshney 2002; Brass 1997; Tambiah 1996). But it does mean that being Indian is simpler than being Chinese. Orthopraxy *is* enough. *It* is the Indian "essence."

IV

Back in the 1950s, India and China were seen by Western politicians through the prism of the cold war. Indian democracy was lauded in contrast to Chinese dictatorship, even though Nehru stubbornly refused to join up with the American-led camp and seemed to some critics at home and abroad to lean over backward toward the Soviet-led camp. Later, during the crisis on the Indian subcontinent that attended the transformation of East Pakistan into Bangladesh in 1971, his daughter Indira signed an India–Soviet Union pact, leading one Indian wit to state that "Neutralism is whatever India does."

Fifty years later in the twenty-first century, there is still a flavor of competition in assessments of the two nations. Which is the better route to global power status: China flooding Wal-Mart with cheap goods or India's interface with U.S. high tech companies? Or are such contrasts simplistic when IBM sells its computer-making branch to a Chinese computer company? Is there any way of forecasting what the contrast will look like in another 50 years?

If one conceptualizes a state in the form of a triangle with a leader at the apex, with one side representing the bureaucracy that follows the leader and runs the state, and the other side representing the national ideology or raison d'être of the state, and the base of the triangle representing the ability of the state to enforce its will, whether through police or military power, then in a democratic nation like India, society can be represented as a circle enclosing the state, ultimately more powerful than the state. The problem for Indian statecraft is to keep the state functioning in tune with society, but not overwhelmed by it.

In the case of pre-Cultural Revolution China, the circle representing society would be enclosed within the triangle, hemmed in and dominated by the state. During the Cultural Revolution, Mao destroyed the bureaucratic side of the triangle, and, though reconstituted by Deng, it has never recovered its old authority. Deng himself destroyed the other side of the triangle, the ideological justification of the state. Mao encouraged the youth to "dare to think, dare to speak and dare to act"; Deng opened up the country to the outside world and its ideas. Society has been liberated and the state no longer has powerful tools other than an ultimate threat of force to ensure obedience. The triangle is now more virtual than real; the circle is enclosed no more.

It will be in the management of the relationship between the state and their vast societies that the competition between China and India will be measured in the next half century. China's leaders continue to act as if the one-party state were still all powerful, but they all at some point have to come to terms with reality, to acknowledge the new relationship between state and society and adapt the political system to reflect it. If not, ultimately they may be swamped by the social forces they have unleashed, and much of what has been won through hard work would be at risk. Such a disaster is far less likely in India because of its more successful development of stabilizing institutions.

Notes

1. He went on to articulate the two great aims of Nehru as democracy and development.
2. Interestingly, in both countries a source of friction was the issue of who should be head of state. Despite the very great differences between Mao and Indira Gandhi as politicians and as human beings, their leadership styles exhibited some similarities. Both were allegedly afflicted by paranoia; both had kitchen cabinets, but held their cards close to their chest even when dealing with their closest supporters; both were avid collectors of tales and gossip; both effectively had courts and personality cults ("Mother Indira," "Indira is India"). For Gandhi, see P. N. Dhar, *Indira Gandhi, the "Emergency," and Indian Democracy* (New Delhi: Oxford University Press, 2000), pp. 133–139; S. Nihal Singh, *Indira's India: A Political Notebook* (Bombay: Nachiketa Publications, 1978), p. 225; Inder Malhotra, *Indira Gandhi: A Personal and Political Biography* (London: Hodder & Stoughton, 1989), pp. 120–129. For Mao, see Roderick MacFarquhar and Michael Schoenhals, *The Cultural Revolution* (Harvard University Press, 2006).

References

Brass, Paul R. (1997). *The Theft of an Idol: Text and Context in the Representation of Collective Violence*. Princeton: Princeton University Press.

Harrison, Selig S. (1960). *India, The Most Dangerous Decades*. Princeton: Princeton University Press.

Kahn, Joseph (2004). "China's Elite Learn to Flaunt It while the New Landless Weep." *New York Times*, December 25, p. A1.

Kothari, Rajni (1970). *India*. Boston: Little, Brown.

Pandey, B. N. (1976). *Nehru*. New York: Stein & Day.

Tambiah, Stanley J. (1996). *Leveling Crowds: Ethnonationalist Conflicts and Collective Violence in South Asia*. Berkeley: University of California Press.

Teiwes, Frederick C. (1990). *Politics at Mao's Court: Gao Gang and Party Factionalism in the Early 1950s*. Armonk, NY: M.E. Sharpe.

Varshney, Ashutosh (2002). *Ethnic Violence and Civic Life: Hindus and Moslems in India*, New Haven, CT: Yale University Press.

3

Two Passages to Modernity

Bruce Gilley

A strong element of coercion remains necessary if a change is to be made [in India].

—Barrington Moore, Jr.

Many thrust their advice upon India, and she remains steady. This is her beauty. It is the sheet-anchor of our hope.

—Gandhi

I

Gandhi wrote the words above in 1909, at a time when he was struggling with the question of India's modernization and how to achieve it. (Gandhi [1909] 1956, 103) Nearly a century later, the words have a deep resonance. Despite decades of calls by outsiders for a more coercive, planned, even revolutionary approach to political and economic development, India has remained steady indeed. Gandhi's hope lay in the idea that repression and violence were not necessary steps on the road to modernity, as Moore and others claimed (Moore [1966] 1993, 410). Today, this hope is being realized as India's constitutional democracy deepens and its poverty rates fall (from 37 percent in 1987 to somewhere between 15 percent and 28 percent by 2002) (Deaton and Kozel 2005).

In this essay, I ponder the nature of India's peaceful transition to modernity.[1] As a narrative device, I dwell on the contrast with China since 1949. Until recently, comparisons between the two countries were found mainly in Western academic works. Neither country's public intellectuals were much concerned with their Himalayan neighbor. Culturally confident and globally expanding China paid strictest attention to its self-declared competition with the United States, and to a lesser extent Japan. Obsessively anticolonial India, by contrast, paid inordinate attention to comparisons with Britain and with its postcolonial rival Pakistan.

Yet for a growing number of people in the media, politics, and the public, the comparison has become irresistible. Asia's two great ancient civilizations and present-day giants are studies in contrasting development. Whether it is ethnic minorities, foreign investment, cultural nationalism, elections, corruption, or technology, it is not just *useful* but *imperative* to understand both countries in order to understand only one. It is not overly bold, I believe, to say that the central issues of political and economic development of our time are nowhere better seen than in the China–India comparison.

I find in this chapter that China's gains in material welfare (income, education, health) in both the pre-reform and reform eras has been among the best of all developing countries, at least as far as we know, based on its official statistics. India however has not been a laggard, achieved two-thirds and then three-quarters of the same gains in the two periods. At the same time, China's performance on rights and freedoms is much worse than most developing countries, excepting those where political disorder cancels out any formal freedoms. Its scoring for "voice and accountability" was only a third of India's score in 2002 according to the World Bank, while in the pre-reform era somewhere between 32 million and 57 million people were killed by Maoist political campaigns.

If there were an empirical tradeoff between rights and welfare gains, then one might still favor the Chinese model because of the life and death implications of welfare gains in a poor country. But there is no evidence of such a tradeoff. Fast gains in China did not depend upon authoritarianism, while average gains in India are not explained by democracy. The reasons for better performance in China concern first a growth trajectory begun in the pre-1949 era and second the economic advantages bestowed by the disasters of Maoism. India's average gains are attributable to the pursuit of a blinkered socialism in the pre-reform era and to its too-slow unwinding of it in the reform era.

In evaluating overall performance, then, we must assume that welfare and freedoms are additive rather than substitutive goods. For the pre-reform period, it is difficult to argue that China did better than India given the moral costs of ongoing "democide" under Mao and the "wound literature" that it spawned. In the reform era, evidence suggests that citizens in both countries consider their states as successes, and thus that the particular mixtures of welfare and freedoms each state has provided are weighted by citizens in each country such as to produce roughly comparable performance. However, a big question mark hangs over the Chinese side of this calculation. Legitimacy measurements there are subject to larger errors and are liable to drastic revisions. As for the future, China faces large transitional costs ahead that India does not, costs that might significantly reduce its overall performance once they are paid. One hopes not. One hopes that China and India will both continue to be success stories. But the most plausible alternative scenario to that is a continued Indian success and a Chinese stumble. If so, then the true costs of dictatorship in China may appear in retrospect much larger than was first imagined.

The contrasting poles of Chinese-style coercion and Indian-style gradualism force us to consider the ends of government, and the tradeoffs among valued moral goods like income, welfare, participation, rights, and procedural justice. Too often, these tradeoffs have been ignored by scholars, or just assumed away. The two countries offer contrasting passages to modernity that highlight the most salient issues for anyone concerned with development. Different conclusions are possible. But the issues need to be clarified.

In the sections below, I first consider the historical discourse on the China–India comparison before examining in detail the pre-reform and reform performances of both countries. I then consider the future and what it may bring. I conclude with some thoughts on the nature of the development discourse itself.

II

Comparisons of China and India are well known to the social sciences and policy circles. The near-simultaneous founding of the two very similar countries, one democratic in 1947 and the other communist in 1949, was seen by world leaders and scholars as an almost perfect natural experiment in proving which developmental approach worked better. This was especially the case since the cold war raised the implications far beyond the countries themselves. As the young John F. Kennedy said in 1959 (Kennedy 1959):

> No struggle in the world today deserves more of our time and attention than that which now grips the attention of all Asia . . . That is the struggle between India and China for leadership of the East, for the respect of all Asia, for the opportunity to demonstrate whose way of life is the better. The battle may be more subtle than loud—it may not even be admitted by either side—but it is a very real battle nonetheless. For it is these two countries that have the greatest magnetic attraction to the uncommitted and underdeveloped world.

From the moment that this battle "to demonstrate whose way of life is better" began, commentators generally concluded that China was doing better. Kennedy himself repeated the widespread misconception that China's Great Leap Forward of the late 1950s was propelling the country into the ranks of the industrialized nations, while India, he said, was beset by uncertainty, political instability, and commodity rationing. Selig Harrison warned in 1960 that in India "anarchy, fascism, and totalitarian small nationalities will each torture this body politic at one time or another in the decades ahead" bringing it finally to disintegration (Harrison 1960). Ronald Segal wrote in 1965 that the plain living, attention to the poor, and wise industrial programs of China's leaders compared to the corruption, politicking, and industrial failures of those in India. "In almost every aspect of industrialization . . . China has advanced further and faster than India," and thus it was China that would serve as a developmental model for the poor in developing countries (Segal 1965, 221).

It seemed no matter what the topic—economic growth, political order, social progress—China was doing better than India. At the outset of the Cultural Revolution, and already a decade into the Maoist nightmare begun in the late 1950s, Huntington could write that the PRC was "one of the most outstanding political achievements of the mid-twentieth century," since it was "a government really able to govern China"(Huntington 1968, 342). Even after the Cultural Revolution the praise continued. China was held up as "the bell-weather for the Third World as whole—and ultimately . . . for the rest of us too" (Sweezy 1976, 13). In an influential 1979 book on social revolutions, American scholar Theda Skocpol praised Mao's China for its "remarkable overall progress in economic development and social equality," especially, she noted, compared to India. China's Leninist regime was an effective Weberian bureaucracy in her view, rather than a troubled dictatorship that induced economic scarcities, relied on repression, and deterred merit through a nomenclature system. "China," she enthused, "from the mid-1950s to the mid-1970s really stands out"(Skocpol 1979, 274, 279). Two years later, the historian L. S. Stavrianos concluded that the Great Leap Forward, the worst famine in human history in terms of deaths, "was not entirely negative in its results" while the Cultural Revolution was "a historic contribution" to Third World development in which "the big winners were the peasants." India by contrast was mired in a failure to "revolutionize" its politics (Stavrianos 1981, 607, 610, 611, 645).

With the launch of economic reforms in China in the 1980s, the latest version of this comparison came into being. Foreign journalists and scholars repeatedly wrote stories of China's success and India's failure (Bradsher 2002; Johnson 1989; Kaufman 1981; Long 2005). Even once India began its own reforms in the 1990s, doubts remained. One scholar of China, writing in 1994, argued that in comparison to China, India's democracy "has been accompanied by enormous social costs in terms of poverty, corruption, exploitation, and insecurity" while "India's democratic institutions are looking decidedly fragile" (White 1994, 79). In their 2000 book *Thunder from the East, New York Times* opinion-makers Kristof and WuDunn, who earlier wrote a book on China's inevitable rise (Kristof and WuDunn 1994), portrayed India as suffering from "mismanagement, bureaucratic paralysis, ethnic antagonisms, and socialist economics." While making steps to follow China's economic reforms, India would not match China's achievements because its "reforms are more tentative, its administration weaker, its savings rates lower, its leaders less commanding" (Kristof and WuDunn 2000, 44–45, 333). Investment bankers who liked the investor-friendly climate in China wrote similar reports (Salomon Smith Barney 2001).

India was a victim of the kind of gloomy paradigms that, the Princeton economist Albert Hirschman noted, had given rise to so much pessimism and, more to the point, inaccuracy, in studies of Latin America. Caught forever in bottlenecks, vicious cycles, dilemmas, and dead-ends, India was fated to disintegrate or be seized by tyrants. Geertz believed that "no general and uniform political solution to the problem of primordial discontent seems possible in such a situation" (Geertz 1973, 289). No one could foresee that minorities could be managed, that Hindu nationalism would be contained, that politicians could direct funds to the needy—that democracy and development could advance together. India, like Latin America, was "constantly impaled on the horns of some fateful and inescapable dilemma" (Hirschmann 1970, 352). Poverty, ethnic divisions, illiteracy—India had it all. An American political scientist, continuing the tradition of scholars wrongly predicting political collapse in India, wrote in 2002 that gender imbalances "furnish grounds for skepticism regarding the viability of democracy in India" (Fish 2002, 35).

By contrast, China has been constantly favored with optimistic paradigms, even in the face of the grave disasters of Chinese Communist Party (CCP) rule. CCP rulers had mobilized and organized society in a way that was heartening. No one could foresee that inequalities and environmental degradation would surpass those of India, that a massive anti-system protest covering 341 of China's 450 cities would erupt in 1989, or that residents in the Chinese empire (Taiwan, Hong Kong, Tibet, and Xinjiang) would bray at Beijing's sovereignty despite the reputed economic benefits.

As one Indian intellectual noted, the wrongful views of India compared to China were not just bad predictions of the future—the danger of all social watching—but a more inexcusable misapprehension of the present. "The other Asian giant, China, shut off the world and began mixing totalitarianism with compassionate economics. India continued her experiment in full public view, leaving all her doors open for anyone to come and examine her warts, even if the visitor wanted to concentrate on the warts to such an extent that he didn't notice the face at all"(Akbar 1985, 97).

III

It is probably fair to say that India and China had roughly similar prospects for political and economic modernization at the time of their founding. Both states were built upon deep historical antecedents, which ensured that state-builders could appeal to shared history to forge unity. India, with a degree of ethnic and religious diversity more than four times that of China (Fearon 2003), was bound to face graver challenges of cultural pluralism. On the other hand, it inherited a greater basis of political organization as a result of colonialism. Both countries had a wealth of potential resources and trade networks. The best estimates of comparative living standards of Simon Kuznets and Angus Maddison said that the two countries had roughly similar GNP per head at the end of World War II (Kuznets 1966, 36). (Swamy, in this volume, puts India's per capita GNP 50 percent higher than China's in 1950, using purchasing power estimates.)

The actual growth performance of the two countries from the mid-1950s until 1980 appears to have been remarkably similar, at about 4–5 percent GNP per year, which would translate into something like 2–3 percent per capita.[2] Previous estimates that suggested a far better performance by China in this period have not withstood scrutiny (Dreze and Sen 1989, 207). India, it turns out, was no more suffering from a low "Hindu growth rate" than China was enjoying a "great leap forward" in the three decades after their founding.

As the Chinese economist Qin Hui has shown, China's economic growth in the early 1950s was not a communist achievement but a return toward the growth trajectory created by the Republican-era state (1911 to 1949) that had been halted by invasion and then civil war in the last decade of the Republican period. However, from the mid-1950s onward, famines, political campaigns, and sclerotic Stalinist economics slowed that trajectory. By 1977, per capita GDP in China was 33 percent higher than in India, little different from the 26 percent higher in 1936. The Republican state, by contrast, had taken over when per capita income was only 3 percent higher than in India (Qin 2005). In other words, the communist state significantly slowed the growth trajectory that began in the Republican era, and thereby eliminated China's natural growth advantage over India until the reform period.

Slow absolute growth in both countries in the pre-reform period was because both countries pursued bureaucratic Leninist command economies—Nehru was as disdainful of economic freedom as Mao. India's problem was not too little state intervention, as both Kohli and Chibber contend, but too much (Chibber 2003; Kohli 2004). It locked out foreign trade and investment, strangulated private enterprise in regulations, and expanded state ownership to become "the most extensive in the non-Communist world"(Rohwer 1995, 177). As Lord Desai notes: "Both [leaderships] considered the state as the engine and the driver of growth and suspected the private sector's initiatives . . . Mao for China and Nehru for India laid down the path from which each country had to deviate, if only because the path led to a blind alley" (Desai 2003, 8).

Nonetheless, China did register more rapid improvements in life expectancy, infant survival, and education. This was primarily a result of the more equal sharing in economic growth resulting from early 1950s land reform as well as local self-help mobilization rather than

Table 3.1 Welfare gains in selected developing countries, 1950–1973 (% gain in log value of Human Development Index)

Mexico	56
Brazil	55
S. Korea	52
China	50
Colombia	47
Turkey	47
Thailand	42
Philippines	36
India	32
Sri Lanka	27
Indonesia	24

the largely mythical Maoist welfare state. India fell behind also as a result of its woeful neglect of education in general and the education of women in particular. Whereas life expectancy in both the countries was around 40 at the time of founding, by 1980 that had risen to around 65 in China but only around 55 in India.

Using the Crafts calculations of the historical Human Development Index (HDI), welfare gains[3] in the two countries from 1950 to 1973, along with those of nine other large developing countries, are shown in table 3.1 above (Crafts 1997). These show that China enjoyed slightly above-average development in the Mao era while India enjoyed slightly below-average development. China's larger gains translated into a notable gap in things like life expectancy, literacy, and nutrition by the mid-1970s compared to India. However, there was no miracle in China, as many scholars claimed, and there was no stagnation in India.

Overstated estimates of Chinese performance in this era won praise from scholars like Schurmann (Schurmann 1968), Skocpol, and Huntington, and advice to India by people like Stavrianos, Segal, and Moore. The common theme of these views was that Indian-style gradualism did not work. Social and economic transformation required an effective bureaucracy and an incorruptible elite. Achieving these was impossible in India in the absence of a violent political transformation. Hence the continued thrusting of advice for radical change upon Indian leaders, not least from Indian intellectuals themselves, that Gandhi had lamented at the turn of the century. The economist Gunnar Myrdal argued of India in his 1968 tome *Asian Drama* that "rapid development will be exceedingly difficult to engender without an increase in social discipline," pointing to reports of stern discipline in China as proof (Myrdal 1968, vol. 2, p. 899).

None of these authors foresaw the downside of Chinese authoritarianism. A significant amount of the superior welfare performance by China must be discounted because of the estimated 32 million to 57 million political deaths of the Mao era, deaths that are not captured in the welfare gains table given earlier. These deaths were mainly from the estimated 20 million to 33 million killed in the Great Leap Forward famine (actual deaths, not including postponed births) (Smil 1999). Claims that the starvation was a result of bad weather or the split with the Soviet Union were long ago revealed to be bogus. The deaths resulted from domestic politics (Kung and Lin 2003). There was another estimated 12 million to 24 million killed in successive political campaigns before and after the famine (including 1 to 3 million in the Cultural Revolution) (Rummel 1991; Shambaugh 1999). Chinese scholars have estimated that one in every nine Chinese citizens was either killed or disabled by Mao's political campaigns (Mao and Zhou 2000).

It is true that China advanced more quickly than India in the 1950s (and indeed overall from the 1950 to 1973 period) but it is untrue that this was a result of collectivization or Maoism. It was rather in spite of it. Thus to say that despite the deaths by famine and murder, China still performed better than India, as do remnant Marxists and Maoists in the West (Patnaik 2003), is to give credit where it is not due.

Moreover, there are important normative reasons why the party's role in these political deaths would cancel out China's superior welfare gains even if they were attributable to the party. The *way* in which outcomes are achieved matters as much as the outcomes themselves. A policy allowing police to randomly shoot 100 innocent people on the streets every year in order to deter crime is morally worse than one in which police unintentionally shoot 100 innocent bystanders per year while pursuing criminals. Indian leaders can be faulted for carelessness, negligence, and even callousness to the plight of the average citizen as they sought to maintain the ruling Congress Party's power by tolerating local village leaders and pursuing a blinkered socialism. Yet that stands in contrast to the actions by China's leaders in willfully covering up and then exacerbating a famine that stands as the worst in human history and in conducting other ongoing political campaigns that led to the murder of millions. Mao and his allies believed that these losses of life were needed to maintain the organizational integrity of the party and its writ over society.

Gradualism in India, by contrast, was a result of the Congress Party's attempts to accommodate pluralism in society. India's failures in welfare and education in this period were a result of attempts by its leaders, both Nehru and Indira Gandhi, to preserve Indian democracy by making deals with entrenched regional and rural elites. It is notable that India in this era is also credited with making the twentieth century's first humanitarian intervention when in 1971 it repulsed Pakistani troops from East Pakistan (later Bangladesh) for a mixture of prudential, strategic, and humanitarian reasons (Walzer 1977, 101). Contrast that to China, which in the 1970s supported the rise of the genocidal Khmer Rouge regime in Cambodia and then attacked Vietnam for removing the Khmer Rouge from power, all the while destroying the social foundations of democracy at home.

India's rights-oriented efforts, note two Indian scholars, "went quite a distance in institutionalizing India's fragile democracy," while sidetracking or undermining valuable development goals. "State capacity to push . . . the Chinese type of radical poverty alleviation was simply missing," they note (Kohli and Mullen 2003, 197, 204). If so, then any attempt to create such capacity might have undermined democracy, which might have ushered in more dire socioeconomic consequences. The notion that India could have forged a "well-organized social-democratic party and a durable ruling coalition at the helm of a more effective state" (Kohli and Mullen 2003, 211) or "greater accomplishments within a democratic framework"(Moore [1966] 1993, 395) may overstate the possibilities for state-led mobilization in a democracy laboring under the quadruple pressures of being poor, populous, diverse, and new. The legacy of a consolidated democracy, on the other hand, may be the greatest gift for development that Nehru and his successors could have left to India.

By contrast, China's "radical poverty alleviation" not only led to the political murder of millions but also undermined the creation of a workable democracy, a result that as the new century began increasingly looked like a greater liability for the poor than India's "soft" state. In any case, Congress had its come-uppance, losing power from 1977 to 1980 and again from 1998 to 2004. The CCP, however, continues to rule China by force and to lie about the causes and consequences of the famine and the Cultural Revolution. If there is a popular signal of this difference, it is the many memorials and "wound literature" in China about the Great Leap Famine and Cultural Revolution that has no parallels in India. The therapy that China continues to undergo with respect to Mao contrasts to the high esteem that Indians bestow on Nehru and, to a lesser extent, the Gandhi family.

On any calculation of overall gains in the pre-reform era, then, it is difficult to see China's modest edge in material welfare gains as decisive. India made somewhat slower material progress but also protected its citizens from revolutionary murder while at the same time consolidating its democracy.

IV

China's nightmare under Mao fed directly into the strength of its economic reform movement. India, which had not suffered from Stalinist horrors, did not have the same impetus to reform. As Rosen shows, the resulting differential performance of the two countries' agricultural sectors—a boom in China resulting from shock therapy reforms prompted by the threat of peasant rebellion versus slow gains in India resulting from gradualism—explains much of their differential economic growth in the 1980s and 1990s. "Unlike China, India neither suffered the shock of a Cultural Revolution to create a major push for reform, nor had a lagging rural economy to provide an initial area of reform from which broad substantial gains in output and income were quickly possible" (Rosen 1992, 123).

For many observers, the comparative achievements of this era were reflected in the journeys into town from the airports of Shanghai and Bombay. In Shanghai, China's business center, the traveler speeds along an elevated expressway past gleaming high-rise buildings, into a city scrubbed clean and festooned with exhortative slogans. In Bombay, India's business center, there is no expressway, barely a road at all, and the path winds through horrendous shantytowns for almost an hour before the breathless visitor arrives shell-shocked at one of the city's few good hotels. North Asia's colossus appeared to be a paragon of efficient government and high growth. Its South Asia counterpart seemed mired in political stasis and sluggish growth. China was held up as a success model that India needed to emulate.[4] Yet a closer reading shows that, in these two decades, India again did almost as well as China in material gains.

Although predating reforms in India, a base point of 1975 can be used to assess the outcomes of reforms in the two countries by the end of the century. Across a range of indicators, the improvements in both countries were impressive (table 3.2), whether it be life expectancy, infant mortality, income inequality, or poverty. Using the all-inclusive

Table 3.2 Human welfare indicators, 2002 (1975)

Indicator	*China*	*India*
Share of income held by poorest 20%	5.9%	8.1%
Gini coefficient (extreme inequality = 1)	0.45	0.33
Under-1 infant mortality	31 (85)	67 (127)
Life expectancy	71 (63)	64 (50)
Human Development Index	0.745 (0.523)	0.595 (0.411)
Welfare gains 1975–2002[a]	**+55% (50%)**	**+42% (32%)**

[a] % change in log of HDI scores. Figures in brackets are gains from 1950 to 1973 using Crafts (1997).

Source: UNDP, World Bank, official figures.

HDI of the United Nations, China's gains over the entire period are at 55 percent, again only moderately higher than India's 42 percent gain. Indeed, in the reform period, India's welfare gains rose to three quarters of the Chinese rate compared to two-thirds in the earlier period.

To be sure, India's per capita GDP growth from 1975 to 1999 was 3.2 percent, less than half of China's 8.1 percent. Yet that only shows what a bad indicator GDP can be in assessing overall welfare. If India's voluntary and education-oriented population-control policies continue to succeed, welfare gains could begin to surpass those of China.

In comparative perspective, other populous developing countries have also done well in enhancing human welfare since 1975 (see table 3.3, in which Nigeria, Egypt, Bangladesh, and Iran are added to the 11 countries from table 3.1). In this view, India's performance is average, on par with Brazil, while China's is above-average, on par with that of Indonesia. The Philippines and Nigeria are poor performers.

V

Material benefits are only one part of what allows people to pursue their life goals. The other indispensable means for this are guarantees of rights and freedoms. On this score, India has clearly outperformed China. While quietly racking up economic and social gains that were only moderately worse than China's, India has remained the world's biggest democracy and has provided its citizens with a great deal of protection for their freedoms.

Chinese are less controlled than they were, but their space is not guaranteed by the state, meaning that it does not constitute true

Table 3.3 Welfare gains in selected developing countries, 1975–2002 (% gain in log value of Human Development Index)

S. Korea	66
China	55
Indonesia	51
Egypt	48
Turkey	46
Thailand	46
Iran	45
Brazil	42
India	42
Mexico	41
Colombia	38
Sri Lanka	38
Bangladesh	37
Philippines	33
Nigeria	32

freedom. It is difficult to speak of the existence of any rights in China given that the party reserves the right to override them all. Beijing's constant jailing of dissidents, religious adherents, environmentalists, and others who threaten the ruling regime compares to India's marvelous tolerance for diverse life goals. In 2002, the latest year for which Beijing revealed figures, 3,402 people were arrested and 3,550 charged under the crime of "endangering state security" (previously called counterrevolutionary activities), a crime that is grossly inconsistent with UN human rights standards (Human Rights Watch/Asia and Human Rights in China 1997). The country's labor camps, where people are sent without a trial, hold roughly 50,000 inmates according to UN. China's annual criminal executions, many carried out the same day as the trial, may be as high as 10,000 people, accounting for 98 percent of the global total (Amnesty International 2004). By contrast, India's execution of a single man in 2004 was the first known execution since 1997, consistent with the strong recommendation in the International Covenant on Civil and Political Rights (to which both China and India are parties) to strictly limit and ultimately abolish the death penalty.

In some cases, rights and freedoms may reduce material benefits. PepsiCo's Indian-born President Indra Nooyi in 2002 praised Chinese officials for their efficient handling of foreign investment projects, an implicit critique of India's tangled FDI approvals process.[5] British investment banker Philip Tose, a central figure in China's 1990s' overseas listings boom, notoriously proclaimed in 1997 that "India's problems can be summed up in one word: democracy."[6] A former Chief Minister of India told students in China in 2004, "We wonder if democracy can deliver at the pace that your system can deliver" (Krishna 2004).

Yet one reason why China was luring more than $40 billion in foreign investment per year compared to India's $5 billion in the late 1990s and early 2000s, in addition to its distorted domestic economy (Yasheng 2003), was that its officials are not accountable. (As Swamy points out, these figures may be more like $20 billion and $8 billion, roughly the same proportions of their GDPs.) They can, and do, chase farmers from their fields and repress union activity to attract foreign investment. They have also been able to stifle the expansion of private enterprise and encourage FDI to take its place as part of a larger political strategy of heading off the rise of a pro-democracy business elite (Gallagher 2002). Cadres looted billions of dollars of state assets and listed them on overseas markets with the help of "foreign friends" like Tose.

More typically, however, rights and freedoms are good for economic and social progress. That is, they have an instrumental value in improving material welfare that is empirically well established (United Nations Development Programme 2000; United Nations Development Programme 2002; Siegle et al. 2005). They make markets more fair and open, give people a stake in the system and ensure policies are legitimate. Indeed, the imperatives of good governance are what forced the CCP to introduce village democracy after 1987, and now are causing periodic renegade elections at the township level as well. India's freedoms have ensured a lively and intense debate on issues such as the extent of poverty reduction in the reform era and the plight of the "untouchable" castes. In China, critics of the government position on such issues are hounded or jailed.

Many prominent Chinese now reject the idea that democracy is bad for growth. As India's economy expands, they are making more direct comparisons between the two countries on this basis. As one researcher working in a Beijing municipal government think tank wrote in an online essay: "At present, Chinese do not pay any attention to India. India's democracy is already quite consolidated. In the worldwide competition for skilled workers, besides the economic advantages of all developed countries, there is political responsiveness in India which provides a strong link between political and technical leaders. In these respects, a China that has set out to become strong through technical education needs to work hard to close these gaps . . . We need to look across the Himalayas and pay attention to our southern neighbor India"(He 2004).

This reflects a broader reevaluation of India within China, detailed elsewhere in this book by Huang Jinxin. Prominent intellectuals in China increasingly want to style their country in the mould of India's open society, with its attention to morality, antimaterialism, and nonviolence. Or put another way, China's intellectuals are rediscovering the cultural similarities that they share with India and that have been obscured by the reform-era violence, environmental degradation, loss of social trust, and hyper-materialist ethos. India provides an example of the road not taken. As one researcher wrote:

> As two ancient eastern civilizations, China and India have long, glorious histories and rich cultures, which place great emphasis on keeping promises and putting principles above interests . . . Both Chinese and Indians are peace loving people. Gandhi's nonviolence traces back to Buddhism's teaching of compassion for all forms of life, a teaching that parallels the ancient Chinese philosophy that advocates non-aggression between nations and a union of all countries . . . A love for peace and a strong dislike for materialism are in the blood of the two peoples. (Lin 2004, 32)

Irrespective of their impact on material welfare, rights and freedoms are an end unto themselves, not just for liberal political philosophers but for billions of citizens around the world. Unlike GDP, we do not have an indicator to show the gains in welfare when an Indian is able to, say, join an ayurvedic health group run by the Hare Krishnas or parent another child. Nor can we measure the loss when a Chinese practitioner of the Falun Gong meditation sect is forced to recant under threat of confinement or a farmer's wife is forced to abort an unborn child. If we did, India would be the "growth miracle," China the "growth debacle." This is the oversight of Ogden who writes that "China has done better than India in terms of [material] human development *and therefore* in terms of creating a fair and just society" (Ogden 2002, 373, italics added). Even if China's material development record were vastly superior this would be untrue. Global citizens repeatedly sacrifice material interests in the pursuit of freedom and dignity. Turnout rates among India's rural electorate are higher than its urban. The poor value the vote. They also value freedom, even amidst material deprivation. "India's democracy has been strengthened by a political process that has facilitated a modest degree of redistribution of power and of other valued resources such as status and dignity, even if not of wealth," writes Kohli (Kohli 2001, 2). The leader of Hong Kong's main pro-Beijing party, Tsang Yok-sing, returned from a trip to India in 2002, "struck by the upbeat outlook that almost everybody seemed to have" despite the country's poverty. He attributed this to the fact that "Indians believe in their system of government" so that "if democracy meant a slower pace of reform, so be it. Indians seem to recognize this as a price worth paying."[7] Development includes expanding choices and personal autonomy. Health, income, and education are part of that, but only part.

Thus, appeals for Chinese-style authoritarianism may obscure the trade-offs that are involved. Ogden laments that Indian governments failed to address "social problems" such as by "mandating a national language" as in China, and notes that China's coercive population policies are "a good example of how a more authoritarian government may at times be more capable of carrying out a policy that is better for society as a whole"(Ogden 2002, 369, 371). Yet Indians value their freedom to speak their own languages and decide on private decisions such as child-bearing. If one adopts a utilitarian perspective on human affairs, as does Ogden, then one needs to accurately assess the moral weights placed on various outcomes by the representative individual (Smart and Williams 1987). Only then can one know what precisely "society as a whole" desires. Indians seem to think their freedoms are valuable, while Chinese have never had an opportunity to make that choice.

Some argue that communal violence in India does not have an equivalent in China. For a start, the levels of communal violence—the incidence of deaths from interethnic violence per capita—has steadily *declined* throughout the history of independent India, consistent with the idea of democracy as a pacifying force in ethnically diverse polities.[8] In addition, India's population is nearly four and a half times as ethnically diverse as China's, meaning that an equal incidence of ethnic violence per capita would lead to far more deaths in India in any case.

India has an indisputable black spot in the form of its institutionalized discrimination against the lowest castes, primarily the "Dalits," not incidentally the one area where Gandhi felt something like a social revolution really was necessary. The "scheduled castes" of historically disadvantaged castes, mainly Dalits, accounted for 16 percent of India's population in 2001 but suffer disproportionately from poverty, malnourishment, and unemployment. Discrimination against them is illegal, and positive discrimination policies exist to help them, but this has not overcome centuries of social oppression. Nonetheless, Dalit political parties have won significant power in many state legislatures and have captured several mayoralties.

In China, communal violence occurs under other names, as the repression of religious believers, ethnic minorities, and the rural poor. In the post–1999 crackdown on the Falun Gong religious sect, as many as 700 adherents were killed in detention, while more than 10,000 were arrested. China also maintains an institutionalized war on its peasants. While India's politicians spend endless weeks in the villages seeking votes, Chinese leaders rarely grace these areas unless they have a team of propagandists in tow to show their "concern for the poor." A prominent Chinese economist describes his country's rural population as "the world's biggest population without political representation."[9] Rural dwellers in China are counted as one-quarter of an urban person in the allocation of seats to the appointed national parliament, even less than the notorious three-fifths of a person that was the measure of a nineteenth century American slave.[10] The advocacy group Human Rights Watch has argued that the treatment of rural dwellers in China amounts to a form of institutionalized racism, or apartheid (Human Rights in China 2002). Beijing has long prohibited the formation of any national or regional peasants association (*nonghui*) on the grounds that it would jeopardize the country's industrial development strategy.

Both countries have failed in minority regions to uphold rights and freedoms. India's poor record in Punjab and Kashmir and China's poor record in Tibet and Xinjiang is pretty much a toss-up—in both places officials and police act with impunity and people are killed and tortured regularly. Overall, then, on any standardized measure, there are grave doubts that group violence would be rated worse in India than in China.

Of course, to be of value as ends unto themselves, rights and freedoms have to be realized in everyday life rather than merely on paper. Any political philosopher will admit that basic liberties are not worth much if they exist within an environment of lawlessness, corruption, and poverty. Indeed, Moore's critique of Indian democracy was precisely that its freedoms were meaningless amidst poverty and disorder. Indian scholars likewise warn of "a million mutinies"

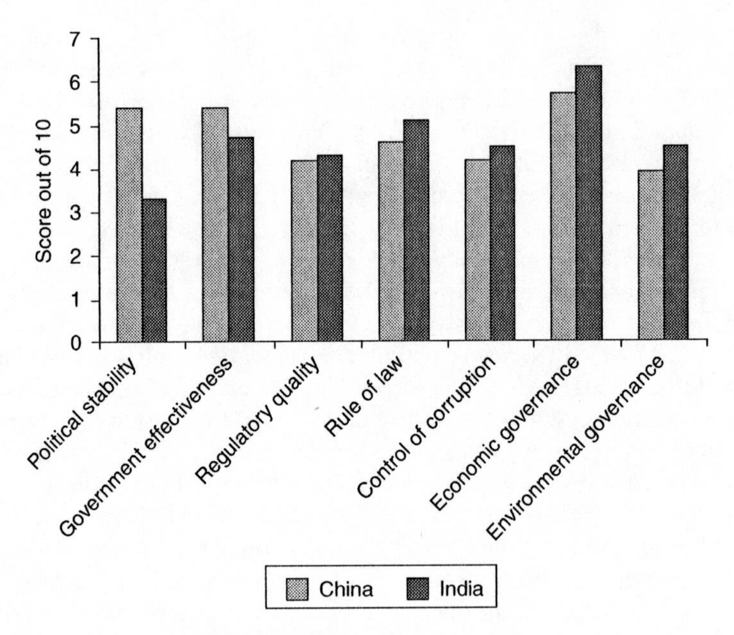

Chart 3.1 Governance indicators, 2004

Sources: Gwartney and Lawson 2004; Esty, Levy et al. 2005; Kaufmann, Kraay et al. 2005.

(Naipaul 1990), or a "crisis of governability" (Kohli 1990). Does disorder in India cancel out its greater freedoms?

To answer this question, I have collected seven different indicators of governance quality, shown in chart 3.1 below, all of them estimated by outside observers using objective criteria.

As chart 3.1 shows, aside from China's advantage in political stability, the two countries perform quiet closely in most indicators, with India having the better rating on five of the other six. As such, it gives lie to the claim that the choice of the two countries is an orderly and efficient China with constrained freedoms and a chaotic and corrupt India with wide freedoms. India provides as good or better "political order" as China and yet has provided freedoms as well, while enhancing material welfare almost as fast as China.

In the reform era, then, as in the pre-reform era, China raced its way from one gust of wind to another, while India continued its slow, straight course. China showed better material welfare gains, but India continued its democratic miracle and backed that up with superior governance in most fields.

VI

Another comparison in the reform experiences of China and India is the way in which decisions were made. This is not just an esoteric concern of political philosophers. The fairness of policy-making is well known to be an end unto itself among those affected. Beyond this foundational value, the perceived fairness of processes has an instrumental value on the legitimacy and thus stability of those policies (Tyler 1990; 1994). Other things being equal, painful economic reform policies will be more durable where they have been shaped and endorsed by the population affected. The fashion in development economics for "participatory development" owes to this insight.

The post-socialist reform period for China began much earlier than in India, in the mid-1970s versus the late 1980s. However, the precise beginning of China's economic reforms is difficult to ascertain. New accounts constantly push the date further back, nowadays to the early 1960s, the recovery from the Great Leap Famine. The reason for this imprecise dating is that reforms in China were society-led, that is, they constituted a form of "everyday resistance" that can cumulatively add up to a revolutionary change (Scott 1985). Private farming rebellions broke out in many rural counties and were winked at by increasingly senior party cadres until eventually the party itself capitulated and announced it had "liberated its thinking" in 1978 (Friedman, Selden et al. 2005; Zhou 1996).

Contrary to popular wisdom about "gradualism" in Chinese economic reforms,[11] the party's response was recurrent doses of shock therapy that put similar rapid reforms in eastern Europe and Latin America to shame. As Rosen noted: "the revolution destroyed the intermediary institutions that might have made transitions more gradual" (Rosen 1992, 32). Communal farming for 800 million peasants was abolished in a single step, raising the proportion of privatized rural farming households from 1 percent in 1979 to 98 percent by 1983 (World Bank 1997, Figure 1.12, p. 9). Rural social welfare was entirely shut down by the mid-1980s. Dreze and Sen noted that "The authoritarian nature of Chinese politics has permitted an abrupt reduction in the social security provisions"(Dreze and Sen 1989, 220).

Elsewhere, whole wastelands of industrial failure emerged in Manchuria and the northwest as the state shut off funding for state enterprises in sectors like textiles, steel, and coal. Sudden price reforms in the 1980s set off inflation spirals, while patriarch Deng Xiaoping's 1992 Southern Tour led to gross overinvestment, both domestic and foreign, and another bout with double-digit inflation. Entry into the World Trade Organization is bringing another wave of sharp change. Just because China's reforms could have been more radical than they were does not mean that they were "gradual." The radical revolutionary approach to modernity of China's pre-reform era continued in its reform era. Cadres who made "decisive and bold reforms" (*guoduan dadan gaige*) became the new Maoists of China.

As one Chinese scholar notes, in this first 15 years of economic reforms, the nonparticipatory approach did not matter much because most people were benefiting (Wang 2000). Farmers may have lost communally organized healthcare but the cash crops they were allowed to grow were selling while family members were earning income as migrants to urban centers or as rural industrial and service workers. This changed in the 1990s. Persistent and systemic losers began to appear—state enterprise workers, women, farmers, and those in inland regions began to experience stagnating or declining incomes. It was then that the fundamental weakness of the nonparticipatory Chinese model began to appear. Economic reform and openness began to create distributive conflicts that are usually resolved through welfare and redistribution. But lacking representation, the Chinese government could not extract enough resources to finance such programs. One might neither add nor could make redistributive decisions that would necessarily be legitimate among the poor in any case. For as Wong argues, the whole notion of markets and why they should be expanded at the expense of state power, and what was the purpose of public policy in a socialist state, was merely decided by fiat from above (Wong 2004).

Contrast that to India, where economic reforms began haltingly in the mid-1980s, at least a decade later than China, and then accelerated in the early 1990s. Easy reforms in areas like licensing, exchange rates, and banking came first. Then the government moved into more difficult reforms in labor, state ownership, and welfare, moving ahead piecemeal unlike the "shock therapy" in China.

The Hindu-nationalist Bharatiya Janata Party (BJP) won office in 1998 for many reasons but one of them was fears that the economic reforms of Congress was already too much an elite-driven, top-down process. Right here we have a startling contrast with China, where there was never any popular voice, much less veto, over economic reforms. The coalition led by the BJP represented a poor people's movement fearful of reforms. Yet when it came into office, the BJP sensibly continued reforms as the best hope for the poor.

Thereafter, India's reforms moved forward by embracing opposition, not bulldozing it (as documented by Manor elsewhere in this volume). The fact that the BJP was criticized not only by business groups for its slow reforms but also by left-wing intellectuals for selling out to "neo-liberalism" shows just how successfully it walked the middle way. Most of the criticism focused on issues where reform was delayed precisely because the losers were not reconciled to change. Reforms in agricultural support, small-scale industry restrictions, labor laws, and privatization were delayed because of the interests affected. Fortunately, the economic reformers ignored advice for more coercive measures and stuck to the country's great democratic tradition. One Indian intellectual referred to India's steady, consensual reform process as "the elephant paradigm," a challenge to the notion that violence and repression are indispensable to progress (Das 2002a; 2002b).

Throughout the BJP government era of 1998–2004, cabinet rifts and a series of antireform strikes chastened the government against moving too fast at the risk of considerable political loss. Its economic transformation was achieved through open processes of reaching a fair and consensual policy. India's trade unions, rural farmers, and petty bourgeoisie middle class all had a say in reforms. In China, notes Long, "communism had beaten both capital and labor into submission" (Long 2005, 8).

The democratic nature of India's economic reforms is frustrating to those who like the lightning-bolt approach of authoritarian China. Yet democracy has ensured that reforms are more just and therefore more enduring in India. Inequality has remained moderate while opportunities have expanded for more people than those in China. The important result, notes a paper by Harvard's Center for International Development, is that "India's political system is more than ever in consensus about the basic direction of reforms"(Bajpai 2002, 2). Or as the columnist Paranjoy Guha Thakurta wrote in *Business Today* magazine in 2003: "While it may be very fine to wax eloquent about the need for so-called economic reforms, unless a political consensus can be arrived at, all such attempts are bound to falter if not fail." Such sentiments are unheard of in influential circles in China, where the whole notion of "politics" is discredited and suspect (Gilley 2004b).

India's more enlightened industrialists are also quick to point out that they prefer reforms that will not face an ongoing poor people's movement, as in China. As a prominent Indian banker told a conference in New York in 1999: "Unless the common man in the street is able to identify himself with the reform process, we will find that the reform is going to be very difficult"(Vaghul 1999). It is difficult, by contrast, to survey the corporate scene in China and find similar voices from executives. The best-known advocates of the poor among business people tend to have been rural entrepreneurs with greater sympathy: farming tycoon Sun Dawu of the Dawu Group in central Hebei province, for example, was a person who set up an (illegal) private bank for rural savers and business who are systematically exploited by the state-run financial system, which he called "worse than feudalism." As he summed up the problem prior to serving a short jail sentence: "(Officials) don't imagine that people at the grassroots level have any power of judgment"(Dickie 2003).

The lack of value placed on things like rights, dignity, social bonds, and freedom by scholars is puzzling given psychological evidence of its importance to human happiness. As Friedman wrote, the crisis of faith in democracy in the West in the 1960s led to an "amoral equivalence" being set between India and China by people like Barrington Moore whose 1966 *Social Origins* represents a major aberration in his own otherwise pro-democracy oeuvre (compare Moore 1978; 1970; and 1954). "Moore's moral equation . . . of all paths toward modernity misled" (Friedman 1998, 120). In the decades since, a similar lack of value placed on democratic procedures and freedoms has been no less evident in comparisons of China and India. India's "Gross Democratic Product" has boomed while China's has stagnated.

Modernity is not a final state obtainable by social revolution or rural violence but a state of mind, a method of managing change obtainable through social reconciliation and respect for human lives as ends unto themselves. It is a process as much as an outcome. As Friedman noted earlier, scholars must reject the allure of "grand narratives of a once and forever transition to modernity" that "assume a final solution to the pains of permanent change" (Friedman 1998, 120, 119). Process, it turns out, matters as well as outcomes.

VII

How do people in China and India evaluate the states to which they belong? The political legitimacy of a state comes from two dimensions of performance, covered in the preceding two sections: the outcomes of public policies; and the processes and institutions that make them. Elsewhere, I have gathered, rescaled, and aggregated legitimacy data

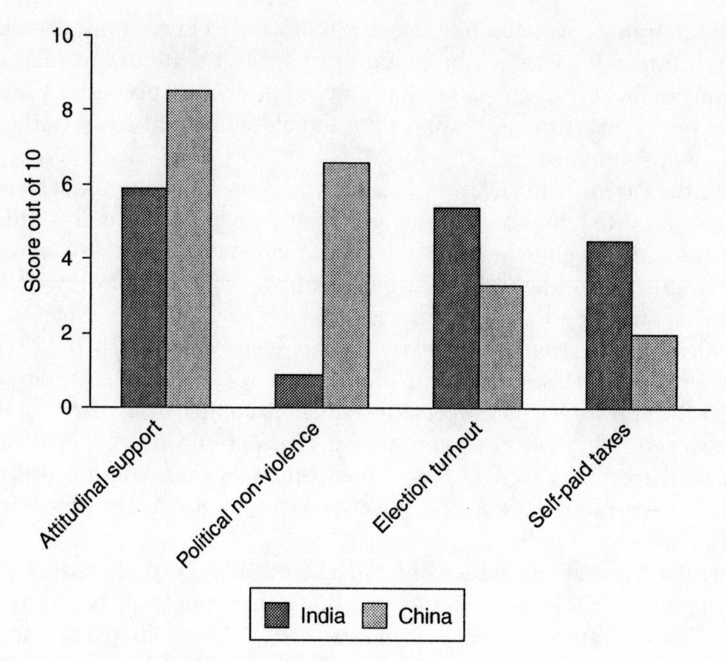

Chart 3.2 Legitimacy indicators, 1999–2002
Source: Gilley 2006.

in a 72-country dataset that includes China and India (Gilley 2006). The scores for the four distinct subcomponents for both countries are given in chart 3.2. Attitudinal support is a composite of views of the protection of human rights, confidence in police, confidence in the civil service, and system support, taken from the World Values Survey IV (1999–2002) and Global Barometer surveys. The three behavioral indicators concern the extent of political violence (the incidence of violence in political protest, taken from the World Handbook of Political and Social Indicators for the years 1996–2000), turnouts to elections (at the village and township level in China's case), and the state's ability to rely on easily avoidable taxes such as those in income and corporate profits.

It is worth noting that *both* India and China outperform the legitimacy scores that would be predicted by their income levels for most of these four categories. This is a reminder that the comparison between these two is intriguing precisely because they have *both* developed and advanced in recent decades, especially compared to the setbacks in

Sub-saharan Africa, and to a lesser extent eastern Europe and Russia. The legitimacy scores for both countries suggest that citizens in both countries believe their states have been moderate successes. China does better on attitudinal support but India does better on two of three behavioral responses.

In the case of China, three decades and more of economic reforms have generated modest legitimacy for the regime. Several studies conclude that regime legitimacy has been enhanced, especially among the more politically salient urban groups, as a result of welfare improvements and a rationalization (which in China's case means a de-ideologicalization) of the state (Feng Chen 1997; Jie Chen 1997a, 1997b; Zhong 1996). It is clear that there is real subjective validity in the oft-expressed view, especially made in comparison to the state deterioration in the former communist states of Europe, that civil and political freedoms were a less valued outcome than continued economic expansion and effective governance in China. At the very least, it has not been a failure.

However, the importance of being skeptical about these results has been pointed out by many observers. Both Zhong and Chen argue that the "performance legitimacy" of post–1989 China in particular is inherently unstable because citizens tend to conflate legitimacy with individual payoffs. As a result, what appears to be legitimacy is in fact merely compliance dependent on payoffs. The post–Tiananmen boom, says Chen, "has not served so much to regain popular confidence in the regime as to divert public attention from political concerns to tangible material interests" (Chen 1997a, 430). Moreover, the nationalism that is based on a rational calculation of national interests means the devotion to the regime is lost in the equation, unlike the nationalism of the Cultural Revolution. Finally, as Saich notes in this volume and Wang notes elsewhere (Wang 2005), the positive evaluations of national government decline steeply for evaluations of local government in China, an inversion of the usual pattern in most states.

China maintains a greater coercive control over society, indicative of a failure to reconcile many citizens to the current regime. What that means is that, as in 1989, the kind of attitudinal approval for the regime that appears so high may conceal more complex attitudes toward the regime, some of which remain falsified until a political crisis erupts (Kuran 1992). Friedman, for example, notes the pervasive unofficial critiques and attacks on the state that suggest underlying unrest, especially outside of Beijing and Shanghai where most opinion surveys are conducted (Friedman 2002). The fact that China underperforms

India on two of three behavioral indicators suggests the degree of dissonance between attitudes and behavior in China. Elsewhere in this volume, Huang and Khanna note how World Bank surveys of experiences of corruption in China are heavily censored.

In India, by contrast, the concealment or falsification of preferences is unheard of (Sen 2006). Indeed, it is the voluminous and strident expression of preferences that has made many wince at the country's democratic experiment. If we are prone to overestimate regime legitimacy in China because of concealed preferences, then, echoing Akbar quoted earlier, we are prone to underestimate regime legitimacy in India because of the cacophony of critical voices that the country's freedoms encourage. As mentioned, legitimacy in India is actually slightly higher than would be predicted by its developmental level. It enjoys above-predicted scores in most of the components above—especially views of rights protections, satisfaction with democratic development, and election turnouts. India suffers mainly as a result of several violent regional insurgencies—especially in Kashmir and the Punjab. Were it to manage those and other ethnically charged conflicts such that its overall nonviolence score was closer to the average for all countries, its standing compared to China would look far better.

These considerations then point to the following conclusions. Concealed preferences and behavioral data in China mean we should discount its attitudinal super-legitimacy. But even then we are left to believe it is considered a moderate success by citizens and certainly not a failure. In India, a deluge of expressed preferences mean that we can take the attitudinal support as reliable, and also as a solid indicator that the country is also not considered a failure by its citizens. Both states can point to achievements in welfare and governance that justify these views.

VIII

Looking ahead, which country will ultimately be judged to have passed to modernity with more aplomb? This requires us to make predictions about the future, a dangerous business in the best of times yet crucial to providing an answer to this question. We can hardly evaluate the passages taken to modernity, the passage from one shore to the next, without making some tentative guesses about when and how India and China will eventually reach the far shore.

China is the world's last major communist state, and one of a declining number of purely authoritarian ones. According to Diamond's typology of regimes, China is one of only 21 "politically closed" regimes remaining in the world of the 150 states with a population of more than one million (Diamond 2002). Thus, of all the predictions one might make about China, a prediction of "no change" seems the least plausible. China's unresolved constitutional question inches closer to some resolution with each passing year. If one had to guess, based on post–Tiananmen events and broader comparative insights, it seems a prediction of an elite-led transition to some form of minimal democracy is the most likely outcome.

What is important is how disruptive the transition and consolidation phases of democratization in China are. In comparative perspective, China has many factors working in favor of a smooth democratization: national cohesion among the Han peoples who make up 91 percent of the population, an emergent rule of law and civil society, an institutionalized state. But other factors work against it: secessionist regions in Tibet and Xinjiang and Taiwan, little experience with elections, yawning income inequalities, and corruption. A middle-range prediction would be then that China's passage to democracy will be turbulent but ultimately successful (Gilley 2004a). A multidimensional model of state fragility developed for the U.S. government in 2005 placed China on the watch list of unstable states (Bennhold 2005).

In India, the political system is as indelibly fixed in society as sitar and tabla ensembles. There is no vast underclass of disaffected farmers and workers threatening to overturn the reforms, or even the political system, as there is in China. India's income distribution is less skewed, its indicators of pollution and environmental degradation less severe, and the permanence of its fundamental political institutions more assured than China's. Rosen noted that economic reform has undermined the political system in China but strengthened it in India (Rosen 1992, 133).

In the mid-1990s, a writer for the *Economist* concluded: "China faces its crucial test in developing an institutional structure to sustain a modern market economy. India has that skeleton in place but so far lacks the dynamism and market-friendly policies that have given China so much economic energy" (Rohwer 1995, 70). That comparison holds true today. But India is finding it easier to implement market-friendly policies than China is to develop an institutional structure. As a result, China's future remains more unstable than India's.

Even if China had achieved some sort of short-term "developmental miracle" compared to India since 1975, there would be real reasons to doubt its long-term feasibility. In the event, it has done nothing of the sort. The idea that China took a better route to modernity by delaying political reforms contains two falsehoods: one is that it has outperformed democratic India so far, something that we have seen earlier is untrue, judged in terms of welfare, freedoms, and procedural justice. The second is the assumption that its constitutional transition, when it happens, will be as painless as the passage of a new stock market law. That is almost certainly wrong. China has end-loaded its transition costs and those costs may be quite significant.

In any case, it may be that China simply should never have paid the transition costs that India did. China does not face the degree of ethnic diversity, the harmful anticolonial obsessions, or the web-like local social powers that India did. China is peopled by a culture famous for its entrepreneurial flair, attention to education, and political pragmatism. To have paid as heavy a price as India for the passage to modernity seems wasteful. To pay more would be pure folly.

IX

Kennedy, in his 1959 speech raised the hope that India would outperform China in the coming decades: "We want India to be a free and thriving leader of a free and thriving Asia." Nearly half a century later, Asia is the world's new economic powerhouse and is largely made up of democratically elected governments (23 of 39 in 2003 according to Freedom House). India, meanwhile, may indeed be emerging as a new leader of Asia, having realized Kennedy's dream of "a real record of performance consistent with our ideals and democratic methods."

To return to our earlier metaphor to which Gandhi's quote gave rise, two great ships of Asia set sail toward modernity with similar cargos and ships. One, India, steered a predetermined course of democratic principle and sensitivity to existing social practice. When storms of advice blew, it furled its sails and dropped its sheet anchor. It moved slowly but ploddingly and, as the twenty-first century begins, appears to be nearing port. Many Western scholars wrung their hands in frustration. The calls for "radical change" in India have resounded from 1947 to the present (Long 2005, 16).

China, by contrast, embraced "radical change" from the start. Its national ship, tacked from one "thought liberation" to another, ravaged the passengers and cargo, and was frequently lured by false winds. Many outsiders cheered its zeal. As the century begins, its ship is leaking and the crew is restless. The port keeps appearing and then receding like a mirage.

By around 2025 or 2030, India will become the world's most populous nation with 1.4 billion people as China's population reaches its peak. A Central Intelligence Agency report argues that India will also "rise" along with China (Central Intelligence Agency 2005). If so, it will have been achieved in both the pre-reform and reform eras through better overall performance and attention to procedural justice.

The belated recognition of India's achievements, if it becomes more commonly accepted, will signal a new maturity in the social sciences. Ever since the modernization theories of the 1950s, the social sciences have considered economic and political development—modernity—in the narrowest of terms. High industrial output and stout political institutions were what mattered. How this was achieved and whether intangible aspects like freedoms and dignity were "produced" were obscured. Only occasional voices—Bendix is one of the few examples (Bendix 1978)—argued that the "production" of rights and freedoms had anything to do with modernization. Yet time and again, regimes that produced welfare gains and political order were overthrown—Suharto's Indonesia, apartheid South Africa, and Pinochet's Chile to name a few. Those that produced "mere" rights and freedoms—and India is the best example—survived despite unstinting predictions of doom. Geertz claimed that India's stability was "something of an Eastern mystery" (Geertz 1973, 292). But when we realize the value that the poor place on freedoms, the mystery dissolves.

Both China and India committed themselves to some form of "socialism" from the start. China's welfare gains have always exceeded those of India, but not for reasons that any Indian leader could or should seek to replicate. China first engaged in a harsh repression of dissent under Mao and then, when that path failed, quickly marketized the economy with little regulations to speak of. In both stages, pre-reform and post–reform, many scholars and thinkers have held up China as a success and India as a failure. Yet only the most tone deaf progressive thinker could have clung to this notion. India recognized early on that, in the words of one American progressive, "without democracy socialism becomes a cruel travesty"(Howe 1976, i). It showed concern for freedom and fairness in its pursuit of modernity. Its reward was a half century of belittlement at the hands of self-styled liberals.

Modernity is less a destination than a journey, an ongoing process of social reconciliation and political fairness. The comparison of India and China takes us right to the heart of this question, challenging everyone to rethink entrenched positions about the meaning of development. We cannot hope to develop a single consensus on which country has done better. But we can hope at least to place the relevant issues on the table.

Notes

My coeditor Edward Friedman was instrumental in encouraging me to develop and sharpen the arguments of this essay. I also benefited from the critical comments of many people, in particular Suzanne Ogden, Prerna Singh, and Jehangir Pocha.

1. On the objective descriptions of modernity and modernization see Ronald Inglehart (1997). *Modernization and Postmodernization: Cultural, Economic, and Political Change in 43 Societies*. Princeton, N.J.: Princeton University Press.
2. Maddison calculates China's annual rate of GDP per capita growth between 1952 and 1978 as 2.4%. Angus Maddison, (1998). Chinese Economic Performance in the Long Run, OECD Development Center.
3. Here and below, welfare gains are measured as the percentage gain in the log value of the HDI index between the two years. Logs are necessary because the HDI is a decreasing function with a limit of 1 and thus needs to be transformed into a linear function in order to calculate percentage change.
4. "Dynamic forces unleashed by the creation of an environment conducive to international business operations have thus played an important role in the process of rapid economic growth and development in China. For the Indian leadership and elite in charge of economic reforms, this is one of the important lessons that can be learned from the Chinese experience with its open-door policy" Jong H. Park, (2003). "The Two Giants of Asia: Trade and Development in China and India." *Journal of Development Studies* 18(1): 64–81.
5. Quoted in News India-Times. http://www.newsindia-times.com/2002/02/22/eco-comp-top.html.
6. Tose's audience in Hong Kong was alumni of the Harvard Business School. See "Banker Blasts Ballots," *The Australian*, April 16, 1997, p.25. Tose was better known for offering to pay the British government to recall Hong Kong governor Chris Patten after Patten introduced democratic reforms in the territory prior to its annexation by China in 1997. Tose's Peregrine Investment Holdings went bankrupt in 1998, the biggest financial failure in Hong Kong in the 1990s, due largely to a loan to a corrupt company in Indonesia. In 2004, Tose was banned from holding any company directorship in Hong Kong for four years for his role in the Peregrine debacle. He continues to speak out against democracy in Asia.
7. *South China Morning Post*, March 1, 2002, 14.
8. By my own calculations, the number killed in communal strife (mostly Hindu–Muslim) per 10 million people for the worst years of 1964, 1969, 1983, and 1992 respectively are 41, 13, 16, and 12. The figure for 2002, the year of the Gujarat riots, is just 8. This is based on official figures compiled by the Bureau

of Police Research and Development of the Ministry of Home Affairs. Although considered conservative, the BPRD data would not affect the comparison if the bias has remained constant over the period. Varshney notes that the trends in his own data, compiled from reports in the *Times of India*, closely match the BPRD figures. Ashutosh Varshney (2002). *Ethnic Conflict and Civil Life: Hindus and Muslims in India*. New Haven: Yale University Press.

9. Hu Angang quoted by Reuters, January 31, 2002.
10. Of course, this vote was given to slave-owners rather than to the slaves themselves. But the semi-human moral standing it implied is comparable to that of rural residents in China.
11. The belief that China's reforms were gradual has been widespread in international institutions. The World Bank noted in its China 2020 report (1997) that "The Chinese leadership . . . had no appetite for dramatic changes in policy"(p.8). See also foreign academic works such as, Steven Goldstein (1995). "The Political Foundations of Incremental Reform." *China Quarterly* 144: 1105–1131, Barry Naughton, (1995). *Growing Out of the Plan: Chinese Economic Reform 1978–1993*. Cambridge: Cambridge University Press.

References

Akbar, M.J. (1985). *India: The Siege Within*. Harmondsworth: Penguin Books.

Amnesty International (2004). Executed "According to Law"?: The Death Penalty in China.

Bajpai, Nirupam (2002). A Decade of Economic Reforms in India: The Unfinished Agenda. Cambridge, MA: Center for International Development, Harvard University.

Bendix, Reinhard (1978). *Kings or People: Power and the Mandate to Rule*. Berkeley: University of California Press.

Bennhold, Katrin (2005). "U.S. Aide Sees 'Internal Strains' Tugging at China." *International Herald Tribune*, March 3, 2005.

Bradsher, Keith (2002). "India Slips Far Behind China, Once Its Close Economic Rival." *New York Times*, November 29, New York, p. 1.

Central Intelligence Agency (2005). *Mapping the Global Future*.

Chen, Feng (1997). "The Dilemma of Eudaemonic Legitimacy in Post-Mao China." *Polity* 29(3): 421–439.

Chen, Jie (1997a). "Assessing Political Support in China." *Journal of Contemporary China* 6(16): 551–567.

Chen, Jie (1997b). "The Level and Sources of Popular Support for China's Current Political Regime." *Communist and Post-Communist Societies* 30(1): 45–64.

Chibber, Vivek (2003). *Locked in Place: State-Building and Late Industrialization in India*. Princeton: Princeton University Press.

Crafts, Nicholas (1997). "The Human Development Index and Changes in Standards of Living: Some Historical Comparisons." *European Review of Economic History* 1(3): 299–322.

Das, Gucharan (2002a). *The Elephant Paradigm: India Wrestles: With Change*. New Delhi: Penguin Books.

Das, Gucharan (2002b). *India Unbound: The Social and Economic Revolution from Independence to the Global Information Age*. New York: Anchor Books.

Deaton, Angus and Valerie Kozel (2005). Data and Dogma: The Great Indian Poverty Debate, World Bank, Washington, D.C.

Desai, Meghnad (2003). *India and China: An Essay in Comparative Political Economy*. IMF Conference on India and China, New Delhi, International Monetary Fund.

Diamond, Larry (2002). "Thinking About Hybrid Regimes." *Journal of Democracy* 13(2): 21–35.

Dickie, Mure (2003). "There's Hope for China, Says Freed Entrepreneur." *Financial Times*, London, P. 2.

Dreze, Jean and Amartya Sen (1989). *Hunger and Public Action*. Oxford: Clarendon Press.

Esty, Daniel C., Marc A. Levy, et al. (2005). 2005 Environmental Sustainability Index: Benchmarking National Environmental Stewardship. New Haven, CT: Yale Center for Environmental Law and Policy.

Fearon, James (2003). "Ethnic and Cultural Diversity by Country." *Journal of Economic Growth* 8: 195–222.

Fish, M Steven (2002). "Islam and Authoritarianism." *World Politics* 55(1): 4–37.

Friedman, Edward (1998). "Development, Revolution, Democracy, and Dictatorship: China Versus India?" in T. Skocpolt (ed.), *Democracy, Revolution, and History* Ithaca: Cornell University Press, pp. 102–123.

Friedman, Edward (2002). How To Understand Public Opinion in China. Washington D.C. Woodrow Wilson International Center for Scholars: 17–21.

Friedman, Edward, Mark Selden, et al. (2005). *Revolution, Resistance and Reform in Village China*. New Haven, CT: Yale University Press.

Gallagher, Mary (2002). " 'Reform and Openness': Why China's Economic Reforms Have Delayed Democracy." *World Politics* 54: 338–372.

Gandhi, Mahatma ([1909] 1956). "Indian Home Rule," in H. Jack (ed.), *The Gandhi Reader*. New York: Grove Weidenfeld, pp. 104–121.

Geertz, Clifford (1973). *The Interpretation of Cultures*. New York: Basic Books.

Gilley, Bruce (2004a). *China's Democratic Future: How It Will Happen and Where It Will Lead*. New York: Columbia University Press.

Gilley, Bruce (2004b). "The 'End of Politics' in Beijing." *China Journal* 51: 115–135.

Gilley, Bruce (2006). "The Meaning and Measure of State Legitimacy: Results for 72 Countries." *European Journal of Political Research*.

Goldstein, Steven (1995). "The Political Foundations of Incremental Reform." *China Quarterly* 144: 1105–1131.

Gwartney, James and Robert Lawson (2004). *Economic Freedom of the World: 2004 Annual Report*. Vancouver, B.C.: The Fraser Institute.

Harrison, Selig (1960). *The Most Dangerous Decades*. Princeton: Princeton University Press.

He, Jiadong (2004). Xia shiji bu neng hushi yindu (We Cannot Overlook India in the Next Century). Beijing Social and Economic Research Institute.

Hirschmann, Albert (1970). "The Search for Paradigms as a Hindrance to Understanding." *World Politics* 22(3): 329–343.

Howe, Irving (1976). "Preface", in I. Howe (ed.), *Essential Works of Socialism*. New Haven: Yale University Press, pp. i–ii.

Human Rights in China (2002). Institutionalized Exclusion: The Tenuous Legal Status of Internal Migrants in China's Major Cities, Human Rights in China.

Human Rights Watch/Asia and Human Rights in China (1997). Whose Security? "State Security" in China's New Criminal Code.

Huntington, Samuel (1968). *Political Order in Changing Societies*. New Haven: Yale University Press.

Inglehart, Ronald (1997). *Modernization and Postmodernization: Cultural, Economic, and Political Change in 43 Societies*. Princeton, NJ: Princeton University Press.

Johnson, Bryan (1989). "India Badly Beaten in Race With China." *The Globe and Mail*, Toronto, p. 8.

Kaufman, Michael (1981). "China Surpasses India". *New York Times*, New York, p. 5.

Kaufmann, Daniel, Aart Kraay, et al. (2005). Governance Matters IL: Governance Indicators for 1996–2004, World Bank.

Kennedy, John F. (1959). *The Basis of U.S. Interest in India: Its New Dimensions*. Conference on India and the United States, Committee for International Economic Growth, Washington, D.C.

Kohli, Atul (1990). *Democracy and Discontent: India's Growing Crisis of Governability*. New York: Cambridge University Press.

Kohli, Atul (ed.) (2001). "Introduction," *The Success of India's Democracy*. Cambridge: Cambridge University Press, pp. 1–19.

Kohli, Atul (2004). *State-Directed Development: Political Power and Industrialization in the Global Periphery*. Cambridge: Cambridge University Press.

Kohli, Atul and Rani Mullen (2003). "Democracy, Growth, and Poverty in India," in A. Kohli, C.-i. Moon, and G. Sørensen (eds.), *States Markets, and Just Growth: Development in the Twenty-First Century*. New York: United Nations University Press, pp. 193–226.

Krishna, S.M. (2004). "21st Century Belongs to India, China, Says Krishna." *The Hindu*, p. 5.

Kristof, Nicholas D. and Sheryl WuDunn (1994). *China Wakes: The Struggle for the Soul of a Rising Power*. New York: Times Books.

Kristof, Nicholas and Sheryl WuDunn (2000). *Thunder from the East: Portrait of a Rising Asia*. New York: Alfred A. Knopf.

Kung, James Kai-sing and Justin Yifu Lin (2003). "The Causes of China's Great Leap Famine, 1959–1961." *Economic Development and Cultural Change* 52(1): 51–74.

Kuran, Timur (1992). "Now Out of Never: The Element of Surprise in the East European Revolution, in N. Bermeo (ed.), *Liberalization and Democratization: Change in the Soviet Union and Eastern Europe*. Baltimore: Johns Hopkins University Press, pp. 7–48.

Kuznets, Simon (1966). *Modern Economic Growth*. New Haven, CT: Yale University Press.

Lin, Limin (2004). "China–India Relations Enter the Fast Lane of Development." *China Strategy* 3: 31–33.

Long, Simon (2005). "The Tiger in Front: A Survey of India and China." *The Economist*.

Maddison, Angus (1998). Chinese Economic Performance in the Long Run, OECD Development Center.

Mao, Yushi and Hongling Zhou (2000). Guanyu Zhengzhi Gaigede Duihua (A Discussion About Political Reform). *2000 Zhongguo Zhengzhi Nianbao (China Political Report, 2000)*. Lanzhou, China: Lanzhou University Press, pp. 191–199.

Moore, Barrington (1954). *Terror and Progress in the USSR*. Cambridge, MA: Harvard University Press.

Moore, Barrington (1970). *Reflections on the Causes of Human Misery and Upon Certain Proposals to Eliminate Them*. Boston: Beacon Press.

Moore, Barrington ([1966] 1993). *Social Origins of Dictatorship and Democracy*. Boston: Beacon Press.

Moore, Barrington, Jr. (1978). *Injustice: The Social Bases of Obedience and Revolt*. White Plains, NY: M.E. Sharpe.

Myrdal, Gunnar (1968). *Asian Drama: An Inquiry into the Poverty of Nations*. New York: Pantheon.

Naipaul, V. S. (1990). *India: A Million Mutinies Now*. New York: Alfred A. Knopf.

Naughton, Barry (1995). *Growing Out of the Plan: Chinese Economic Reform 1978–1993*. Cambridge: Cambridge University Press.

Ogden, Suzanne (2002). *Inklings of Democracy in China*. Cambridge, MA: Harvard University Asia Center.

Park, Jong H. (2003). "The Two Giants of Asia: Trade and Development in China and India." *Journal of Development Studies* 18(1): 64–81.

Patnaik, Utsa (2003). On Measuring "Famine" Deaths: Different Criteria for Socialism and Capitalism? China Study Group, March 10, 2005.

Qin, Hui (2005). "China's Economic Development Performance under the Pre-Reform System." *The Chinese Economy*, 3 parts, 38 (4, 5, and 6).

Rohwer, Jim (1995). *Asia Rising*. New York: Simon & Schuster.

Rosen, George (1992). *Contrasting Styles of Industrial Reform: China and India in the 1980s*. Chicago: University of Chicago Press.

Rummel, R. J. (1991). *China's Bloody Century*. New Brunswick: Transaction Publishers.

Salomon Smith Barney (2001). China and India: Different Tunes.

Schurmann, Franz (1968). *Ideology and Organization in Communist China*. Berkeley: University of California Press.

Scott, James (1985). *Weapons of the Weak: Everyday Forms of Peasant Resistance*. New Haven: Yale University Press.

Segal, Ronald (1965). *The Crisis of India*. London: Jonathan Cape.

Sen, Amartya (2006). *The Argumentative Indian*. London: Penguin Books.

Shambaugh, David (1999). "After 50 Years of Communism." *The Independent* (October 1): 4.

Siegle, Joseph, Michael Weinstein, et al. (2005). *The Democracy Advantage.* New York: Routledge.

Skocpol, Theda (1979). *States and Social Revolutions.* Cambridge: Cambridge University Press.

Smart, J. C. C. and Bernard Williams (1987). *Utilitarianism—For and Against.* Cambridge: Cambridge University Press.

Smil, Vaclav (1999). "China's Great Famine: 40 Years Later." *British Medical Journal* 319 (7225): 1619–1622.

Stavrianos, L.S. (1981). *Global Rift: The Third World Comes of Age.* New York: William Morrow.

Sweezy, Paul (1976). "Socialism in Poor Countries." *Monthly Review* 20(5): 1–15.

Tyler, Tom (1990). *Why People Obey the Law.* New Haven: Yale University Press.

Tyler, Tom (1994). "Governing amid Diversity: The Effect of Fair Decisionmaking Procedures on the Legitimacy of Government." *Law & Society Review* 28(4): 809–832.

United Nations Development Programme (2000). Annual Report: Human Rights and Development.

United Nations Development Programme (2002). Annual Report: Democracy and Development.

Vaghul, Narayanan (1999). India's Economic Reforms: Positive Developments, Underlying Concerns and the Big Picture. Center for the Advanced Study of India, University of Pennsylvania.

Varshney, Ashutosh (2002). *Ethnic Conflict and Civil Life: Hindus and Muslims in India.* New Haven: Yale University Press.

Walzer, Michael (1977). *Just and Unjust Wars.* New York: Basic Books.

Wang, Shaoguang (2000). "The Social and Political Implications of China's WTO Membership." *Journal of Contemporary China* 9(25): 373–405.

Wang, Zhengxu (2005). "Political Trust in China: Forms and Causes," in L. White (ed.), *Political Legitimacy in East and Southeast Asia.* Singapore: World Scientific.

White, Gordon (1994). "Democratization and Economic Reform in China." *Australian Journal of Chinese Affairs* 31: 73–92.

Wong, Linda (2004). "Market Reforms, Globalization and Social Justice in China." *Journal of Contemporary China* 13(38): 151–171.

World Bank (1997). *China 2020.* Washington, D.C.: International Bank for Reconstruction and Development.

Yasheng, Huang (2003). *Selling China: Foreign Direct Investment During the Reform Era.* New York: Cambridge University Press.

Zhong, Yang (1996). "Legitimacy Crisis and Legitimation in China." *Journal of Contemporary Asia* 26(2): 201–220.

Zhou, Kate Xiao (1996). *How the Farmers Changed China: Power of the People.* Boulder, CO: Westview Press.

II

Economic Reforms

4

The Causes of Differential Development: Beyond Regime Dichotomies

Joydeep Mukherji

I

Successful economic modernization in China and India is crucial for the success of the global economy. This chapter reviews the course of reform in both countries and assesses the main challenges they face in becoming developed nations. Although China and India account for only 4 percent and 2 percent respectively of global GDP, they account for two-fifths of humanity. Failure to modernize in one or both of these countries would risk confining the successfully "globalized" part of the planet to large pockets in the West and East Asia, excluding half the world's people and potentially threatening the stability of the global economy.

China and India are global success stories in reducing poverty and moving toward a prosperous market economy. Since starting its economic reforms in 1978, China has more than quadrupled its national income. Indian per capita GDP has doubled since the country began to liberalize its economy in 1991.

Both countries have advanced at their own pace, following different economic strategies within very different political systems. India has invested more in political development, compared with China, and created a plural and open society. China has focused more on economic modernization and shunned political pluralism. Popular comparisons of the economic performance of the two countries often focus on the advantages or disadvantages of democracy for poor countries.

However, a closer examination of the recent history of both countries shows that a variety of economic outcomes could have been possible in democratic India and in authoritarian China. Much of the difference in economic performance can be attributed to particular factors in each country, undermining any simple conclusions about the impact of democracy on development. Any evaluation of their performance needs to describe the criteria for successful development, the relative importance of personal freedoms, and assess the very different risks they face going forward.

II

Domestic forces largely drive economic reform in both countries. China and India are led by cautious elites determined to improve the status of their countries. After a quarter century of reform in China, and over a dozen years in India, both political systems and political elites were largely intact. The sequence of reform measures is different in either country, influenced to a large extent by their very different pre-reform legacy.

China embarked upon economic reform in 1978 following decades of ideological experimentation that culminated in social disorder. The massive upheaval of the Cultural Revolution (1966–1976) threatened the legitimacy of Communist Party rule. China's paramount leader, Deng Xiaoping, understood that the survival of the party would depend increasingly on economic results as its ideology was discredited. Deng created a political consensus within the party that combined an open mind on economic restructuring with strict political control to maintain social stability. Over time, the party leadership became obsessed with economic growth and modernization as the prerequisites for staying in power. Unlike in the past, the drive was no longer based on ideological formulas but increasingly on pragmatism and a willingness to experiment with market forces.

A remarkable feature of China's recent history is the ability of its party elite to agree on working rules that have kept internal conflicts from shattering its cohesiveness. Under Deng's guidance, the party created rules to facilitate turnover in key party and government positions, regularly injecting new blood. New rules for recruitment and retirement were complemented by less harsh methods for dealing with political opponents inside the party, in contrast with the fate of those who lost intra-party struggles in the past.

Over the years, the party has allowed much more internal debate, enlarging the role of technical experts in policy matters. The leadership has also sought feedback on the impact of new economic policies, through internal channels and through independent research by technical experts reporting directly to top leaders. The main subject that remains off-limits for public discussion is the party's unchallenged right to rule.

Membership in the party has grown impressively toward nearly 70 million in recent years, now formally including new groups like rich farmers, urban middle class, and entrepreneurs. Their presence reflects an emerging social contract in China; the party helps people get rich and gives them more autonomy in economic, social, and even cultural matters, but demands acquiescence to its monopoly on power.

Governance in China has become more troublesome at the village level, where the lack of accountability of the local party and the imposition of illegal taxes on farmers have led to unprecedented riots. The party has responded in part by holding village elections, hoping to keep control by having elected leaders at the bottom rung of government. Similar elections have been held in urban neighborhoods, and could spread very slowly to other levels of government.

The circumstances that led China's political leadership to mobilize so energetically for economic modernization, and its willingness to receive feedback that typically comes through open elections and a free media in other countries, may not be repeatable elsewhere or in China at another time. The obsession with economic growth is similar to the focus on rebuilding in Japan after the Second World War. It springs as much from immediate past memories and events as from strong leadership. The reform path was not inevitable and it is difficult to imagine that China would have embarked on it so decisively absent Deng's leadership. More than two decades of material success has provided China's governing elite with political capital, especially in the perception of the growing middle class. Political dissidents and other opponents of the party are generally weak and divided.

China's achievement in combining economic dynamism with political continuity in recent decades is matched by India's achievement in constructing a stable democracy that has accommodated growing social mobility. Modern India emerged from a negotiated withdrawal by Britain, not through war or a revolutionary movement as in China. Modern China began with a social revolution that overturned the hierarchy and distribution of assets in every village and town in the country. India experienced religious violence at independence but no social revolution.

India's new leaders were devoted to parliamentary democracy, creating rules and institutions that would be used by groups at the middle and bottom of the social and economic hierarchy to gain power at the elite's expense over the subsequent decades. India's social revolution, shifting power toward the lower castes and the poor, has been happening largely peacefully through the ballot box since 1947. The pace of social change accelerated in the early 1990s, coinciding with an economic crisis that nearly led the government to default on its debt in 1991.

The economic success of other Asian countries, including China, and the failure of the Soviet Union had convinced a significant portion of India's leadership that its economy had to be liberalized in order to catch up. The 1991 crisis provided an opportunity for reformers to revamp the country's development strategy but it was a mild shock in political terms. India's leaders sought to modify but not discard the old economic system after 1991. The crisis did not threaten the very existence of Indian political parties or its system of governance, unlike the failure of the Cultural Revolution in China. Hence, the political impulse for reform was weaker in India in 1991 than it was in China when Deng Xiaoping came to power. Over the years, the consensus behind economic liberalization has strengthened in India but the pace of reform has been modest compared with that in China.

India began reform at a time of growing political pressure to devolve power from the national government to the states. Political decentralization has been accompanied by the growth of regional and caste-based political parties, reflecting India's social cleavages. Only about half of the total votes in recent national elections went to the two political parties with a national presence, the Indian People's Party (BJP) and Congress. No Indian leadership, even a dictatorship, could avoid grappling with the turbulence arising from the rapid social changes under way in a country with as much diversity as India. Hence, a singular focus on economic development, as in China, is not politically possible in contemporary India.

Coalition governments, which have governed India in recent years, give more political leaders the ability to exercise a veto, complicating the process of liberalizing the economy. Almost every party in the government at the national level faces some election somewhere every year, making them hesitant to approve policies that could imperil local electoral calculations. Both the BJP and Congress, and almost all of the more than thirty smaller parties, have served in either the national or state governments during the reform years. None has opposed reform when in office. However, the divisions within the parties over economic issues tend to be bigger than the divisions between parties, further constraining the pace of change.

The main political risks in India are poor implementation of policies and too slow a pace of reform that could undermine economic growth prospects. Under such a scenario, a combination of slow GDP growth and rising fiscal deficits could boost the Indian government's already high debt burden, weakening its creditworthiness. The biggest political challenge facing China over the medium term is to close the gap between economic modernization and political modernization without severe disruption.

III

China is following the East Asian growth path of mobilizing low cost capital for massive investment, often with a low return. India's fiscal weakness and more market driven financial sector force it to follow a different path. China has enjoyed faster economic growth than India, with GDP growing at an average rate exceeding 8% in the last decade, compared with around 6 percent in India. Growth may accelerate modestly in India, and decelerate in China over the next decade but China's lower population growth rate will likely ensure that it continues to enjoy slightly higher per capita growth.

Sustained productivity growth, based on a stable macroeconomic environment and an increasingly educated labor force, distinguish both countries from many other parts of the world in recent decades. Table 4.1 indicates the positive experience of both countries with long-term trends in labor productivity, which has grown faster in Asia than elsewhere. According to IMF estimates, the biggest factor behind growth in China was added use of capital, contributing proportionately more than twice as much to GDP growth as in India. Total factor productivity grew well in both countries but about 50 percent higher in China than in India (Weng 2003).

Higher worker productivity has translated into lower poverty. More than 200 million Chinese have been lifted out of poverty in recent years. Poverty has become largely regional; two-thirds of the poor live in western provinces. Poverty reduction has been slower, but still impressive, in India, where the poverty rate fell to 26 percent

Table 4.1 Mean growth rate of output per worker

	1980–2000
China	7.9
India	3.6
East Asia (incl. China)	4.1
Latin America	−0.5
Middle East	1.5
Industrial Countries	1.5

Source: IMF "*Why India Can Grow at 7 Per Cent a Year or More: Projections and Reflections*," Dani Rodrik and Arvind Subramanian, *World Politics*, 4:118, July 2004. From table 1, which uses data from "*The Empirics of Growth: An Update*," an unpublished manuscript by B. Bosworth and S. Collins, Brookings Institution.

in 2000 from 36 percent in 1993 and 45 percent in 1980. As in China, poverty in India is becoming more regional, with over half the poor located in four large states (Bihar, Uttar Pradesh, Madhya Pradesh, and Orissa). About two-thirds of India's poor live in rural areas, mainly working in agriculture. Chinese are richer on average than Indians but the distribution of income may be more skewed in China (UNDP 2003). While measuring inequality is difficult, most analysts agree that income distribution has worsened in China during the reform years (even if absolute incomes have risen for almost everybody), reflecting in large part the growing gap between urban and rural development.

China began economic reform in agriculture, giving farmers fixed term land use rights in the late 1970s and moving toward giving them full property rights in recent years. Irrigated land, which has more potential for increased output, accounts for about 45 percent of China's farmland, compared with about 30 percent in India. Better prices and better land tenure for peasants sparked an agricultural boom in the 1980s in China, substantially reducing poverty by boosting farm wages. The "Green" revolution on the farm led to a "Grey" revolution as rural wealth sparked the growth of rural industries that allowed tens of millions of farmers to leave the land for better-paying jobs. Output from new "township and village enterprises" (TVEs), formally owned by local collectives and townships and enjoying a comparatively light regulatory burden, grew about 20 percent per annum and employment by 15 percent in 1985–1995. TVEs became the largest contributors to GDP growth and employment growth from the mid-1980s, transforming the countryside and setting the stage for subsequent reform of politically sensitive state-owned enterprises (SOEs). TVEs started to decline after 1996, shedding labor, due to growing financial difficulties and greater competition from other sectors. However, other sectors of the economy, especially the private sector and foreign ventures, had grown by then to a sufficient scale to absorb labor and sustain economic growth.

India began its reform with industry and largely ignored agriculture until recently. Hence, it has not benefited from a substantial increase in productivity and income on the farm, which would have reduced rural poverty at a faster rate. Similarly, India lags China in the development of rural and agro-industry, due in part to restrictive industrial policies and to poor rural infrastructure (i.e., roads, electricity). Unlike in China, most rural income in India comes from the farm (except in a few pockets where irrigated land has facilitated pockets of Chinese-style Green and Grey revolutions).

Another distinguishing feature of China's development strategy has been massive public investment in infrastructure, such as roads, power, railways, and ports, financed partly by government-owned banks and various levels of government. Such development was deliberately directed to promote special economic zones and the coastal regions at the expense of the rest of the country. The strategy, combined with liberal policies to attract foreign direct investment (FDI), successfully transformed much of coastal China in the course of two decades into a powerful export platform. In the 1990s, when the gap between the advanced coast and the backward interior became very big, the government directed more public investment to the less developed provinces.

In general, China has pursued a pragmatic approach to reform without any master blue print, best described as "crossing the river by groping for the stones one at a time." It often involves using pilot projects and experiments to test new policies before implementing them nationwide. It has also permitted flexible arrangements for the use of land and labor in the non-state sector, explicitly following a dual track approach. Such institutional flexibility, as well as an explicitly regional approach, is not as politically feasible in India or in most countries, where interest groups and the unfavored regions would oppose it.

India has been a democracy for nearly six decades but not a market-oriented one until barely a decade ago. The country's large private sector enjoyed property rights but operated in a largely controlled economy till recently. From 1991 onward, India has created competitive market conditions for much of the private sector, reducing legal and bureaucratic restrictions on production and investment. Reform began with liberalizing the industrial sector and lowering barriers to FDI and trade, with peak import tariff rates dropping to 20 percent in 2004 from 155 percent pre-reform. The results have been impressive. The regulatory system has gradually facilitated private sector investment and production. Many markets that were once dominated or exclusively served by SOEs are now dominated by the private sector, such as telecommunications, airlines, and mutual funds. Foreign trade now exceeds 35 percent of GDP, compared with 21 percent in 1991–1992.

The budgetary problems of India's central and state governments have denied them the resources needed for investing in physical infrastructure, in sharp contrast with China. Indian public sector investment has declined from over 9 percent of GDP in 1991 to below 7 percent a decade later, while capital spending by Chinese governments, as well as by SOEs, has increased impressively. Poor physical infrastructure has slowed the pace of economic growth and deterred domestic and foreign investment, even in sectors where India has more liberal policies than China.

China did not undertake large-scale layoffs from its bloated SOEs until other sectors of the economy started hiring new workers, almost a decade and a half after reforms began. Since 1998, SOEs have shed 30 million workers while the government has been building a rudimentary social safety net to take care of those who could not find a new job. Private sector off-farm employment growth has been slower in India than in China, making it more difficult politically to downsize its bloated SOEs.

China's national government has focused its resources on 500 or so key SOEs that it supports and nurtures in order to make them internationally competitive. Most of the other hundreds of thousands of SOEs, largely small and medium sized, have been shifted to local government control, to be modernized, subsidized, sold, or closed. Fiscal pressure is driving more local governments to sell part or all of their shares in SOEs in order to pay for current expenses. The central government, by contrast, has not sold its ownership in the key SOEs below 51 percent but has listed many of them on stock exchanges domestically and abroad. Beijing recently established a State Owned Asset Supervision and Administration Commission to assume ownership rights over the largest several hundred SOEs, trying to strengthen their management autonomy and financial performance. This may result in a more diversified ownership of larger SOEs and the privatization of some of them. The recent privatization of much of China's urban housing stock was perhaps the biggest shift of assets from public to private hands in recent history.

Privatization has been less dramatic in India and continues to meet political resistance. The national government has transferred ownership and control of several SOEs in telecom, energy, and mining to the private sector and will be forced to do more in coming years by fiscal necessity. Many cash-strapped state governments have privatized or closed some of their enterprises. However, the size of SOEs in India is much smaller than in China and the challenge of privatization is proportionately less important.

Chinese producers face greater domestic and external competition compared with their Indian counterparts. The competitiveness of the Indian private sector is constrained in part due to high trade barriers and to "small scale reservations." The peak customs tariff in India is 20 percent, compared 10.4 percent in China, and about 13.4 percent for 105 developing countries surveyed recently by the World Bank (2003, p. xi). Lobbying from powerful private sector companies in India (who enjoy more political clout with government than their Chinese counterparts) has slowed the pace of liberalizing restrictions on imports and FDI.

India continues to "reserve" the production of around 500 consumer goods to small firms employing limited amounts of labor and capital. Designed to promote labor-intensive growth, the policy limits investment, hurts product quality due to inadequate machinery and the small scale of operations, and stifles the growth of competitive medium-sized enterprises. It also hinders exports. The Indian policy of artificially propping up small firms, which is now being slowly reversed, contrasts with China's policy of sheltering the biggest firms, indicating very different political priorities.

China's physical infrastructure is much better than India's, boosting the competitiveness of Chinese firms. However, India has an advantage in "soft" infrastructure, such as its legal and regulatory systems and the rule of law. China has more flexible labor practices in general than India but it continues with a residential registration system that makes it difficult for people to move to new locations, hindering labor mobility. Although it is being diluted slowly, the registration system in effect offers greater access to public services to those who are registered as local residents, discriminating against migrants to the cities. India also has a dual labor market, with rigid labor laws for the barely 10 percent of workforce in the formal sector and little protection for the rest. The markets for goods and services are more developed in India than that for land, where various restrictions mean that politics sometimes determines prices more than economics.

Changing the nature of the economy is a bigger challenge for China than for India, which has always had property rights, a private sector, and the rule of law. The extent of economic transformation in China is impressive. The "non-state" sector now produces 60 percent of GDP, including two-thirds of the value added in industry (compared with less than one-third in the late 1970s). China is successfully building the architecture of a modern market-oriented economy. Nevertheless, its economy remains a hybrid of market forces and considerable state control, with much work to be done in creating a viable legal system, genuine markets in land, labor, and capital, and an effective regulatory system for financial markets. The discretionary rule of the party is being withdrawn from the commercial sector quite rapidly but is not being fully replaced by a functioning system of new laws and rules that are adequately enforced. Strengthening the courts and regulatory bodies, and making them more independent, would help insulate the economy from possible negative political developments in future. China's accession to the World Trade Organization, indicating a strong political commitment to deepen reform, augurs well for institutional development.

India has largely met the broader institutional challenge, despite weaknesses in its legal and regulatory system. Its bigger challenge is to build physical infrastructure, improve the provision of public services, liberalize trade, and deregulate domestically to create a genuine national market for goods and services.

The distinct economic structures of the two countries reflect differences in their pre-reform legacy, their reform strategies, and the sequencing of reform. The leadership in both countries realizes that job growth is coming from the private sector and that government policies have to encourage it. The Communist Party enhanced the constitutional status of the private sector in 2003 to acknowledge this reality. Indian political leaders of all stripes are promoting policies to boost private investment for the same reason.

IV

Neither China nor India enjoy much fiscal flexibility. Annual budget deficits of around 10 percent of GDP and a government debt reaching

80 percent of GDP constrain India's sovereign credit rating (both figures are for consolidated government, netting out intra-government transfers and debts). The equivalent numbers for China, a deficit of 3 percent–4 percent of GDP and debt around 38 percent, appear to be much better. However, fiscal activity is more transparent in India. In contrast, much of China's future government debt has been piling up as bad loans in the financial system. The cost that will ultimately be borne by the government resulting from the contingent liabilities of the financial system is the main constraint on China's sovereign credit rating.

Much of China's bad loan problem reflects the role of financial institutions as fiscal agents of the government during the earlier years of reform. Government-owned banks have played key role in delivering resources to favored sectors of the economy and to favored companies. The strategy has been costly, with nonperforming loans estimated to exceed 40 percent of total loans. But, in the absence of a modern administrative system to directly compensate those who would be hurt by the massive economic dislocation that comes with rapid reform, the strategy may have been politically prudent.

A high domestic savings rate, about 40 percent of GDP, has allowed China to pursue rapid growth without depending on foreign loans. It has also provided the banks with ample deposits to maintain their liquidity, buying time until the government helps to strengthen their balance sheets. The ultimate fiscal cost of nonperforming loans is difficult to determine; they could boost general government debt to 100 percent of GDP. Adjusted for the potential cost of government guarantees and of contingent liabilities from its own banking system, India's general government debt would likely reach a similar level.

China has a higher level of contingent liabilities than India but its government also has more assets. Various estimates suggest that the value of the government's holdings in SOEs could be 50 percent or more of GDP (IMF 2004). The proceeds from the disposal of such assets would appear gradually, and may be largely devoted to meeting SOE debts to lenders, workers, and pension funds. Successful management of the debt problem depends on fiscal reform to raise tax revenues, continued economic growth, and financial sector restructuring.

Tax reform has been largely successful in China, laying the foundations of a modern tax system. General government revenues are projected to reach 20 percent of GDP in 2004, compared with only 13 percent in 1998 (actual revenues are modestly higher because of the persistence of "off-budget" funds, mainly at the local level). China's value added tax (VAT) accounts for about one-third of total tax revenue, providing a solid base for tax buoyancy as the economy grows.

India's fiscal system is more transparent than China's. Government support for key sectors is usually provided through the budget, typically as subsidies. However, general government revenues have stagnated around 18 percent of GDP over the last decade, contributing to massive fiscal deficits. India's general government debt is about four times the level of its annual revenues while China's debt is less than twice its revenues. However, adding estimates for contingent liabilities to the debt level would sharply narrow the difference. Unlike China, India does not have a VAT but has proposed introducing one at the state level in 2005. Extending the tax into a comprehensive national VAT would strengthen public finances in India. A domestic savings rate of around 24 percent of GDP allows India to fund its budget deficits domestically, containing recourse to external debt. However, the cost of fiscal deficits appears in rising domestic debt and foregone public spending on basic services and infrastructure, constraining GDP growth.

China's higher savings rate provides enough funds for productive investment that generates a higher rate of economic growth than in India, despite the massive misallocation of resources through China's inefficient banking system (appearing later as nonperforming loans). India saves and invests the equivalent of around 24 percent of GDP annually to achieve a nearly 6 percent GDP growth rate while China saves a higher share of its GDP (around 40 percent) to achieve a modestly higher growth rate (around 8 percent). India gets "more bang for its buck" but China has more bucks.

China will continue to rely heavily on FDI for growth, partly to compensate for the misallocation of capital by its domestic financial system. India will rely largely on domestic investment but should get more FDI in future as its infrastructure and regulatory policies improve.

India enjoys more monetary flexibility than China, thanks to more sophisticated financial markets and a flexible exchange rate. Indian policy-makers have more supple instruments for conducting monetary policy, due to better-developed financial markets linked by interest rates that largely reflect market conditions. Interest rates are largely set by the government in China, forcing the government to rely on administrative measures to influence the flow of lending. Indian authorities, in contrast, can apply monetary policy tools like the central bank's lending rate or open market operations to influence market behavior. The poor quality of bank loans, and the fear of the impact of potentially higher interest rates on cash-strapped SOE borrowers, has delayed the liberalization of interest rates in China.

Financial markets in both countries are deep enough to give policy-makers discretion in calibrating the pace of integration with global markets. Such policy discretion stands in contrast with many countries whose low domestic savings rate forces them to depend on foreign capital for economic growth, restricting their policy options. The bulk of government debt in both India and China is in the local currency, insulating them from exchange rate volatility of the kind that plagues Latin American sovereigns with a large external debt burden denominated in foreign currency.

V

Both India and China have successfully inserted themselves into the global economy, gaining external flexibility. China was more isolated from the world economy than India when it began to reform in 1978 but is now more integrated. Today, trade accounts for about half of China's GDP, compared with about one-third for India. China accounted for about 6 percent of world trade in 2003, compared with 1 percent in 1979 (IMF 2004).

Much of China's export success is due to its ability to attract FDI, which has transformed its coastal provinces into an export platform for multinationals. Electronic parts and products account for just over half of China's imports and exports. About two-thirds of China's manufacturing exports are electronic products and textiles, indicating China's success in shifting away from commodities and natural resources (in contrast with much of Latin America). China has received more FDI, around $50 billion according to official figures, in recent years than any country in the world other than the United States. Even discounting for statistical problems, the level dwarfs India's FDI level of around $4 billion. Foreign ventures are estimated to account directly and indirectly for about 60 percent of China's exports, often through tying up with local suppliers.

China has excelled as an exporter of goods while India has done better in exporting services, ranging from information technology (IT) to business processes like data management and call centers. India's service exports grew at an average annual rate of 17.3 percent in the

1990s, compared with 15.8 percent in China and 5.6 percent for the world on average. India's skilled workforce in science and technology attracts FDI related to research and development. According to World Bank estimates, foreign firms account for about 27 percent of exports from IT and related services, less than the foreign share in Chinese exports of goods (World Bank 2004, 19). The different ways the two countries have entered the global economy are likely to converge over time, with India developing its capacity for exporting goods and China its capacity for exporting services.

The importance of export success goes well beyond the numbers. Both countries have accumulated record levels of foreign exchange reserves after opening their economies to global forces, overcoming a major political fear of vulnerability. Higher reserves give confidence to leaders to try new reforms in trade and other sectors to insert their countries into global production chains. The pace of economic reform would have been much slower in both countries absent export success. Increased openness has brought new business practices and technology into both countries. In China, it has created massive employment along the coast, making it easier for the government to proceed with reforms that displaced many workers. FDI and export production has provided resources to local and national governments to pay for the costs of reform elsewhere.

In India, the success of IT exports did something similar but on a smaller scale. The industry serves as a model of private sector wealth creation that is socially acceptable in a country where many years of a controlled economy had led people to associate wealth with corruption and connections. The political impact of IT and related services is bigger than its direct economic impact (i.e., the $14 billion in remittances sent home every year by Indians working abroad still exceeds total exports from IT and related services in 2004). Success has inspired confidence and created momentum to introduce similar policies to promote private investment in sectors such as auto parts and pharmaceuticals.

Both countries enjoy ample external flexibility. China has higher foreign exchange reserves and export earnings than India. However, foreign exchange reserves vastly exceed short-term debt in both countries. Both countries impose controls on capital flows across their borders in order to protect their weak banking systems and avoid instability. However, India has looser rules for capital flows, especially for investors in its stock and bond markets. China, which has fixed its currency to the U.S. dollar, faces greater pressure to appreciate its exchange rate as its foreign exchange reserves reach record levels. India has a floating exchange rate and greater discretion in undertaking monetary policy.

VI

The difference in economic performance in the two countries reflects in part the differences in the capacities of their subnational governments. City, village, and state governments are responsible for most public services that are visible to people, such as electricity, health, education, roads, and law and order. Subnational governments account for more than 85 percent of public spending on health and education in India and more than 90 percent in China. China's subnational governments are generally stronger than their Indian counterparts, providing a better level of public services and contributing to the country's faster growth rate. Both countries need to reform local government; India needs to strengthen it so it can provide basic services while China needs to make it subject to the rule of law and reverse the decline in services in some areas.

China is more decentralized fiscally than India. Table 4.2 shows that Indian states collect a lower share of consolidated government revenues than Chinese provinces and also account for a lesser share of consolidated spending. Interestingly, Indian states are closer in revenue and spending shares to their counterparts in many other federal countries. A large share of India's consolidated government fiscal deficit is at the state level, in contrast with China where provincial finances are in better shape.

Table 4.2 Decentralization in comparative perspective local government share (average 1990–1997)

	Spending	*Revenue*	*Fiscal deficit*
India	56.7	39.1	36.7
China	81.5	59.7	−0.9
United States	44.4	42.1	−48.2
Canada	58.8	53	3.8
Argentina	45.6	39.1	177.4

Source: IMF, "*India: Selected Issues and Statistical Appendix*," August 2003, table IV.2. The figures indicate the share of general government revenue and spending that is accounted for by sub-national governments.

Sub-national governments in China have done a better job than their Indian counterparts in raising resources to provide local services. Local officials see the direct benefit of attracting more investment into their area, leading them to be pragmatic in establishing the working rules for foreign and domestic investors to compensate for the uncertainty that would otherwise arise from China's weak legal framework. The stronger revenue base of China's provinces reflects their right to collect turnover tax, corporate income taxes levied on enterprises they own, and a share of the national VAT. Starting in 1994, China established the basis for a modern tax system at the central and provincial level. Indian states have failed to widen their tax base and impose adequate user charges on basic services such as electricity consumption. While India's proposed VAT could strengthen state revenues over the medium term, most states are not likely to garner enough resources to invest substantially more in basic services in the near term.

The weaknesses of India's sub-national governments largely explain the poor state of the country's infrastructure and its low level of human development. The revenues raised directly by Indian states often cannot pay for salaries and pensions, leaving little available for development activities. India's complicated administrative system weakens the authority, responsibility, and accountability of local governments, giving them little incentive to improve services, raise more of their own resources, and make their own investments, compared with their Chinese counterparts. Elected city and rural government politicians in India enjoy less power than their nonelected counterparts in China, as the bureaucracy and state level leaders largely control them. Local political leaders have little ability to change policies and implement them through the bureaucracy. The occasional successful initiatives at the city level usually result from prodding by state leaders or from national civil servants posted in top city government jobs. The failure of local governments is reflected in the slum-like appearance of much of urban India, which looks worse than cities in other countries at the same level of wealth.

China's rural governments are coming under serious financial stress, especially in poorer provinces. They are generally overmanned and their authorized revenue base is not enough for their payroll and for the provision of public services in some parts of the country. As a result, the public health system is declining in many rural areas, and life expectancy stagnating in some of the poorest counties, even as China makes great progress in health care in most parts of the country. Rural governments typically seek more money by collecting illegal taxes from farmers, imposing a heavy burden on some of China's poorest people. Peasant protests against such arbitrary taxes have become common in recent years, leading the central government to experiment in a few districts with fiscal reform to lighten the local burden.

India has moved slowly to strengthen rural governments, amending its constitution in 1992 to establish local bodies called "panchayats." Most states have yet to implement the reform properly, but panchayats are beginning to make a difference in a few states. However, they do not provide anything near the level of services provided by Chinese communes and collectives in the past and by rural local bodies today.

Chinese fiscal federalism faces many challenges. Its complicated system of revenue and spending assignments needs modernization to deal with the growing income gap between provinces. China's richest province enjoys more than ten times the average per capita income of its poorest province. The tax system for provinces favors those with an industrial base and penalizes those with a larger agricultural base. Both rich and poor provinces are becoming increasingly burdened by new social welfare responsibilities such as health, education, and pensions, much of which used to be provided by SOEs to their workers in the past. Local governments often avoid restrictions on incurring debt by issuing guarantees and by borrowing through enterprises under their control, as in India. The central government does not want to bear the cost of more transfers to rural governments and has great difficulty in getting cash-strapped provinces to transfer more money to them.

India is more decentralized politically than China. The decentralization of political power in the recent decade, and the active participation of state-level political parties in national coalition governments, has strengthened India's ability to smoothly devolve more tax revenues to states and from states to local governments. The process of modifying the architecture of federalism and reassigning tax and spending powers will be cumbersome but should not disrupt the political fabric of the country.

China's more decentralized fiscal architecture may be more conducive than India's current system toward delivering public services in a large country. However, the high level of decentralization in China in government tasks is combined with an extreme form of centralization through the rule of the unified communist party. Absent the glue that comes from one-party rule, China's formal government structure may come under severe pressure and reveal a weak national government with limited resources at its disposal.

VII

China and India are following different approaches to globalization. The failure of "forced march" modernization, such as in the Great Leap Forward and the Cultural Revolution, has shaped China's current pragmatic strategy. China is entering the global economy rapidly under a determined leadership that is increasingly open-minded about economic policies. India is moving at a slower pace, with less disruption.

Both China and India have avoided "shock therapy." While dramatic economic shocks may quickly tame inflation or change people's expectations, they may cause more harm than good for countries seeking to build new institutions or managing complex political forces whose consent is needed for reform to continue. A gradual and pragmatic approach has allowed both countries to make the adjustments that are needed to sustain change, both economically and politically, in the absence of many of the institutions (especially in China) that normally characterize a modern market economy.

India possesses the political liberty, pluralism, and institutional framework needed to successfully enter the global economy. It suffers from poverty, poor physical infrastructure, and fiscal weakness. China has good infrastructure, a high savings rate, a reform-minded leadership, and is well integrated into the world trading system. It has serious problems in its financial sector and faces a long-term political challenge. Indian democracy faces no threat from globalization but China's system of governance is likely to change over the medium term.

Comparisons of the economic performance of the two countries usually center on the advantages or disadvantages of democracy for poor countries. Such debates often overlook many other factors that explain economic performance. For example, Indians have long enjoyed political freedom but little economic freedom until barely a decade ago. Much of India's backwardness can be attributed to its "non-market" democracy for much of its recent history. In many ways the gap in economic performance between the two countries today reflects the fact that China started economic reforms about a decade sooner than India.

A comparison of the economic and human development record of the two countries may tell us more about the consequences of different federal systems, or local political factors, rather than the consequences of democracy and dictatorship. Would democracy in India have produced better economic results if the country had moved sooner toward strengthening state and local governments to facilitate better provision of basic public services? The huge gap in economic and social performance within India shows that a broad range of outcomes is possible within a democratic framework. For example, some states like Kerala enjoy a lower birth rate and a comparable literacy rate with China while others like Bihar fail badly on both counts. The flaws of Indian state and local governments are due to many factors and it is not evident that they would be fixed by less democracy.

Indian political parties today are highly factionalized, complicating governance in the recent era of coalition governments. Such conditions were not present for most of India's history since independence and need not persist forever. Nor are they inherent in a democracy. Conversely, one-party states typically enter into stagnation because of the inability to change leadership and policies smoothly. They often persist with policies to an excessive degree and stop receiving feedback from their own people.

China's Communist Party has displayed such faults in the past and could well do so in future. For example, environmental problems are likely to be identified and publicly acknowledged sooner in pluralistic India than in China. The obsession with rapid economic growth and the tight political control enjoyed by the party leadership is likely to worsen the extent of environmental damage and delay the response to it, compared with India where civic society and the courts are active in the environmental movement.

An evaluation of the experiences of the two countries needs to specify the definition of "success," the time frame for measurement, and the relative importance of economic versus political goals. India has invested heavily in political development, adopting democracy at an earlier stage of development than other countries. As a result, its leaders faced pressure for redistributive and populist policies at an earlier stage of economic development compared with many East Asian countries. Only recently have Indian leaders given more priority to faster GDP growth through market forces and on reducing, or at least containing populism. In attaining a comparatively more mature level of political development, India has solved the biggest long-term challenge facing China.

India is not likely to follow the path of East Asian tigers, such as Korea, Taiwan, or even China in attaining very rapid growth rates over a prolonged period of time. It will continue to grapple with identity politics but may develop a stronger political consensus on economic reforms. It may follow the path of Thailand or Italy, which experienced good economic growth and falling poverty, thanks to a dynamic private sector and despite many years of squabbling coalition governments (until very recently). Or, its growth rate could falter due to macroeconomic mismanagement and debt crises, as happened in Brazil (another large country whose economy grew 9.5 percent annually during 1965–1974 before falling to around 3 percent on average in the following 25 years).

China may follow a path similar to that of Taiwan or Korea, countries that grew rapidly under authoritarian governments that developed the institutions of a market economy, including more secure property rights, before holding fair elections and changing governing parties. Some Chinese in the leadership prefer the Singapore model, where one-party rule continues despite economic modernization. China may succeed in "ruling by law" but there is no sign yet of the party submitting to the "rule of law".

The Communist Party is changing rapidly from an ideological vanguard to a broad tent that encompasses old and emerging elites, looking more like its civil war opponent the Kuomintang in its composition and outlook. However, its continued intolerance of any organized opposition or civic groups may foreclose the option of following the example of Taiwan or Korea, where opposition parties were allowed to grow and provide a viable alternative to the ruling party. A closed political system may show beneficial results by helping to focus China's leadership on economic growth but may not always be the best long-term practice. The lack of a viable alternative could raise the risk of eventual political disruption, potentially resulting in a serious economic setback.

India is a politically open society that is slowly embracing the market economy. China is a politically closed society moving from a semi-market to a market economy. China may achieve first-world status before India but it will have to avoid a political hard landing.

Note

Some of the material in this essay originally appeared in Standard & Poor's Credit Week and is reproduced with permission of Standard & Poor's, a division of The McGraw-Hill Companies, Inc.

References

International Monetary Fund (2004). China's Growth and Integration into the World Economy: Prospects and Challenges. Occasional Paper 232.

United Nations Development Programme (2003). "Human Development Report 2003."

Weng, Tao (2003). China: Economic Performance and Policy Challenges. IMF Conference on India and China, November. 23, New Delhi.

World Bank (2003). India: Sustaining Reform, Reducing Poverty.

World Bank (2004). Sustaining India's Services Revolution—Access to Foreign Markets, Domestic Reform and International Negotiations.

5

Chasing China: Can India Bridge the Gap?

Subramanian Swamy

I

In the 1960s and 1970s, Indians were told how much better the Chinese authoritarian system was doing than India. There was no poverty, inflation, or unemployment in China. China was growing at 8 percent per year while India was stuck with the Hindu rate of 3.5 percent. This was because we were not socialist the way China was.

Then, in 1980, came the Deng Xiaoping revolution in China and the first accurate information about that period. India and China over the three decades of 1950–1980 had actually grown at the same rate of 3.5 percent, and their per capita incomes in 1980 were about the same. There had been a terrible food shortage in China during 1959–1961 due to commune formation, and about 30 million people had died. No such thing had happened in India. We had democracy, and China did not. China had labor camps to which intellectuals with wrong ideas were sent to dig ditches. India did not.

Nonetheless, the advice to emulate China continued. China was doing well because of Deng's reforms. Indian ministers came back from short tours to China all too easily impressed. They have steadily proclaimed that China has outperformed India since 1980. Again, there is a need to study this question in depth to sort out claims from counterclaims.

Three questions will be asked to put the China–India comparison into perspective: First, did the two countries begin from the same initial conditions? Second, does there exist today a significant measurable gap between the two? If so, to what should that gap be attributed? Third, is this gap bridgeable within a short period? If so, what policies will rapidly close the gap? That third question has profound consequences for the future of the global economic system. If China and India both rise rapidly, it will redefine the global economy.

The conclusion reached is that while India may have had a lead over China at the time of their independence, that lead was lost in the pre-reform period to 1980 mainly due to faster population growth. In the reform era since then, the comparison is a mixed story, but China has grown faster due to higher investment and more openness. The future will be decided by which country undertakes necessary structural reforms, which in China must include political reforms.

II

Many similarities existed when India achieved independence in 1947 and the Communists assumed power in China in 1949. Each had already made modest beginnings toward industrialization. Modern factories in both were devoted to "light" consumer goods, particularly textiles. A large percentage of industrial production was still from cottage and handicraft industries, with little "heavy" industry. The Japanese development of heavy industry in Manchuria had not become integrated with the Chinese economy. Much of the equipment was removed by the Russians during their postwar occupation of Manchuria. In 1952, therefore, neither country had made much progress in advanced industry.

The relative position of China and India is reflected in appendix table 5.6. In 1952, China was ahead in agriculture. Back in 1870, China and India were on par. In 1952, India, however, was ahead in industry and transportation. Overall, India's per capita income measured in PPP dollars in 1952 was about 54 percent higher than China's.

Because Indian agriculture was a shambles, India should have paid more attention to agriculture. It was a monumental error for India to have pushed for industrialization in a command socialist model without first having laid the foundation for agricultural progress. India learned this lesson the hard way in the mid-1960s, when a drought led to near famine conditions. China learned in an even harder way. The irrationality of Mao's Great Leap Forward policies caused over 30 million deaths during 1959–1962. In both countries, this led to a change in agricultural strategy, but more in China than in India.

Even more than a decade after economic reforms began in India post–1991, agriculture remains an albatross employing over 65 percent of the labor force mostly in low value production. China, on the other hand, created an agricultural boom during 1980–1985 and then followed it up by an industrial expansion that has absorbed much of the labor released from the dismantled collectivist system.

During 1952–1980, in the command economy era before reform, although China outstripped India in physical outputs of 19 key industrial commodities, the two Asian giant countries grew at about the same GDP rate, about 4 percent per year. The Chinese and Indian per capita incomes in 1980 were approximately equal. Lower population growth in China wiped out the 54 percent difference in per capita income levels in India's favor in 1950.

In 1952, China's population was 57 percent higher than India's. In the 1990s, it was just 28 percent higher. At present, China's population is growing at less than 1.0 percent per year while India's population is expanding at 1.8 percent per year. At these rates, India will overtake China in population by 2025.

China initiated economic reforms a decade earlier than India. As a consequence, China grew at double the rate of India during the 1980s. Since 1992, there has, however, been a slowdown in Chinese growth. Since 1991 there has been acceleration in growth in India. On corrected data, the average difference in growth per capita of China and India, at the turn of the millennium, is marginal, equal to the difference in population growth rates of the two countries. The head start that China had in economic growth in the 1980s put China significantly ahead.

III

China's 1980s reform growth led to significant advances for China over India in areas like health, technology, and income (see appendix table 5.7).

The comparative India–China growth rates are given in table 5.1. A comparative international perspective of China's and India's growth rate is in table 5.2. Although we do not share the alarmist view that the Chinese authorities cook their statistical books, nevertheless, officially released data require reworking to bring them into conformity with international practice. Some reworking of Indian data is also essential. Correcting Chinese data leads to a lowering of its growth

Table 5.1 Growth rates in GDP of China and India (1980–2004) (corrected data)

	Percent per year		
Period	*China (1)*	*India (2)*	*Ratio: (1)/(2)*
1980–1992	8.4 (1.4)	5.8 (2.0)	1.4 (0.7)
1992–2004	7.1 (1.0)	6.7 (1.8)	1.1 (0.6)
1980–2004	7.6 (1.3)	6.3 (2.0)	1.2 (0.7)

Note: The growth rates were calculated on compound rates basis using the three year moving average centered. Figures in brackets are those of annual average population growth rate. We have in making the corrections followed the methodology outlined in Samuelson and Swamy (1974) and Swamy (1984). Raw data for 2001–2004 are from IMF Article IV documents and my corrections are tentative.

Source: Swamy (2003), p. 47 and IMF (imf.org; country reports).

Table 5.2 Selected countries: growth performance (average, in percent per annum)

	Real GDP growth 1992–2004	*Per capita GDP growth 1992–2004*
India	6.7	4.9
China*	7.1	6.1
Asian developing countries**	4.2	2.4
ASEAN-4**	3.8	2.1
All developing countries**	5.4	3.8

* Corrected in this study.

** 1992–2000.

Source: World Economic Outlook (WEO) 2002 database.

rate estimate, increased inequality, reduced Foreign Direct Investment (FDI) inflows, and a less impressive export performance.

Because of its earlier reforms, China spurted ahead and has kept its lead intact. China is ahead of India, in PPP-based corrected income per capita by 44 percent. However, India has, since its reform effort began in 1992, halted the widening of the gap. The post–1992 leveling in growth rates has implications for development theory. India has achieved this high growth while maintaining a vibrant democracy. Treating democracy as an obstacle to growth, the East Asian model (which already suffered a blow in 1997, because of the Asian financial crisis that devastated authoritarian Indonesia) stands further devalued by India's performance. Moreover, while China had one major national famine since liberation (in 1959–1961) that caused massive starvation, India suffered no mass famine. Democracy in India made the difference. The social cost of authoritarianism is high. India's performance since 1992 is a deathblow to the proclaimed benefits of authoritarian structures for growth.

How does one explain the continued rapid growth of these two giant nations? For China, there are three main factors: (1) A sharp rise in the rate of investment, fueled first by rising incomes in the rural sector following decollectivization of agriculture, and later by a fivefold rise in FDI; (2) Galloping exports from $20 billion in 1980 to $200 billion in 1999, which introduced new technology and modernization of the industrial system; (3) A supporting diaspora providing two-thirds of China's FDI and reallocating industries, offering China access to finance and marketing know-how. Still, deficit financing and bank-financed credit expansion in a soft budget constraint framework have bolstered demand since 1993. This reckless expansion of credit cannot be sustained.

In India, the 1980s spurt in growth from 3.5 percent to 5.8 percent per year was primarily due to (1) external commercial loan-financed imports; (2) bank credit-pushed public investment that built industrial capacity; and (3) the rise in exports of textiles, gems, and chemicals. This growth came at a heavy cost. Accumulated short-term debt caused a balance of payments crisis in 1990–1991. Following deregulating reforms, by utilizing the excess capacities built in the 1980s, industrial production rose and so did the service sector (now nearly 50 percent of GDP). By the twenty-first century, the Indian economy grew at an impressive rate, nearly 7 percent. But the hard reforms were not implemented. As a result, industrial growth slumped and the scandal ridden financial system milked by crony capitalism and ill-served by poor supervision was on the verge of a crisis. In China too, reform of the bank fund-guzzling State Owned Enterprises (SOEs) and the financial system is over due.

In the 1980s and 1990s, both countries reduced population growth. China's annual population growth rate fell from 1.9 percent in 1960 to 1992 to 1 percent from 1992 to 2000, while India's fell from 2.2 percent to 1.8 percent. China has achieved this by drastic authoritarian steps, while India has achieved reduction with no coercion. A pure economic calculus has no way to measure how life is enhanced for Indians by freedom from authoritarian coercion on the most intimate of matters.

Faster growth in China was also made possible by much higher investment, which averaged from 35 percent to 40 percent of GDP in the 1980s and 1990s compared to 20 percent to 25 percent in India. Chinese rates of domestic savings and investment are high by international standards. Investment (as a percentage of GDP) rose from 35 percent in 1980 to 40 percent in 1999. Household savings rose from a 2 percent rate in 1978 to 22 percent in 1994, offsetting a decline in government savings during this period. China's rate of growth of GDI during the 1990s was 2.27 times the rate in India. The wide gap between India and China in per capita income (which gap was about zero in 1980) was due more to a greater investment effort than lower population growth.

India cannot close this per capita income gap by 2020 without a much faster GDP growth rate (e.g., 10 percent per year), for which an even greater effort to raise the level of investment (coupled with a greater efficiency in the use of capital) would have to be made. Yet, since 1995, GDI rate has been falling. Increasing consumption enhances the quality of life. But it comes at a cost to growth, unless efficiency in capital use is enhanced to a compensatory extent.

The China–India gap can be closed if India designs its fiscal architecture so investment rises to above 30 percent of GDP from the present 23 percent, and if India reduces the ICOR (incremental capital output ratio) from 4.0 to 3.0. At the same time India has to maintain macroeconomic stability in respect of interest rates, exchange rates, inflation, fiscal policy, and balance of payments.

Although India had a superior infrastructure in 1950, China closed the gap by 1980. It has raced ahead since then (see appendix table 5.8). Indian ports are bottlenecks. The cost of handling cargo at ports is lower in China. Turnaround time at Shanghai is less than two days, while Kandla in India can take eight to nine. A trucker can do a 600-km stretch in China in 10 hours. An Indian transporter will need three times as much. In a retailing world in which it is crucial to make "season," Indian suppliers are notorious in their inability to meet deadlines. Power in India is about two and a half times as expensive as in China. Power supplies in India are also more erratic and subject to staggering theft (40–50 percent T&D losses). Consequently, input costs in manufacturing are about 30 percent less in China. China's efficiency in its use of infrastructure, however, is lower. China's energy input per output is much larger than India's, partly due to the enormous inefficiency of China's state-owned enterprises. China has almost three times India's capacity in electricity generation, but its electricity consumption is four times that of India's. In per capita consumption of electricity, China uses nearly three times as much as India.

In terms of human development, China had a higher ranking in the Human Development Index (HDI) than India. In life expectancy, literacy, and infant mortality, China did better. Landed elites in much of rural India have had the power to grossly underfund health and education for the poor. Yet, since India began to reform, the gap has narrowed. And as Gilley calculates elsewhere in this volume, the overall gains in human development in India from 1975 to 2004 were not that far behind those in China.

Income inequality was much higher in China, where the Gini coefficient measuring the degree of inequality rose from 0.33 in 1979 to 0.46 by 1999. In India, the Gini declined from 0.42 in 1979 to 0.34 by 1999. In China, urban–rural disparities account for more than half of the inequality. The World Bank estimates that urban–rural disparities also explain 75 of the increase in income inequality. With urban incomes rising at 6.4 percent per year, and rural income crawling at 2.1 percent per year in China, intensifying inequality in China is ever worse than India. Also, in regional inequality terms, comparing coast and hinterland, the regional income dispersion is wider in China at 0.25 versus 0.23 in India, although the figure has worsened in both countries since 1980. Comparing China's transition to other formerly Leninist countries shows China's Gini coefficient, a measure of income inequality, substantially higher than eastern Europe.

The size distribution of incomes has widened in China. Unlike India, in China, intra-rural inequality (0.34) measured by an official-based Gini ratio is higher than the level in urban areas (0.28).

High inequality can impede growth, delegitimize reform, and contribute to social tension. Chinese leaders worry that the current growing labor unrest and increasing protests have the potential of spiraling out of control. The increasingly skewed income distribution in China since reforms era signals an unsettling and deep structural transformation in the distribution of assets and the returns on these assets made possible by the unaccountability and non-transparency of an authoritarian regime.

Chinese and Indian levels of inequality fall between egalitarian Denmark (0.25) and polarized Brazil (0.60). According to Xinhua, China's 1999 Gini ratio is 0.46. But the *Economist* (June 26, 2001) quotes economist He Qinglian to place it at 0.60. Economist Thomas Rawski has established that Chinese statistics understate how bad it is for the worst off in the country side. This magnitude of inequality signals a distribution of assets on behalf of the entrenched party far more extreme than even Russia where "oligarchs" seized wealth in the era of privatization. Whereas a more open India was seen as the epitome of poverty, malnutrition, and inequality, in fact, neither India nor China has been successful in addressing the rich–poor gap.

In terms of environmental parameters there is also little to choose between India and China in terms of deforestation, air and water pollution, and carbon emissions. Both countries have experienced environmental degradation in the reform era. The annual deforestation rate in China is slightly higher (0.7 percent) than in India (0.6 percent). Ecological problems are likely to increase in both as they pursue developmental strategies with scant regard for the environment—as did the industrializing countries of western Europe and North America. But the implications for the global environment will be far graver.

IV

Globalization may be defined as the process of relocation, restructuring, and outsourcing of productive economic activity characterized by more cross-border movement of factors of production, knowledge, technology, and services, and by the interaction effects of such movements. The success of Chinese exports is largely due to globalization. India's success in IT software is also due to globalization. With WTO and new communication technologies, globalization is likely to intensify for both.

Globalization has five dimensions: internationalization of production, liberalization of regulations, standardization of weights, measures, and quality, de-territorialization, and homogenization of tastes. It is important to make the process socially tolerable and morally adequate. Unbridled, it could erode community, interpersonal trust, and a family-based acceptance of responsibility for underprivileged relatives that are the hallmarks of Indian and Chinese societies. Successfully dealing with globalization requires skill empowerment to absorb new technologies. How India and China change to seize the opportunities provided by globalization, and how the two manage globalization's volatility will decide winners and losers in the twenty-first century. The key element in globalization is openness.

China has outperformed India because of the greater openness of the Chinese economy. In 1980, trade constituted 13.6 percent of India's GDP as against 12.6 percent for China. But in the reform era, China's external trade grew at a much faster pace; it accounted for 39.8 percent of GDP as against India's 19.3 percent in 2002. Similarly,

Table 5.3 Openness indicators

All figures are 2000, unless otherwise noted	*China*	*India*
Share in world trade flows	3.7	0.7
Exports of goods and services (in % of GDP)	25.9	13.1
Imports of goods and services (in % of GDP)	23.2	16.0
Average tariff rate (China 2001, India 1999)	15.3	32.9
Effective tariff rate (1998)[1]	2.8	23.0
Share of tariff revenue in total government revenue (1998)	6.3	20.1

[1] Tariff revenue/import value.

Sources: Government Finance Statistics; International Financial Statistics; and Fund staff estimates.

in 1980 the share of exports in India's GDP (5 percent) was on par with China's (6 percent). But India's exports recorded a growth of only 7.4 percent per annum as against 13.0 percent per annum for China during 1980–1990, and 14.9 percent for India and 21.2 percent per annum for China during 1991–1999. Over the 20 years, China's export share became six times that of India.

Exports and imports as a share of China's GDP rose from negligible amounts in the 1970s to nearly 25 percent in 2000 (table 5.3). The average tariff rate in China fell from well over 50 percent to about 15 percent, less than half of that in less open India. The collection rate, that is tariff revenue as a percent of import value (effective tariff rate), in fact is less than 3 percent in China. In protectionist India, it is 23 percent. Also, foreign invested enterprises based in China contributed substantially to China's export growth, accounting for 40 percent of exports. In India, it was less than 8 percent of total exports.

The WTO framework requires transparent participatory institutions that promote a stable economic environment and the rule of law. Democratic India has the necessary political structure in place. But India is infected by a fear of what is alien that has hurt its trade and FDI.

China's trade has two components: (1) imports that are processed and reexported and (2) "domestic" or "own" trade, that is, exports of goods primarily originating in the domestic economy, and imports for domestic consumption and production use. The former reflects China's rising role as a labor-intensive processing and assembly center, fueled by outsourcing and external final demand, while the latter is more strongly influenced by domestic economic trends. China's trade surplus is due completely to the positive balance on the processing trade, that is, value added in China before reexporting to final-destination markets, which reached US$40 billion in 2002. China's own domestic trade is increasingly in deficit, with the balance declining from a positive level of nearly US$20 billion in 1998 to a deficit of the same magnitude in 2001 because of rapidly growing domestic imports, a testament to import liberalization, openness.

With the opening of the Chinese economy and the continuing rise of the ASEAN nations, the regional division of labor has changed. Capital goods are now shipped from Japan to Taiwan and Korea, which then send capital-intensive inputs to China and ASEAN for labor-intensive processing and assembly before reexporting to developed markets. Each new link, recorded as surging intra-Asian trade, need not raise the final value of goods exported to end markets outside of Asia.

This means that a good part of China's rapid trade growth is "double-counting." Because China has become a main exporter to the EU, Japan, and America, it appears as though China is grabbing world trade share at a phenomenal pace. Yet, the PRC has recorded an ever-increasing trade deficit with the Asian NICs, reaching US$40 billion in 2001, and an ever-increasing surplus with the United States. Thus, America remains essential to Chinese growth. But if Chinese labor becomes relatively expensive due to rising demand for labor, then the processing trade could shift to other countries such as of those South Asia. Then China's trade surplus with the West would fall below its deficit with East Asia causing a drain on China's foreign currency reserves. If that is not contained, then China could face a crisis.

In contrast, India's foreign trade is not structured on the processing trade. But India's trade suffers from a shackled system of high tariffs and regulations. For India to fully benefit from globalization, its anti-export bias must be eliminated.

During the pre-reform near-autarkic socialist period, neither India nor China encouraged FDI. Since reform, both have welcomed FDI, with China's FDI seemingly ten fold that of India's. But India underestimates its annual FDI massively. Based on the IMF definition, India's FDI rises from $2.32 billion to as much as $8.00 billion. Inflows into China, excluding "round-tripping capital" (i.e., funds sent out of China and brought back via Hong Kong) would only be $20 billion, not the official $40 billion. Indians experience "round-tripping," too, especially via Mauritius, but it is insignificant.

A study by the International Finance Corporation using comparable definitions of FDI finds that FDI constitutes 1.7 percent of India's

GDP, and 2.0 percent for China. Real estate and construction account for 28 percent of FDI in China while in India it is near zero. Until recently FDI in real estate was banned in India. In sum, while China attracts more FDI than India, it is the impact on upgrading technology that is more to India's disadvantage.

The share of takeovers and mergers in FDI varies. China has restricted it to 25 percent. In India, its share in FDI is 40 percent. While greenfield investment implies a wholesale transfer of technology, in the case of takeovers and mergers, it will mean, at most, modernization of existing industrial firms.

China's advantage over India in foreign investment lies in the content (more direct and less portfolio) and the deployment of FDI for development through export earnings. China has done much better. With foreign investment making China a global leader in light manufacturing, it has distanced India in per capita income, power availability, telecom subscribers, bandwidth, and exports, but, most important, in technology upgrading. China requires that firms with foreign participation export a substantial portion of output.

Why then are FDI inflows into India low despite large domestic markets and a low cost labor force? The greater enthusiasm among foreign investors for China suggests Indian underperformance in return and risk and China's lower transaction costs. For India to attract more FDI requires streamlining procedures and developing modern infrastructure. That India has not really tried to compete is shown by how little it does to attract NRI (non-resident Indians) FDI compared to what the PRC has done to court diasporic Chinese. Also, China inherited a locational advantage. Nearly 58 percent of its FDI comes from richer neighbors. India does not have more developed neighboring countries. Non-Hindu Pakistan, Bangladesh, and Burma are India's neighbors, but are all poorer.

Nevertheless, India has great potential to attract FDI. Its educated middle class can provide the demand level to sustain rapid growth. India already has an impressive industrial base and a tradition of private enterprise with 7,000 listed companies. It is accustomed to the rule of law, English is widely used, property rights defined, and financial systems conform to international standards. India's capacity to absorb FDI especially in knowledge-based products can make it an attractive destination for FDI, and could put India ahead of China. Achieving this requires more welcoming conditions in terms of infrastructure and labor laws. India's future therefore rests on its politics and policy choices. The task is clear and attainable.

V

The world is littered with examples of countries that had miraculous spurts of economic growth, only for the "miracle" to fizzle out. Success or failure hinges on the appropriateness of the financial architecture. In both China and India, government control still dominates the financial sector and nonmarket factors shape the sector, guanxi in China, cronyism in India. Both suffer from "soft budget constraints" that severely distort the conditions essential for the efficient allocation of scarce resources. Government banks in both suffer from high ratios of non-performing loans (NPLs), though much less in India. The Chinese banking system is under much greater financial strain and threat of bankruptcy. The four major banks, which account for two-third of the country's financial assets and 90 percent of bank assets, are tied to loss-ridden State Owned Enterprises (SOEs) to which they have a very heavy exposure. Of the four major banks' loan portfolios, 25 percent are nonperforming, according to Chinese government statistics. Independent observes have placed NPLs at 40 percent, with the net worth of the four state banks actually negative. In India, NPLs are about 15 percent, by international norms.

Both claim that their high level of foreign exchange reserves is a firewall against a foreign exchange crisis. China and India have avoided a financial crisis due to macroeconomic fundamentals being sound, and not because the financial architecture is well designed. Unlike others, what China and India have attracted is predominantly FDI rather than short-term portfolio capital. Second, the present value (PV) of foreign debt as a ratio of GDP stood at 14 percent of GDP for China and 16 percent for India, well below a debt level that is risky. More than 82 percent of China's foreign debt outstanding is long-term, in sharp contrast to Thailand, Indonesia, and Korea in 1997. Also, the two nations pursue relatively closed capital account policies that offer a firewall protecting the currency from speculative attacks. Finally, the biggest difference lies in current account positions. Between 1993 and 1997 China turned a current account deficit to a surplus while India reduced hers, whereas other Asian countries incurred high levels of imbalances. China and India also steadily built up their foreign exchange reserves.

While many analysts conclude that China is the next "bubble" waiting to burst, the fundamentals of both China and India for averting a 1997 type Asian meltdown are actually strong. They, however, could weaken if financial reforms are not continued.

VI

Computer-enabled new techniques, information technologies have the potential to become a major source of accelerating growth and raised productivity. For China and India, IT can (1) cut transaction and inventory costs; (2) increase employment through backward and forward linkages; (3) accelerate growth through a rise in factor productivity.

India has achievements in IT software, China is ahead in hardware. India scores in quality. Of the Fortune 500, 185 outsourced to India. Of the 23 software companies with SEI-CMMS Certification, 16 are Indian. Of the startups in Silicon Valley, 40 percent had Indian partners. Because of Indian quality, GE and Google set up R&D centers in Bangalore, India, to benefit from low-cost world-class Indian engineers and scientists. Fluency in the English language and excellent institutes of technology make Indian software engineers world class. Hence, in IT-enabled services and outsourcing, India may long retain its advantage. India hopes for $87 billion in gross sales by 2008. IT would then constitute 7.8 percent of GDP, as high as the United States in 2003. China lags behind India on most counts of software development, as tables 5.4 and 5.5 show.

China is already ranked third in IT hardware supply to the world. A lower cost physical and telecom infrastructure gives China a competitive edge. Turnover in the Chinese computer industry is around $50 billion and rising rapidly.

In the five years after 1996, the number of main telephone lines in India and China rose from about 12 million and 57 million respectively to around 34 million and 164 million lines respectively in 2001. In mobile phones, China has around 165 million units while India has

Table 5.4 Information technology capacity: India and China (2002)

	India	*China*
PC Population (million)	6.5	16.3
Internet users (million)	9.8	30
Fixed line phones (million)	32	189
Cellular phones (million)	6	165
C&S households (million)	37	75
International bandwidth (Gbps)	1.5	50

Source: Nasscom, Morgan Stanley, CLSA, China Telecom, *Business Week*, October 21, 2002.

Table 5.5 Software industry: India and China (2002)

	India	*China*
Software exports	$6.2 billion (+37.78%)	$0.85 billion (+112.5%)
Software exports as a % of total exports	14.17%	0.37%
2005 software exports growth target	$20.42 billion	$15 billion
IT professionals graduating each year	73,218	50,000
Current IT professionals	522,000	150,000
Demand for IT professionals	400,000	350,000
Number of software companies	3,000+	6,000+
Domestic software sales	$2.06 billion (+31%)	$4.3 billion (+55%)

Note: Percentage increase/decrease figures in brackets are for a one-year period.

only 6 million. China hopes to reach 400 million mobile phone users by 2006, 800 million by 2010. China, by outsourcing to Taiwan, Korea, and Singapore, has outstripped India in IT hardware. India's target for 2010 is only 50 million mobile phones, but recent deregulation of the Telecom Sector in India has raised hopes of a sharp acceleration, and possible closing of the gap with China.

The IT sector's growth in India has been driven largely by the private sector. Government support in terms of IT infrastructure investments, duty-free access to hardware for software exporters and hitherto zero taxation of export profits has helped. In China, in contrast, the share of government-owned IT enterprise spending is over 80 percent.

India's software thrust, based on cheap skilled labor is akin to earlier waves of Indian migration by doctors, nurses, and blue-collar workers. The "net foreign exchange remittances" to India from migration of the old kind, is in the range of $10–12 billion. The gross foreign exchange revenue from software exports at the outset of the new millennia is just around $8 billion.

The Chinese government fosters telecom infrastructure and power grids. Chinese telecom facilities are at least 10 years ahead of India. Chinese engineers are at least at a par with Indian engineers. And the Chinese government is promoting English language learning. Expatriate Chinese in the United States are heading back to China as entrepreneurs. India's English fluency alone will not protect it from competition.

Aiming at the high end of IT manufacturing, Beijing University patented China's first 32-bit and 16-bit microprocessors, and the General Research Institute of Non-Ferrous Metals has developed an 8-inch mono-crystalline silicone chip. Copying America, China is deploying abundant R&D funds to its universities to create high-end technical manpower. China has already proved its economic and technological capacities through the success of indigenous telecom giant Huawei Technologies, which has established offices in India sensing the opportunity to develop India's telecom infrastructure.

India and China could work together in IT because China is a front-runner in hardware and India in software. But the two nations are still behind in R&D. To complete the hardware–software–R&D "triangle," Israel would be an ideal choice. Otherwise, there will remain an "IT innovation deficit."

VII

Economic progress in China and India has falsified prophecies of doom. Both have fed huge populations and earned enough to buy inputs for continuous economic upgrading. In GDP (PPP$ terms), China is today the second largest nation (after the United States) and India is fourth (after Japan).

Prospects for China and India as economic superpowers collide with obstacles to new reform. These problems include poverty, inequalities, and the financial sector. The two are also shackled by structural weaknesses including banking systems saddled with NPLs, fiscal deficits crowding out private investment, pervasive corruption, and bloated and difficult-to-reform "public" or SOE sectors. Nevertheless, most signs are positive: sustained high growth, adequate food, foreign reserves and a rising HDI. China and India have become front-runners in cutting-edge technologies: IT, mass communications, biotechnology, pharmaceuticals, and nuclear and space sciences. The two have a vast pool of scientific personnel and technologists with proven capacity for original research.

Because China recognized that the export of labor-intensive manufacture could stimulate growth through technological upgrading, it has outperformed India, which faces major competitive disadvantages. Privately owned Chinese companies and foreign invested or owned companies can hire and fire workers at will, while firms in India are restricted by socialist-era laws and unions that contest layoffs in protracted litigation. In the pre-reform era, companies added to their workforce to appease politicians and secure their patronage. The Chinese face this problem in SOEs. While Indian wage rates are generally lower, productivity is higher in China. China also has the advantage that it shifted a considerable proportion of labor out of low value agriculture to industry, building up a rural industrial base with higher labor-intensive exports.

The Chinese government has decentralized, permitting regional decision-making, whereas, in India, the center's regulation nightmare continues, facilitating much greater local FDI for China. Deregulation of the non-state industrial sector, reform of labor and land laws, and entry and exit policy for firms have also gone further in China. And China's special economic zones (SEZs) were far more successful in promoting trade and attracting FDI than India's due to welcoming neighboring diasporic Chinese and from India's failure in building infrastructure.

Lastly, money is far more expensive in India. China has kept the prime lending rate (PLR) at a relatively low 8 percent and the interest rate spread between lending and deposit rates confined to 2.6 percent. In India, the PLR has been not less than 12 percent since the 1980s while the interest rate spread is 3.4. China's money management is more conducive to domestic investment. Even though Indian stock markets were established much before China's, in market capitalization China is ahead at $231.3 billion, 2.20 times that of India's. Marginal tax rate on corporate incomes is at a maximum of 30 percent in China; in India it is 40 percent. Even in fiscal decentralization, Beijing transfers 51.4 percent of tax revenue to the provinces; in Delhi it is 36.1.

The wide gap between India and China in per capita incomes since 1980 was due to greater investment and openness. India cannot close this gap without investment, and adapting to the needs of globalization, which require "second generation" reforms.

Yet Chinese growth must slow. Neither export nor investment growth can be sustained. And China too needs a second generation of financial reforms (see chart 5.1) But in authoritarian China such reforms could weaken the Chinese Communist Party's control. Hence some see a major upheaval coming either from failed reforms leading to a financial crisis as in East Asia in 1997, or successful reforms that facilitate a political upheaval. The risks of globalization amplify when the financial sector is weak and the economy liberalizes, as shown by the 2001 meltdown in Argentina.

Hence, if India deepens its reforms, the gap with China could be quickly bridged. But can India's political leadership shift from divisive internal politics to meet the hard challenge of globalization? If both India and China deepen reform, both could grow much faster. This would return the global order to the balance of the late eighteenth century when China and India were the top two world economies. Politics will decide.

Chart 5.1 Four scenarios

		CHINA	
		Financial & Political Reforms	*Status Quo*
I N D I A	*Second generation reforms and secular polity*	India & China grow together and become developed countries.	India overtakes China
	Status Quo	China widen gap in performance with India	The bubble bursts. China and India in quagmire

Appendix: Additional Data Tables

Table 5.6 Key economic indicators: China and India (1950)

Indicators	*Unit*	*Year*	*China*	*India*	*Ratio*
1. Per capita GDP	1970$	1952	101	154	0.66
2. Population	millions	1952	574.8	367.0	1.57
3. Birth rates	per 000	1950	37.0	40.0	0.93
4. Death rates	per 000	1950	18.0	28.0	0.64
5. Life expectancy	years	1950	40.0	32.0	1.25
6. Infant mortality	per 000	1950	175.5	190.0	0.92
7. Adult illiteracy	percent	1950	25.0	20.0	1.25
8. Calories	per capita	1952	1917.0	1540.0	1.24
9. Foodgrains	million tons	1952	163.9	69.9	2.35
10. Yield	tons/ha	1931–1937			
	Rice		2.5	1.3	1.90
	Wheat		1.0	0.6	1.56
11. Sugar	tons	1952	0.5	1.8	0.25
12. Irrigation	percent	1949	20.7	14.6	1.42
13. Cropping	Index	1949	20.7	14.6	1.42

Continued

Table 5.6 Continued

Indicators	*Unit*	*Year*	*China*	*India*	*Ratio*
14. Ammonium Sulphate	000 tons	1951	129.0	53.7	2.40
15. Cotton textiles	million spindles	1956	7.2	12.4	0.58
16. Coal	million tons	1952	66.0	39.3	1.68
17. Electric power	billion kW h	1952	7.3	6.1	1.20
18. Crude oil	million tons	1952	0.4	0.4	1.01
19. Cement	million tons	1952	2.9	4.1	0.71
20. Railways	00 kms	1950	25.7	54.8	0.47
21. Highways	000 kms	1949	130.2	391.8	0.33
22. Literacy	percent	1951	14.3	16.7	0.86
23. Students enrolled in higher education	(000s)	1954	253.0	594.1	0.43
24. College graduates percentage in technologies subjects	%	1954	31.4	17.8	

Source: Swamy (2003), p. 7.

Table 5.7 Selected ratios in China and India comparisons (2000)

	China (1)	*India (2)*	*Ratio: (1)/(2)*
1. Land area (million sq. km)	9.33	2.97	3.14
2. Arable land (% of land)	10.00	56.00	0.56
3. Irrigated area (1000 sq. km)	498.72	480.00	1.04
4. Population (billions)	1.26	1.01	1.24
5. Birth rate (per 1000)	16.12	24.79	0.65
6. Death rate (per 1000)	6.73	8.88	0.76
7. Infant mortality (per 1000 births)	28.92	64.90	0.45
8. Life expectancy (at birth, years)	71.40	62.50	1.14
9. Literacy (Age 15 & over)	81.50	52.00	1.57
10. Railways (1000 kms track)	65.65	62.92	1.04
11. Highways (million kms)	1.21	3.32	0.36
12. Mobile phones (million)	23.40	1.90	12.32
13. Televisions (million)	400.00	63.00	6.35
14. Internet service	3.00	3.00	1.00
15. Electricity (trillion kW h)	1.16	0.45	2.58
16. Exports (US$ billion)	194.90	36.30	5.37
17. External debt (US$ billion)	159.00	98.00	1.62
18. GDP (PPP$ trillion)*	3.86	2.15	1.80
19. Poverty (% below PPP$/day)	16.00	35.00	0.46
20. Per capita income ($)*	3063.00	2129.00	1.44

* Corrected data *World Development Indicators*, 2001, The World Bank, Washington D.C. for 1999 projected to 2000.

Table 5.8 Infrastructure in China and India (1999)

		India	*China*
Electricity			
Electricity generating capacity	1000 MW	89.17	258.00
Electricity generation	billion kW h	417.00	1166.00
Transmission and distribution losses	billion kW h	91.11	79.09
T&D loss in total output	%	23.40	6.80
Electricity consumption	billion kW h	280.00	1080.00
Per capita consumption	kw h	350.00	1000.00
Cost comparison*			
Electricity tariff	$/100 kW h	7.53	4.30
Diesel	$/MT	356.00	298.90
Port			
Freight handled	million MT	251.73	922.37
Number of major ports	nos.	12	17
Railways			
Route	kms	62,809	57,566
Double track route	%	24.80	33.10
Route electrified	%	21.90	20.90
Freight handled	million MT	420.92	1697.30
Freight km	billion MT km	282	1309.70
Freight to total traffic	%	32.70	34.20

* At official exchange rate.

Sources: China:- *Statistical Year Book* (2000), National Bureau of Statistics, Beijing.
India:- *Infrastructure Report* (Oxford University Press), 2000.

References

Sachs, Jeffrey et al. (1997). Economic Reforms in China and India: Selected Issues in Industrial Policy. Harvard Institute for International Development, Discussion Paper, No. 580.

Samuelson, Paul A. and Subramanian Swamy (1974). "Invariant Economic Index Numbers and Canonical Duality." *The American Economic Review* LXIV (4): 566–593.

Swamy, Subramanian (1984). "Samuelson's Analytical Notes on International Real Income Measures." *The Economic Journal* 94: 265–266.

Swamy, Subramanian (2003). *Economic Reforms and Performance: China and India in Comparative Perspective*. Delhi: Konark Publishers.

Zhang, Z., Liu, A., and Yao, S. (2001). "Convergence of China's Regional Incomes 1952–97." *China Economic Review* 12(2/3): 243–258.

6

India's Reform Strengths

James Manor

I

Why does China receive so much more international attention than India? China is the world's most populous nation, but the gap is shrinking. For a long time, China's economy was growing much faster than India's, but that gap too has closed substantially. In recent years, China has received vastly more foreign direct investment (FDI) than India, but India does almost as well with nonethnic Chinese investors. Indian imports still lag behind China's, but have begun to increase as China's did after the first few years of its economic reforms. While China struggles with political liberalization and decentralization, India has long had a resilient democracy, a federal system and—since 1993—a somewhat more decentralized political system. This chapter explains why India was taken less seriously by the outside world and why that situation has begun to change.

Some realists might say that India began to be taken more seriously after it tested nuclear weapons in 1998. But that is only a small part of the story. Goldman Sachs finds that by mid-century, not only will India be a formidable force in world affairs but it will also be one of the world's three largest economies, behind the United States and China. It has become both an attractive place to invest and a huge future market. Its services industries have taken off. A boom is on in outsourcing and information technology. There are now 20,000 more techies at work in Bangalore alone than in Silicon Valley.

There was also a delay in taking China's prospects seriously after it started to reform. It took years of sustained changes before the outside world appreciated what was happening in China. Hyperbole turned to horror following the June 1989 Beijing massacre of activists in a democracy movement headquartered in Tiananmen Square and the collapse of European communism in 1989–1991. But foreigners' enthusiasm soon returned. India's reforms, more gradual and limited than China's, have been maintained only since 1991. India's economy was hardly wounded by the 1997–1998 Asian financial crisis. India had been cautious about opening financially because of the dangers that global forces represent. Since the Asian financial crisis, growth rates to the east of India have again picked up, but India still competes respectably with even the best of Asian tiger economies. Sustained growth rates of around 7 percent now seem achievable.

Cynics held that India's rambunctious political system would stifle growth. But five general elections since the reforms began have produced little retreat. When these trends persist, the outside world's still somewhat guarded interest in India and its economy is likely to grow. India already has a working democracy and well-tested federal structures for governing the decentralized system necessary in large market economies. China's decentralization, discussed here in the chapter by Sinha, is not as institutionalized. Some Indian states have developed impressive experiments with democratic decentralization to lower levels that deepen democracy and foster creative synergy with civil society (Manor 2002). The state governments in India's federal system have often taken the lead in economic reform, something the World Bank's strategy for the country has recognized. India has a well-established system of law—not least commercial and contract law—and (albeit slow-moving) judicial institutions. Unlike China, India does not make irredentist claims on its neighbors' territory and it is far more transparent about military matters. As a result, India has better prospects of moving smoothly toward greater interdependence with the outside world than China. But all of these hopes depend on sustaining economic reform and managing the ensuing political challenges.

II

India's economic reforms began in mid-1991, at the time of a severe financial crisis. But the crisis did not require the reforms to go as far as they have. Prime Minister P. V. Narasimha Rao and Finance Minister

Manmohan Singh—who returned as prime minister in 2004—saw an opportunity to introduce a new development strategy and resolved to pursue it much further than their immediate problems demanded, or than their previous careers had led people to expect. Narasimha Rao had long been associated with Congress Party governments that had mainly pursued state-led approaches. Singh had served on India's Planning Commission and later with the South Commission (the developing world's response to the Brandt Commission of the early 1980s), which certainly had not prescribed the reforms he espoused after 1991.

It is important, however, not to exaggerate the extent of the recent reforms. Economic liberalization has, by Indian standards, gone quite far. But by comparison with the prescriptions of neoliberal economists or with the "big bang" approach that was adopted in Poland, Indian reforms are quite cautious and limited. They visibly slowed once the BJP-led coalition took power in 1998, and they remained slow after it achieved a working majority at the election of 1999. Indian officials were responding pragmatically to a sense of looming bankruptcy. As a consequence, the liberalization of certain sectors of the economy was matched by continuing subsidies on a vast array of goods, which are now recognized as a serious problem by leaders of most Indian parties. Wasteful subsidies have left governments without the money required for badly needed infrastructure, education, or basic health. The modest receipts from India's very cautious program of privatization (or, more often, partial disinvestment of shares in state companies) were often used to fund subsidies, not to increase efficiency. India's leaders, unlike China's, have never trumpeted slogans such as "to get rich is glorious." The result has been very gradual, still somewhat limited—and some would say hobbled—economic reform.[1]

Nevertheless, major progress has been made in industrial deregulation, in removing impediments to domestic and foreign private investment, in liberalizing trade, in reforming the exchange-rate system, and in promoting partnerships between private firms (Indian and foreign) and Indian state-owned enterprises in certain key sectors. Savings rates are up, as is the ratio of exports to gross domestic product (GDP). But successive governments—under the Congress Party (1991–1996), the United Front (1996–1998), and especially the BJP-led coalition (1998–2004) held back from politically tough decisions that not only neoliberals, but also social democrats, who are less enchanted with market forces, have urged upon them. This has happened, for example, with reductions in subsidies in various sectors and in policy toward loss-making public enterprises.

Narasimha Rao—who, despite his quiet manner, always maintained the upper hand in economic policy-making—understood and refused to accept all-out pro-market approaches. In early 1992, he stated flatly that "I do not believe in trickle down economics."[2] His hero was not Margaret Thatcher, but Willy Brandt. Like a European social democrat, he wanted to open space for market forces to generate wealth, not in order to discard the welfare state, but to sustain it. He knew the market would not provide primary education, health care, or safety nets for the poor. Narasimha Rao sought to reduce the state's often costly role in areas where the private sector could perform more effectively so as to be able to use government revenues (which, amid growth, might increase) in spheres where only the state could be effective.[3]

Narasimha Rao and Singh orchestrated the reforms brilliantly. Changes were almost always modest, occurring one at a time. The reforms unfolded gradually, but relentlessly—at least until late 1994, when spending was increased to court popularity before the parliamentary election in mid-1996. One interest group would be faced with an unwelcome new policy, but then it would be left alone for a considerable time (often with a few political concessions to ease the discomfort of liberalization) while the reformers made changes that affected other interests. This partly explains why opponents of reform could never mount major public demonstrations against liberalization.

The other part of the explanation for the reforms' political sustainability in the crucial first half-decade after 1991 lies in Narasimha Rao's reluctance—indeed, his intense aversion—to policies that would severely injure any major interest. In China, self-serving reforms by unaccountable rulers caused far more pain and suffering to powerless victims. Several prominent economists urged Rao to begin extracting the government from its commitments to loss-making public enterprises, to develop an "exit policy." They argued that public-sector workers who would lose their jobs were few in number and constituted a cosseted labor aristocracy. The sell-off would liberate massive resources that could be used to cut the budget deficit, build infrastructure, or assist the nonunionized poor who greatly outnumbered organized workers (Dhar 1987).

These arguments all have substance, but the prime minister steadfastly refused to act, for three reasons. First, he staunchly opposed confrontational actions of any sort, although this created trouble when Hindu extremists took advantage of his hesitancy and destroyed the Babri Masjid (mosque) at Ayodhya in December 1992. But Narasimha Rao, in the 1980s, had been so appalled by the dire consequences of the Indian government's confrontational actions in Punjab and Kashmir with religious minorities that he was determined not to outrage any major interest group. Unionized workers had the ability to mount disruptive agitations across urban India. Second, he was acutely aware that organized labor formed an important force within his own party. Finally, as he told the World Economic Forum in Davos in early 1993, he did not have the moral right to throw large numbers of people out of work. However unfamiliar Chinese might be with hearing their prime ministers discuss the moral limits on their power, Rao's statements must be taken seriously. They are genuine.[4]

His reluctance to cause pain to any major interest, and the hesitant approaches of his successors, have meant that relatively few Indians have experienced severe suffering as a result of liberalization. This has been a matter of heated debate in, for example, the pages of the major Indian journal, *The Economic and Political Weekly*. But since 2002, those debates have subsided in the face of evidence that growth has reduced the number of people living in poverty. India has witnessed nothing comparable to the destruction of the livelihoods of perhaps 100 million Chinese peasants, the result of Beijing's economic reforms since 1979. Rao's reluctance, and his successors' even greater restraint, largely explains why India's reforms have been cautious, limited, *and* politically sustainable (Manor 1994).

Analysis of economic liberalization suggests that it is essential for reformers to create a constituency in favor of change. Narasimha Rao's view of this challenge was rather diffident. He never sought to "sell" reform (until desultory attempts during state elections in 1995), even among his party colleagues in the supposedly crucial early years. In 1993, only one of the cabinet ministers from the prime minister's own party in the state of Karnataka had the remotest idea of what the central government was up to, a minister who had studied economics at Cambridge. Rao's way worked. By late 1994, most chief ministers in India's states had concluded that liberalization was not a bad idea because it offered clear benefits within a very limited but crucially important sphere. It made foreign investment possible in key infrastructural sectors—road-building, telecommunications, port facilities, and, above all, electricity generation. It offered hope of reducing the hugely unpopular power cuts—ask the farmers who have to sit up all night next to their pump, waiting for the power to come on—which were a crippling drag on economic development and their governments' popularity. Without foreign investment, little could be accomplished.

To bring electricity supply into line with rising demand over the next few years will require an investment equal to India's entire public-sector outlay under the current five-year plan.

Since every major party in India governed at least one state in the early-to-mid-1990s, the backing from chief ministers ensured that an important voice in every major party favored economic reform—up to a point. In India's federal system, this process ensured a wider base for reform and offered the prospect that, even if support for reform might falter in Delhi, there would be supporters in the regions. When growth and reform wavered, states, particularly on the coast, experimented with foreign investment. Orissa and Andhra Pradesh pioneered privatization in the power sector. Maharashtra invited P&O to set up a billion-dollar port, thereby undermining obstructionist officials at the federal level and conservative workers in the state. In a democratic and federal system, this complex process of creating regional stakeholders in reform seemed necessary and even useful.[5]

Narasimha Rao's caution indicates the type of consensus that exists in favor of economic reform among India's political elite, which is not yet matched by a popular consensus.[6] The elite consensus is not based on a conversion of leaders to a free-market strategy. Only one senior politician in any party in the subcontinent today can be regarded as a committed free marketeer, the finance minister during the late 1990s, P. Chidambaram, who became finance minister again in 2004. The elite consensus is pragmatic and has a very limited range of concerns, mainly regarding infrastructural constraints. This may not inspire the people at the Harvard Business School who taught Chidambaram, but it provides a reasonably firm foundation for sustaining liberalization. Pragmatism outweighs ideology in India's politics.

If high growth rates continue, a broader constituency in favor of reform is likely to develop, even if slowly. The existing elite consensus—which at a minimum supports most reforms that have occurred thus far and at least a few further steps—is strong enough to make an outright policy reversal extremely unlikely. (The failure in most states to bring power generation projects to fruition provides a further spur to change.) The main threat to liberalization is not a U-turn, but fiscal indiscipline—budget deficits that result from overspending by ministers. India's overall fiscal deficit (of state and national governments combined) is very high, around 10 percent of GDP in 1992, but should decline. Thus far, however, this has not become a severe problem. The national government's pressure on states to curb their deficits has produced greater results than its efforts to curb its own deficit. This has bred a degree of complacency, although sizeable deficits keep the cost of borrowing high and handicap India's private sector.

The elite consensus extends to most leaders in India's two main communist parties, the Communist Party of India and the Communist Party of India (Marxist), and also in the Hindu-nationalist BJP. One of the subcontinent's most distinguished and market-friendly journalists, Swaminathan Aiyar, said before the 1996 general election that the best possible change for liberalization would be the elevation of communist leader Jyoti Basu to the post of prime minister, something that nearly happened.[7] He said this because, when Basu sustained economic reform, it would become evident that the changes would stay. Most senior communists oppose certain changes—a rise in petroleum product prices, privatization and labor flexibility—that would affect the poor. But they are not inclined to roll back the reforms. In 2004, they began to govern in a coalition with less left-wing parties.

Thus, the democratic process in India matters enormously when we consider the kind of policy-making that affects economic performance. India's economic reforms since 1991 have been consistently cautious and incremental—because politicians have hesitated to take actions that would injure interest groups with numerical strength or economic power. This has meant that many reforms have occurred piecemeal or—in the case of action to reduce vast subsidies and the dangerously large fiscal deficit—not at all. This has produced two main results, each of which offers contrasts to China. Indian growth has been slower than China's, and the ensuing social dislocation in India has been far less severe than that in China.

This bears upon the question of whether India will "catch up" to China in terms of economic growth. On present trends, the answer appears to be a firm "no"—especially because India's swollen and unaddressed fiscal deficit will continue to be a drag on growth. The only way that it might "catch up" is if China loses its huge gamble that it can cope—through a combination of growth and coercion—with the massive social dislocation that is occurring. Because democratic compulsions have made Indian leaders so cautious, it has taken no such gamble. Economic reform in India has produced social dislocation, but on a puny scale by Chinese standards. It jeopardizes neither the stability of the political order nor economic reform policies.

India's most thoughtful social scientists argue that slower growth is a price well worth paying if it implies far more limited social dislocation than China faces. They do not want the sort of society that is emerging in China—with vast numbers of people leaving the land in the sometimes vain hope of better lives in the great cities, and with new, yawning inequalities. Nor do they want to see the Indian state exercising the kind of aggressive political control that they believe is necessary to cope with the social tensions that arise when any country allows (or encourages) massive social dislocation to occur. For them it is quite enough that India should be growing faster than almost every country on earth except China. Their concern, and the concern of India's more judicious leaders, is not with the counterexample of China but with the sociopolitical health of India. For them, social and political conditions matter at least as much as the economy.

China and India thus present other less developed countries with two alternative models. Many of those countries may prefer the Chinese approach—and they are being pushed in that direction by international aid agencies, which share the excessively economistic preoccupations of the Chinese. But they may find that for them, that model does not work—because they have no overseas Chinese to pour in huge amounts for FDI, and because they do not possess the kind of efficient coercive apparatus that in China has kept the lid on the social tensions and conflict, which growth has spawned.

India's hesitant, ambiguous, sometimes halting approach lacks the clarity of China's, and offers slower growth. Nor is it being touted by donor agencies. So it is unlikely to be seized upon at the level of theory by other less developed countries. But in practice, things may be different. Even if those countries set out to follow the Chinese example, the compromises that most will have to make—not least because most are more open polities than China—will mean that they end up resembling India more than China. The Indian model may become more popular by default rather than by design. If that implies that they take fewer hair-raising risks with social dislocation than China has done, it may be a messy but happy outcome.

III

The cautious and limited nature of India's economic reforms has, as noted, made them politically sustainable by avoiding the serious social dislocation, which China's leaders use carrot and stick to repress. India has not experienced anything remotely on the scale of the colossal migrations that reform has caused in China, where 120 million or so villagers have left the countryside, and a further 300 million are expected to move in the decades ahead. Far more cautious than the Chinese ruling groups, Indian leaders are too alarmed by the

potential of massive change to produce disorder or unexpected electoral outcomes or both to contemplate policies that would trigger such a disruption.

Given this caution and gradualness, in contrast to many liberalizing countries, the reforms in India have been largely a nonissue in state and national elections since 1991. They did little either to help or hurt ruling parties (Yadav 1997). Incumbent governments did badly at some (indeed most) of those elections because they had governed poorly, especially at the state level. Opinion-polling indicates that the public is, for the most part, neutral about economic reform, thereby reinforcing Robert Wade-Gery's point that Indians use a false "democratic alibi" (discussed in Friedman's chapter) to argue that reforms are constrained by Indian democracy.[8]

As outlined later, there are aspects of the Indian political system that make reforms slow and limited, but the problems lie more with the elite and bureaucracies than with public opinion and the democratic system. But with India reaching growth rates of around 7 percent for three years in the late 1990s, after which they have declined somewhat only to bounce back—and with Aiyar (who once had his doubts) now saying that growth at near 7 percent is probably sustainable—slower growth is not a severe problem.

It is sometimes said that India, and democracies more generally, are less effective than authoritarian regimes at liberalizing their economies. However, evidence from India indicates that the opposite is true. In several important respects, democracies are better equipped to undertake reform.[9] Although democracies enjoy advantages over authoritarian regimes, this element of the story has received little attention from scholars (Gaddis 1997). In countries like India, with a long experience of democracy, huge numbers of political operatives acquire skills and attitudes that make it easier for a political system to adjust to change, whether it be liberalization or something else. Their ability to arrange political bargains and build new coalitions is invaluable when conditions change. Their skills at representation and easing discontent prevent groups that experience stress from becoming dangerously alienated from democratic politics. An eventual implosion is far more likely in China than in India because in China brutally corrupt and unaccountable local leaders can be hated in ways that are inconceivable in democratic India.

This point refers not just to senior politicians, but also, and more importantly, to activists at lower levels in the system. India has a vast army of such people who constitute an unrecognized but vital national resource that is certainly not matched by China. Such political "fixers" are found in strength in every region of India and in every significant Indian party, with the exception of the *Shiv Sena* in Maharashtra.

These fixers are on the political make, seeking to ingratiate themselves with groups of potential grassroots supporters and with higher-level politicians, often in the hope of gaining some minor office or at least some sort of, usually legal, income from office-holders in exchange for political services. They often represent the view of communities in areas remote to politicians, offering to ensure their future support in exchange for politicians' responses. They tend to lack polish. This, plus their earnestness to get ahead, sometimes causes middle-class people and ordinary folk to treat them as figures of fun. There is a popular expression in Kannada to describe these fixers: "towel over armpit." It refers to their habit, while shuttling between city and countryside in hot buses, of wearing a cotton towel over one shoulder with which to wipe the sweat from their brows.

But, however comical these operatives may appear, they perform badly needed services, especially given the organizational decay that has afflicted most parties in India since the late 1980s. They provide politicians with channels to groups of constituents, through which explanations of changes (such as those associated with liberalization) can be supplied, and compensatory largesse can be distributed to ease the resentments that some groups feel. They help to arrange bargains and to build and sustain coalitions of support (Manor 2000). They have, among other things, made it possible for India to achieve a more thorough democratic decentralization than almost any developing country (Crook and Manor 1994, Manor 1998). They play a significant role in deepening India's democracy, and in making governance in India responsive and resilient.

Federalism, a democratically constrained center with autonomous locales, also advantages India, which has a large number of arenas in which political conflict occurs in each state and also within the country's federal system as a whole. Contests frequently take place for the national parliament and state assemblies, for seats on councils at lower levels, and for positions of influence in a number of quasi-official and nonofficial boards, cooperatives, associations, and so on. The existence of so many opportunities to capture at least some power tends to persuade parties, senior politicians, and small-time "fixers" to remain engaged with the politics of elections and bargaining. They tend strongly to do so even when they suffer defeats, or when they or their supporters experience hardship as a result of economic liberalization.[10] Democratic stability at a broad and wide base is quite in advantage in tranquilly transiting through the potential traumas of reform.

The above, plus the skill with which politicians have orchestrated economic reform, have ensured that democracy facilitates a quiet adjustment to liberalization. Many state-level leaders have been as adroit as politicians at the national level when faced with the often painful dilemmas posed by the new policies.[11] Indeed, some state governments have devised significant innovations that will be adopted in other states when they prove successful. Several states have begun privatizing elements of their state electricity boards, and have unbundled power generation, transmission, and distribution to set the stage for a more efficient management of this problem sector. Rajasthan has revised its taxation system in ways that appear to lower the tax burden while enhancing government revenues. Karnataka has achieved something similar with a reform of urban property taxes. The states in India's multilayered democracy are often creative partners in the fraught business of adjusting to a new economic logic. It is for this reason that the World Bank and other development agencies have often concentrated on assisting promising state governments.

Many commentators express concern that India may succumb to religious extremism. These worries should not be dismissed lightly. India's sociocultural complexity and heterogeneity offer substantial reassurance here, however, one reason for the BJP coalition's defeat in national elections in 2004. Societies within India's various regions are also highly complex. Its heterogeneity has contributed to a strong tendency among citizens to shift their preoccupations from one to another of the many identities that they have available to them, often and with great fluidity. Depending upon circumstances and recent events, they may fix for a time on their *jati* (the caste group in which people marry), or *jati*-cluster identities; on their *varna* identity (another, much larger caste category); on their local, subregional, or national identities; on their class, linguistic, religious identities; or on sectarian identities that fragment Hindu, Muslim, and other religious groups. But they seldom fasten ferociously and tenaciously on any one of these in some us/them polarization.

This is frustrating for those on the Indian left who would like people to cleave to their class identities, and for those on the Hindu right who would make religious identities preeminent. This penchant for fluidity and mutability is not diminishing in the face of recent complex trends.[12] This tenacious cultural complexity reduces the severity and longevity of most social and political conflicts because it prevents tension and conflict from building up along a single fault line (Manor 1996a). Identity politics have, so far at least, distracted Indian voters from the issue of economic reform, which has helped the liberalizers. This tendency toward fluidity has also limited the damage that identity politics, however inflamed they may be at any one time, can do to the democratic process. The presence of a BJP-led coalition government in New Delhi from 1998 to 2004 led some to argue that a benign form of identity politics would not persist. But Hindu nationalism has not gained ascendancy, and there is little chance that it will anytime soon. Indeed, it lost votes in the 2004 parliamentary elections.

Finally, we need to consider three grand themes that have dominated India's recent political history: awakening, decay, and regeneration. Since the late 1960s, a gradual popular political awakening has been evident. Social groups of every sort, poor as well as prosperous, have become more politically aware, more assertive and demanding of politicians. This has made India a more robust democracy, but also a more difficult country to govern. At the same time, the decay of political institutions—informal party institutions and the formal institutions of state—has weakened the instruments through which politicians seek to govern, even though those politicians were the main instruments of decay.

If awakening and decay were the only two trends at work, India would be sliding inexorably toward disaster. But a third theme has become apparent, especially in the 1990s—a capacity for political regeneration—which serves as a counterweight to decay. This regeneration is evident in a number of ways. It includes the ability to rebuild damaged institutions and expand the remit of existing institutions or create new ones so that they perform much-needed tasks; the ability to assert norms, rules, and laws that had fallen into disuse or had never been asserted; and the ability to restore the properly nonpartisan character of institutions that had been turned to partisan purposes (Manor 1996b). The struggle between decay and regeneration is far from over. But India has come a long way since the 1980s, when the political outlook was far more depressing. Economic reform has been accompanied by political reform.

IV

Indian foreign policy has traditionally been an elite concern. Under Prime Minister Jawaharlal Nehru, foreign policy was theoretically based more on the norms of nonalignment. But managing Pakistan and great-power politics were two major concerns. In Indira Gandhi's time, following the defeat by China in the 1962 war, Indian foreign policy could be described as more assertive, more "Gaullist." Pakistan was cut in half with the formation of Bangladesh, and relations with the Soviet Union grew much closer. In the 1980s, India learned through its failed attempt to bring peace to Sri Lanka and the depressing drama of Kashmir that there were limits to its ability to order South Asia. Talk of India as a "superpower" faded.

When the cold war ended and the Soviet Union collapsed, India found that few people outside the region cared much about India. It neither had economic influence nor risked becoming a major source of instability, the two most important bases for earning foreign attention. The troubled relationship with Pakistan was a drag on India's claim to be a player in global affairs. At first, China turned its back on India, focusing instead on East and Southeast Asia. Russia was no longer a useful ally and America thought India's continuing obsession with nonalignment quaint and irrelevant. When the outside world looked at Asia, it fixated on the economic boom in Pacific Asia and threats to that growth, which could result from instability in the part of Asia bordering the Pacific Ocean.

Then under Narasimha Rao after 1991, Indian foreign policy changed. Economic reform was accompanied by foreign policy reform. The major source of the change was internal. Had the Indian economy been prospering in the late 1980s to early 1990s, there would have been little desire to change foreign policy. As with China a decade earlier, domestic economic reform and the opening to the outside world were driven by the need to find new solutions to a failing domestic economic system. To be sure, part of the rationale for change was an appreciation of the experience of rapidly growing states in Pacific Asia and a recognition of the need to compete in the global market economy, rejecting previous notions of nonalignment and "dependency." It was one thing for Americans to tell Indians, as they had for decades, that without an opening to the global market economy there could be no prosperity. But when other Asians who used to subscribe to the norms of nonalignment also began to praise the world market, to liberalize and to grow rapidly, then sections of India's elite began paying attention.

This combination of domestic difficulties and regional examples of a better way ahead has led to a more pragmatic foreign policy that offers striking parallels to China in the early 1980s, and some contrasts. In the decade after 1985, Indian defense spending fell as a percentage of GDP by 0.5 percent to 2.5 percent (Gupta 1995). Indian defense planners still paid attention to Pakistan and rhetorical hyperbole about a worsening balance of power remained in evidence. In truth, however, India was more secure than at any time since independence and, unlike China, lived in a region where most of its neighbors' economies were too weak to sustain an arms race. Also, unlike China, India had no immediate great-power rivals. Beijing, Moscow, and Washington all downgraded their interest in South Asia and the Indian Ocean in the 1980s. China and India agreed to some limited confidence-building measures along their disputed frontier in the early 1990s, and Washington and New Delhi increased the level of their military-to-military exchanges. Pakistan and India remained deadlocked over Kashmir, but the breakup of the Soviet Union meant that Pakistan now had far more to worry about in a destabilized Central Asia.

It took some time for India to see the possibility and the need for a new approach to its region. The Narasimha Rao government began this process, haltingly, but then under Foreign Minister and later Prime Minister Inder Kumar Gujral, between 1996 and 1998, there were signs of an approach to foreign policy that was neither Nehruvian nor Gaullist.[13] The so-called Gujral doctrine included preemptive concessions to neighbors—such as to Bangladesh over water use in 1997—to stimulate goodwill that would also eventually satisfy some Indian desires, for example, Indian transit rights through Bangladesh.[14] This doctrine could be described as a common-sense policy for a regional hegemon. India need not overtly bully its neighbors because everyone—perhaps even Pakistan—knows that it is the preeminent regional power and that the great powers cannot change that. In domestic political terms, such a strategy and the response it invites from neighbors also made sense as a way of demonstrating to Hindu nationalists that a more confrontational strategy, especially with Muslim neighbors, would be counterproductive.

The BJP-led coalition, which succeeded the Gujral government in 1998, however, shelved this approach and adopted more assertive postures within South Asia. Its early decision to test nuclear weapons was meant to be a clear indication that things had changed. But that government, and especially Prime Minister Vajpayee (who had been an accommodative foreign minister between 1977 and 1979), also sought to ease tensions with Pakistan. Vajpayee's first overtures in the late 1990s foundered because of continuing infiltration of militants from Pakistan into Indian-ruled Kashmir and, more especially, because of incursions by Pakistani forces into territory formerly controlled by

India in the Kargil region. India ejected them by force. When a military coup in October 1999 brought General Pervez Musharraf, whom many Indians saw as the architect of the Kargil incursion, to power in Pakistan, distrust deepened further, and dangerously.

After Islamic militants attacked the New Delhi parliament in December 2001, with most of India's political elite inside the building, India mobilized for war, or perhaps more accurately, for coercive diplomacy. Pakistan responded and the standoff along their border came close to armed conflict during May–June 2002. The intercession of the U.S. State Department can probably be credited with averting war, but the armies remained poised for many months thereafter. Another, less widely recognized close call followed, but then in December 2003, Vajpayee astonished his party colleagues by making one "last" unilateral effort to ease the tension, doing so in part to curb the burgeoning power of Hindu extremists in his own camp. This has gradually produced positive results, and ties are being normalized. But serious risks remain, especially if yet another assassination attempt by Islamic extremists against Musharraf were to succeed and destabilize Pakistan.

India and Pakistan are still in the early stages of learning to have a mature balance of nuclear deterrence while managing raw sores of conventional conflict, such as Kashmir.[15] No Indian defense planner can afford to ignore the Pakistan problem, but India does not benefit, as Vajpayee learned, when paranoia is allowed to distort priorities. Pakistan is an inferior power and will remain so with a minimum of Indian effort. Most Indian leaders recognize the importance of rising above the hostile entanglement with Pakistan, to enable India to play a more influential role on the global scene, and to encourage a more economistic (and benign) concept of national security. They therefore are prepared to make adjustments to conditions in and to the status of Kashmir, which will be attractive to Pakistan,[16] although it will not be easy to make headway on this front.

India has slowly drawn away from the illusory virtue of the type of South–South cooperation envisioned in the nonaligned movement from the 1950s to 1980s. It has begun to reformulate cooperation in new, more relevant ways. The states of Pacific Asia demonstrated that economic growth comes initially from an outward orientation to the global market economy. Only with the sustained prosperity of newly industrialized economies that learn to become service economies do the prospects for economic cooperation with neighbors eventually increase. While absorbing this message, New Delhi also began to make common cause with other governments from the south, including Brazil, South Africa, and China, in ways that may hold promise for those potent players and for other less formidable developing countries.

These trends have persuaded India that its interests will be served if it can ease the impasse with Pakistan, worry less about South Asia, and develop a more wide-ranging foreign policy. Hence Vajpayee's overtures for a reduction in tensions with Pakistan. Hence India's pursuit of closer ties to the Association of Southeast Asian Nations (ASEAN, and some of its members, notably Singapore) and to America, the European Union (EU), Iran, and Israel. And hence the recent substantial improvement in relations with China. Trade has soared, border issues are being seriously addressed by both sides. China has begun to acknowledge India's concerns over Sikkim, and India has accepted Chinese control in Tibet. All of this indicates that Indian leaders, even the Hindu nationalists, understand that the country cannot base economic prosperity or global influence on its region alone.

Given the recent wars and the continuing tensions over Kashmir, this enlightened global approach is still afflicted by difficulties. But, just as the UK has found with its domestic concerns about Ireland, local concerns need not preclude countries from pursuing global interests. A broader, more outward vision is, and is now seen by most leaders in New Delhi to be, an essential feature of an Indian foreign policy that the outside world can take more seriously.

A key to sustaining such a vision is the need to be "rewarded" for change. When India—and not Pakistan—was invited into a closer relationship with ASEAN and the Asian Regional Forum (ARF) in 1996, it was explicitly in recognition of its new role as a more outward-looking Asian country anxious to learn from the experience of Pacific Asia.[17] Some ARF members welcomed India as an implicit counterweight to China, others as a way to dilute the presence of Anglo-Saxon states and the EU in the region. Whatever the motive, India was the only South Asian state thus honored. It sent New Delhi a clear message that it can find new foreign friends in Pacific Asia. India's current desire to join the Asia-Europe summit process (ASEM) is evidence of both a wider Indian vision and a sense that its strategy of more open and economic forms of multilateralism may be working. Without a string of such successes, India stands no hope—despite its sterling record in United Nations peacekeeping operations—of a permanent seat on the UN Security Council.

Success for any government in New Delhi will depend on developing what must lie at the heart of any more outward-looking policy, a new attitude to the global market economy. As seen from the challenge of integrating China into the global economy, weaving webs of interdependence is a fraught process. Large continental countries like China and India (and America) are more inclined to believe that they can manage the constraints of interdependence. Certainly, poor continental nations feel that they should be spared the most severe constraints of the global economic system. They tend to argue against intellectual property rights that hurt their pharmaceutical industry, on subsidies for state-owned industries, against limits against restrictions on child labor or environmental abuse. They believe these rules should not be applied to a poor, developing country, or at least not without a long adjustment period.

V

These attitudes manifest themselves in various aspects of India's struggle with its opening up to the global economic system. There is more than a residue of "dependency-school" suspicion of the global economy. However neat the BJP slogan of "micro-chips but not potato chips," it reflected a desire common throughout the part of the developing world that is integrating with the global economy to manage interdependence.[18] It is true that, in order to obtain power-plant technology from major international companies, there is no necessity to have a Dunkin' Donuts in Delhi. But, as the spread of doughnuts and potato chips in Pacific Asia demonstrates, the confidence of international investors is restrained when developing countries are too selective about certain elements of the global economy.

In recent years, India's senior officials have understood the need to sell the virtues of their economy to the world economy's key players. Indian delegations at the World Economic Forum in Davos have tended to be larger and more impressive than those from China. The Indian delegations include the heads of state governments in India's federal system seeking to be salesmen to investors. Indian officials are regularly more accessible and realistic than their Chinese counterparts. They are frank about the slowness and complexity of their legal system, but point out that, whereas McDonald's in Beijing, when the Communist Party government chose to throw it out of its desirable location, had no recourse to a court of law to settle its disputes with local authorities in 1996, Kentucky Fried Chicken in Bangalore eventually obtained legal satisfaction in the very same year.[19] The rule of law is far better established in India. Where foreign investors stagger blindly through the non-transparent, corrupt maze of personal networks that is center–province relations in China, India's federal system is reasonably transparent, and becoming more so as the central government openly imposes conditionalities on state governments to homogenize and reform before releasing massive funds to the states. Indians are aware of their problems and are sensitive to the need to explain how foreign investors can cope with them. Nonethnic Chinese investors are beginning to understand that, while China is one of the world's riskiest emerging markets, India is among the five least risky.[20] The survey that first indicated this was conducted before it became apparent that the Indian economy would escape serious damage from the Asian financial crisis, because its liberalization had been cautious. That caution offers reassurance to investors on some fronts, even though it inspires frustration on others.

Signs for the future of India are more reassuring. Indian leaders in every conceivable ruling party are aware of the need for further reforms. A snail-like bureaucracy ranks high on international investors' lists of complaints, as does the need to make the rupee fully convertible, although existing controls helped India to weather the East Asian financial crisis of the late 1990s relatively well. The World Bank has been deeply unhappy about the state of the Indian banking sector since 1991, although the necessary reforms are acknowledged to be complex.[21] Those reforms began in the new century, but caution again has bred as much exasperation as hope. On the other hand, India's banks are saddled with far less bad debt than many counterparts in China, where official data place default loans at 25 percent of the total, and private agencies suspect that it may run as high as 45 percent.[22]

The tense negotiations of India with America and the EU about tariff reductions in the World Trade Organization (WTO) demonstrated both India's ability to work adroitly in both political and economic terms within the system and the strong and strengthening external pressures for further reform. The increase in World Bank aid to India in 1997 was seen as a reward for, and a vote of confidence in, New Delhi's economic reforms.[23]

India's economy has performed reasonably well since the mid-1990s when the openings after 1991 began to pay dividends. China has continued to outstrip India in foreign direct investment (FDI). But 85 percent of the Chinese foreign capital comes from ethnic Chinese and, at a comparable point in the process of the opening by China, the Indian and Chinese totals are nearly the same. Nevertheless, even if we optimistically conclude that India will do relatively well with international investors, the lack of an equivalent "ethnic-Chinese" dimension will make India's task more daunting and the need to deal with Organisation for Economic Cooperation and Development (OECD) investors more pressing. But the outlook, despite the familiar ambiguities,[24] is still quite promising.

Goldman Sachs made an optimistic prediction about India's economy, referred to at the start of this chapter. Such expectations seem rather overblown. They exaggerate the promise of information technology and outsourcing. These account for only a tiny portion of Indian output, although services more generally now account for more than half of GDP. And they certainly underestimate the difficulties involved in tackling two critical problems: cutting subsidies and reducing the fiscal deficit. They also underplay the damage already done by a lack of sufficient investment in infrastructure and by the bungling that has largely ended hopes of foreign investment in the crucial electricity sector, without which current shortfalls will persist.

But Goldman Sachs' optimism is not wildly inflated. India is likely to continue opening only slowly to the global economy, so that its growth rates will not take off at the 9 percent levels the government seeks. But India should remain at least equal to the ASEAN average and well ahead of almost the whole of the rest of the world. India will also benefit from foreigners' dissatisfaction with the China market, because of corruption, China's lack of legal protection, and perhaps something that is a real threat in China but not gradualist India, social unrest. The need of Indian domestic politics for complex coalitions is very likely to constrain plans for growth (although we must remember that the biggest burst of reformist initiatives in early 1997 came under the United Front government, a coalition). India has made a clear break with its past and substantial economic benefits are pouring in. Reform is now as difficult in domestic political terms to stop as it is to accelerate. If reasonable growth rates are sustained (which is very likely) and more employment results from it (which is less likely and has not yet happened), then large numbers of people will depend on growth and foreign investment for their jobs. As a result, political leaders will increasingly find that reelection depends on delivering the economic growth produced by an open economy.

This will be an India that the international business community and overseas investors will gradually take more seriously. Indeed, they may do so well before foreign governments and academic specialists, as with China in the early 1980s. That is already happening in certain sectors. The issue is how far it will spread. India's task will be made easier by worries in OECD countries about trade deficits with China and Beijing's resistance to, or its inability to implement, international economic agreements. Both Asian giants will suffer from corruption, but given India's free press and assertive judiciary, and its voters' patent willingness to punish malfeasance, foreigners may come to favor the Indian market, as a corrupt Brezhnev-like party further entrenches itself in China.

VI

Assuming that these trends are correct, it is likely that other dimensions of policy toward India will also change. With a growing business lobby in the OECD nations favoring good relations with India, the relative absence of disputes over Indian human rights and arms exports, and no international anxiety about the country's nonexistent desires to seize neighboring territory, much closer ties to India than to China seem quite possible for the already industrialized democracies. Disputes between India and the developed world about nuclear-weapons policy are already nearly as benign as current attitudes toward Israel's clandestine nuclear arsenal. The arguments favoring technology transfer to India as opposed to China are growing stronger, and closer defense collaboration—foreseen in the late 1990s (Sidhu 1997)—has begun to happen. As China grows militarily formidable, a greater coincidence of interests is emerging between India and America in thinking about a more effective balance of power in Asia.[25] Those Asian countries such as Japan or Indonesia that are also becoming more worried about China also increasingly welcome a constructive Indian alternative in both economic and security terms. As a result, India's prospects of winning a permanent seat on the Security Council—still less than likely—will grow.

If India is to have any hope of achieving these objectives and shaping its own destiny outside its home region, it will have to do more to forge a bargain with the global economy because greater independence of action for India requires greater interdependence by India. If India refuses, it should not be surprised if it again faces neglect. If India accepts that compromise—and it has moved a long way in that direction—at a minimum the outside world will be challenged to take a successful India still more seriously.

Notes

This is a substantially revised version of a paper that originally appeared in *Survival* (Summer 1998), pp. 53–70. Since then, my coauthor Gerald Segal has passed away. He is sorely missed by people who take Asia seriously.

1. As Swaminathan Aiyar, Consulting Editor of the *Economic Times*, also points out, subsidies (defined as the unrecovered cost of services provided by the state) in 1997 were 15% of gross domestic product (GDP) and tax revenues 16%. These figures are roughly what they were a decade earlier. See his "Prospects for Economic Reform," paper presented at the IISS conference "Rethinking India's Role in the World," Neemrana Fort, India, September 1997.
2. Interview with P. V. Narasimha Rao, New Delhi, February 11, 1992.
3. *Ibid.* It should be noted that Narasimha Rao also hoped to use government revenues to sustain the politics of "resource distribution"—bestowing political spoils on social groups in exchange for their electoral support—on which the Congress Party had long depended.
4. These comments are based on encounters during February 1992, when the prime minister permitted one of us to observe his and his staff's routines for a working week.
5. See Swaminathan Aiyar, "Prospects for Economic Reform"; and Andrew Taylor, "Survey: Asia—Infrastructure, Power and Water," *Financial Times*, September 23, 1997.
6. We owe this distinction to Ashutosh Varshney of the University of Michigan.
7. Interview with Swaminathan Aiyar, New Delhi, April 7, 1997.
8. Comments made by Sir Robert Wade-Gery at the IISS conference "Rethinking India's Role in the World," September 1997.
9. This analysis draws on recent research by Rob Jenkins of Birkbeck College, University of London, on the political management of economic reform at the state level in India, and by James Manor on the survival strategies of India's state-level chief ministers. See Jenkins's *Democratic Politics and Economic Reform in India.* Cambridge: Cambridge University Press, 2000.
10. This is Rob Jenkins's insight.
11. See, e.g., S. Guhan's treatment of this in Balveer Arora and Douglas V. Verney (eds.), *Multiple Identities in a Single State* (New Delhi: Konark, 1996).
12. See Yogendra Yadav, "Reconfiguration in Indian Politics"; and interview with Yadav, New Delhi, August 7, 1996.
13. For a different view of India's evolving foreign policy, and a fuller description of the "Gujral doctrine," see Bhabani Sen Gupta, "India in the Twenty-First Century," *International Affairs*, vol. 73, no. 2, April 1997.
14. "Asia: India's Chaos-as-Usual Politics," *The Economist*, April 26, 1997.
15. Sumit Ganguly, "Stalemate in the Valley," *Harvard International Review*, vol. 18, no. 3, Summer 1996.
16. These plans are imaginative and well developed. One of us was shown detailed evidence of this by the Indian authorities in the mid-1990s.
17. "India Looks East," *The Economist*, March 8, 1997.

18. On these issues and a changing India, see Ian Jack, "Introduction," *Granta: India!* no. 57, Spring 1997.
19. For a less positive view of this case, see Jonathan Karp, "Foreign Firms Try to Avoid India's Labyrinth of Laws," *Asian Wall Street Journal*, July 11, 1997.
20. See the DRI/McGraw Hill survey of emerging-market risk in Stephen Fidler, "China One of the Riskiest Emerging Markets," *Financial Times*, July 10, 1997.
21. Vivek Y. Kelkar, "India Back in World Bank Favour," *Asia Times*, May 21, 1997, p. 1. For a taste of the extraordinary complexity, see Percy S. Mistry, "Financial Sector Reform in India: Hesitant Pursuit of an Incomplete Agenda," in Robert Cassen and Vijay Joshi (eds.), *India: The Future of Economic Reform* (Delhi: Oxford University Press, 1995), pp. 167–208.
22. See the chapter by Mukherji in this volume.
23. Pia Copper, "World Bank Rewards India Reforms with Aid," *ibid.*, June 27, 1997.
24. See "A Survey of India," *The Economist*, February 21, 2004.
25. In its 1996–1997 national security report, the Indian Department of Defence directly expressed concern about the growth of China's military power. See Sanjeev Miglani, "New Delhi Puts its China Cards on the Table," *Asia Times*, April 29, 1997.

References

Crook, Richard, C. and James Manor (1994). *Enhancing Participation and Institutional Performance: Democratic Decentralization in South Asia and West Africa.* London: Overseas Development Administration.

Dhar, P. N. (1987). "The Political Economy of Development in India." *The Indian Economic Review*, January–June.

Gaddis, J. L. (1997). *We Now Know.* Oxford and New York: Clarendon Press and Council on Foreign Relations.

Gupta, Shekhar (1995). India Redefines Its Role, Adelphi paper 293. Oxford: Oxford University Press for the IISS.

Manor, James (1994). "The Political Sustainability of Economic Liberalization", in Robert H. Cassen and Vijay Joshi (eds.), *India: The Future of Economic Reform.* New Delhi: Oxford University Press, pp. 341–363.

Manor, James (1996a). " 'Ethnicity' and Politics in India." *International Affairs* 72(3) (July): 459–476.

Manor, James (1996b). "Political Regeneration in India," in D. L. Sheth and Ashis Nandy (eds.), *The Multiverse of Democracy: Essays in Honour of Rajni Kothari.* New Delhi and London: Sage Publications and Thousand Oaks, pp. 230–241.

Manor, James (1998). *The Political Economy of Decentralization.* Washington D.C.: World Bank Publications.

Manor, James (2000). "Small-Time Political Fixers in State Politics in India: 'Towel over Armpit,' " *Asian Survey* (September–October): 816–835.

Manor, James (2002). "Changing State, Changing Society." *South Asia* (August): 231–256.

Sidhu, Waheguru Pal Singh (1997). Enhancing Indo-US Strategic Cooperation, Adelphi Paper 313. Oxford: Oxford University Press for the IISS.

Yadav, Yogendra (1997). "Reconfiguration in Indian Politics: State Assembly Elections, 1993–1995," *Economic and Political Weekly*, 31(2–3) (January 1996): 2, 133–143, reprinted in Partha Chatterjee (ed.), *State and Politics in India*. New Delhi: Oxford University Press, pp. 177–208.

III

Subnational Factors

7

The Persistence of Informal Finance

Kellee S. Tsai

I

Regardless of regime type, most developing countries face the challenge of providing credit to lower-income portions of their rural populations (Bouman and Hospes 1994; Hoff, Braverman, and Stiglitz 1993). China and India are no exceptions. Due to perceived deficiencies in the formal financial system, in both countries the state has attempted to alleviate rural poverty by establishing government microfinance programs. Even with such programs, however, small business owners and farmers in both China and India rely primarily on curb market finance. Indeed, in some cases, the scale of informal finance actually increases in communities targeted with more official credit. One of the reasons that even an expanded supply of formal finance is insufficient to meet demand is because state policies are seldom implemented properly. Furthermore, the reality of segmented credit markets at the local level means that government microfinance programs often fail to reach their intended clientele. Developmental outcomes often deviate from state intentions due to complex political and economic dynamics at the local level.

Both China and India have relied on directed credit and encouraged microfinance programs. Both countries have established credit cooperatives, commercial banks, and poverty alleviation microfinance programs. But for neither have these displaced informal and semiformal sources of credit.[1] In this realm, there is no sense in the notion that China is a success and India a failure. To the contrary, the fact that nongovernmental groups have greater independence in democratic India suggests greater potential for microfinance institutions to operate in a financially sustainable, rather than policy-driven manner.

II

After India's independence in 1947 and the establishment of the People's Republic of China in 1949, both regimes promoted growth without exploitation and fostered grassroots-level savings and credit institutions to serve farmers. Although India inherited a network of credit cooperatives, in 1951, 93 percent of rural households relied on informal finance (Bouman et al. 1989, 12–14). This inspired a commitment to establish alternatives to curb capital, viewed as exploitative and "evil." Throughout the 1950s and 1960s, India promoted cooperatives "to provide a positive institutional alternative to the moneylender" (RBI 1954, 481–482) to expand agricultural credit and to alleviate rural poverty. In the mid-1970s, India established regional rural banks, a hybrid between cooperatives and commercial banks, farmers' service societies, and more nonbanking finance companies. By 1998 India had 64,547 regional rural banks branches, one for every 17,000 to 21,000 rural citizens. However, the regional rural banks proved financially unsustainable and inefficient (Bhatt and Thorat 2001).

Shortly after the founding of the People's Republic of China, the communists closed private finance and banned curb market financing, including pawn broking and "loan sharking" (Hsiao 1971). During the 1950s, China set up a network of rural credit cooperatives. But these served state purposes and were not commercial credit-granting institutions. It was not until reform began in the late 1970s that credit cooperatives functioned more as grassroots banking institutions that served rural households. The credit cooperatives, however, were technically insolvent. Over time, central banking authorities have injected approximately US$4 billion in recapitalization funds into the credit cooperatives system (Watson 2003).

Microfinance programs try to bridge the gap between the supply and demand for rural finance. In both India and China, microfinance has taken the form of subsidized loans in government-supported poverty alleviation programs, and various donor and NGO-led endeavors. The relative effectiveness of the two forms of microfinance is similar. Subsidized micro-loans in government-supported poverty alleviation programs tend to have low repayment rates and seldom reach the intended clientele. NGOs are somewhat more effective in reaching poor clients.

Subsidized loans to low income rural areas have a record of ineffectiveness (Adams, Graham, and von Pischke 1984; cf. Morduch 2000). In India, an Integrated Rural Development Programme was established in 1978 to extend microloans through the banking system to the impoverished. In its first two decades, it extended Rs 250 billion (US$12.3 billion) worth of subsidized loans to 55 million families with an annual income of less than Rs.11,000 (US$305). The repayment rate was only 25 to 33 percent. Regional rural banks and primary agricultural credit societies have not performed better. The banks have been saddled with soft loans to priority sectors, while primary cooperatives have served mainly as tools of political patronage.

State-subsidized microfinance in China began about one decade later than in India. Introduced in 1986, it targeted collective enterprises at the township and village levels (Rozelle et al. 1998) charging only 2.88 percent annual interest when official interest rates ranged from 8 to 10 percent. Distributed to politically important enterprises and higher-income households, the repayment rate was about 50 percent (Park 1999). Subsidized loans to households were introduced in 1993 for the poorest counties. In 1996 many counties adopted the Grameen Bank model whereby groups of five borrowers mutually guarantee repayment (Bornstein 1997; Holcombe 1995; Khandker, Khalily, and Khan 1995). Loans ranged from 1,000 to 2,000 RMB (US$120–240) and were subsidized at the official lending rate of 2.88 percent. The loans were disbursed rapidly, almost quota style. By 2000, the government had disbursed US$775 million worth of subsidized microloans (Tsien 2001). By 2002 nearly US$3.7 billion (or half) of Beijing's poverty-relief funds went to poverty-relief loans (Xinhua March 2, 2002). Repayment rates were less than 60 percent. The loans were treated more as one-time fixes rather than sustainable microfinance (Cheng 2003).

The central bank prodded credit cooperatives to extend microloans to households. As of 2002, they had extended 78.9 billion RMB (US$9.54 billion) in microloans, and 25 percent of rural households had received loans (CIIC November 5, 2002). As of year-end 2003, nonperforming loans ran at nearly 30 percent (SIC January 14, 2004), an unsustainable rate.

III

NGOs function differently in democratic India and authoritarian China. India has promoted self-governing NGOs and encouraged domestic development finance institutions to collaborate with them. China's "NGOs" are government-run. India's NGOs have had a more extensive reach in microfinance than those in China. In both countries, few microfinance institutions are financially sustainable.

In India, microfinance NGOs take three forms: (1) self-help group programs linked to banks, (2) cooperatives, or (3) Grameen-style banks (EDA 1996). Self-help groups consist of 10 to 12 people with similar socioeconomic and demographic characteristics (e.g., low-income women in rural areas). They help members save on a regular basis to create insurance for emergencies, to empower, and to make uncollateralized loans to members (Hannig and Katimbo-Mugwanya 1999, 7). As of 2002, there were 1 million self-help groups with 17 million members (Ashe 2002, cited in Wilson 2002, 221). Since 1992, the National Bank for Agriculture and Rural Development (NABARD) has lent through them, reaching almost 8 million low-income households by March 2003 (NABARD 2002, 2003). The bank aims to reach one-third of rural Indians through one million bank-linked self-help groups by 2008 (Bansal 2003, 24).

In addition, over 500 NGOs serve as financial intermediaries to low-income borrowers. Also, a handful of cooperatives such as the SEWA Bank, the Indian Cooperative Network for Women, and cooperative credit societies associated with the Cooperative Development Foundation provide microfinance. About ten organizations are Grameen-style banks, the largest being SHARE, Activists for Social Alternatives Trust, and Rural Development Organization, Manipur (Sinha 2000, 70).

These institutions have not been subject to stringent regulation, ignoring the prohibition against savings mobilization without central bank permission. Liberalization since 1991 has loosened interest rate controls on microcredit. The institutions therefore can structure their loans in a financially self-sustainable manner. With flexibility comes self-sustainability because low-income borrowers can then afford commercially viable interest rates.

In contrast to democratic India, China restricts NGOs. They must have an official government sponsor (Saich 2000). In 1994 the Grameen model was extended to China. Researchers from the Rural Development Institute of the state-run Chinese Academy of Social

Sciences, with international funding, established the Funding the Poor Cooperative in Yixian, Hebei (Tsai 2002, 200–202). As of March 2003, the cooperative was operating in three counties, serving 15,244 borrowers (Du 2003). Repayment rates ranged from 95 to 99 percent, even with loans covering operational costs. There are plans to expand their outreach. International donors have initiated over 200 microfinance programs (Cheng 2003, 123), all implemented with local governmental partners, but usually as projects with a limited lifespan (Cheng 2003; IFAD 2001, 20–21; Park and Ren 2001).

IV

Despite these successes in the formal financial sector, informal finance remains a major source of credit for farmers who obtain four times more credit from the curb market (IFAD 2001, C11). In small business the curb accounted for up to three-quarters of private sector financing during the first two decades of reform (Tsai 2002, 36–37). In India, a 1992 survey revealed that nearly 40 percent of rural households rely on informal finance, agricultural moneylenders, professional moneylenders, traders, relatives and friends, and others (RBI 2000, table 5). Table 7.1 outlines the primary forms of informal and semiformal finance in both countries and notes the extent to which they are prohibited. In both countries, private transactions with high interest rates violate banking regulations. In practice, however, the curb market in both China and India has adapted and flourishes.

In China, small business owners frequently borrow money from friends, relatives, and neighboring shopkeepers to meet short-term liquidity requirements. Wholesalers deliver goods to retailers on 10-day or even 30-day credit. This is not illegal if interest rates do not exceed those in state banks. Private commercial banks are scarce in China and the central bank works to shut down private money houses. In sum, curb capital can be found in both prosperous and impoverished parts of the country (Tsai 2002, ch. 5).

Pawnshops exemplify Beijing's ambivalence toward informal finance. Eliminated in the Mao era, the first private pawnshop opened in 1987. By 1993, there were over 3,000. Most were run by branches of government (Li 2000), some registered as ordinary private businesses. They were legitimated as "a medium for normal commodity circulation . . . [aiming] to serve the people and social production" (Zhongguo yinhang 1993, 240–243). Despite this more favorable evaluation of pawnshops, it became increasingly apparent that many

Table 7.1 Legal condition of informal finance in China and India

Type	*China*	*India*
Interpersonal lending—loans extended among friends, relatives, neighbors, or colleagues	*minjian jiedai*—financial authorities do not interfere with casual, interest-free lending	Financial authorities do not interfere with casual, interest-free lending
Trade credit—merchandise credit between wholesalers andretailers	*hangye xinyong*—neither sanctioned nor prohibited	Trade credit, forward sales
Moneylenders, loan sharks—loans from professional and nonprofessional money brokers, typically at high interest rates	*gaolidai*—all high interest lending is illegal	Mahajan and Chettiar bankers—Some are registered as finance companies, trusts, banks, and partnership firms
Rotating savings and credit organizations (ROSCAs)—indigenously organized savings and credit groups	*huzhuhui, hehui, biaohui, chenghui, juhui*—permitted in localities where they have not collapsed	Chit funds—registered as companies, partnerships, and sole proprietorships
Pawnshops—extend collateralized loans with interest	*diandang, dangpu*—permitted when operated according to regulations	Legal if licensed
Indigenous banks, money houses, finance companies—mobilize savings and extend collateralized loans	*siren qianzhuang*, private money houses—regarded as private banks, which are illegal; most operate underground now	Deal with short-term credit (*hundis*) combined with trade for financing trade—committees have made efforts to formalize them
Rural cooperative foundations	*nongcun hezuo jijinhui*—approved by MOA until closure by PBC in 1999	n.a.
Social organizations, mutual benefit funds—registered entities that are supposed to serve lower-income populations	*huzhuhui, hezuo chu jijinhui* (mutual assistance societies, cooperative savings foundations)—registered with MCA, but not supposed to engage in for-profit financial intermediation	Nidhi companies, mutual benefit societies, permanent funds (mainly in Tamil Nadu)—committees have recommended that they be regulated more stringently

were (illegally) mobilizing savings deposits from the public and offering high rates of interest. As a result, in 1994 a crackdown on illicit financial institutions closed over half.

Rotating savings and credit associations (*hui*) are largely unregulated. When *hui* involve relatively small groups of people, typically women pooling monthly contributions and rotating the pot of money, local governments usually consider them a productive form of mutual assistance.

The establishment of Rural Cooperative Foundations under the Ministry of Agriculture further exemplifies the ambiguities (Cheng, Findlay, and Watson 1998; Du 1998). By the early 1990s foundations had been established in about one-third of townships. By 1998 there were over 18,000 foundations with over five million depositors (Holz 2001). Not permitted to mobilize deposits or extend loans like formal financial institutions, the foundations used euphemistic terms for comparable transactions. Instead of paying interest on deposits, they sold "shares" (*rugu*) or extended "capital use fees" (*zijin zhan feiyong*). In March 1999, the central government announced the closure of poorly performing foundations and placed better performing ones within credit cooperatives.

Some nongovernmental financial institutions have operated above ground, registering as social organizations, dubbed mutual assistance societies, or cooperative savings foundations. The credit societies are supposed to be nonprofit organizations that serve the poor. In practice, they operate like private money houses. They mobilize savings, extend credit to private entrepreneurs who may be well off, and offer interest rates higher than the central bank. They should be distinguished from organizations oriented toward poverty alleviation via microfinance.

India's formal financial sector is more liberalized than China's and its informal financial sector is more likely to take corporative forms. Yet, India has made repeated efforts to track, regulate, and create

Table 7.2 Sources of informal finance in rural India over time

Type of non-institutional sources	*1951*	*1961*	*1971*	*1981*	*1991*
Landlord	3.5%	1.1%	8.6%	4.0%	n.a.
Agricultural moneylenders	25.2	47.0	23.1	8.6	6.3
Professional moneylenders	46.4	13.8	13.8	8.3	9.4
Traders and commission agents	5.1	7.5	8.7	3.4	7.1
Relatives and friends	11.5	5.8	13.8	9.0	6.7
Others	1.1	7.5	2.8	5.5	4.9
Unspecified	n.a.	n.a.	n.a.	n.a.	3.8
Informal credit as share of total household debt	92.8%	82.7%	70.8%	38.8%	39.6%*

*1991 figures do not add up to 39.6% even though Table 5 of the 1991–1992 AIDIS report clearly states that non-institutional agencies account for 39.6% of total rural household debt.

Source: Reserve Bank of India, All-India Debt and Investment Survey, various years.

institutional alternatives to the curb. In China most informal financing activities are simply banned.

Informal credit has declined over time, and the share of moneylenders in informal credit has declined even faster (see Table 7.2). Some moneylenders, however, went underground while others were reclassified (Bell 1990). Landlords, agricultural moneylenders, and professional moneylenders are hardly distinct.[2] And "traders and commission agents," known as indigenous bankers, broker funds between banks and their clients, usually traders (Schrader 1994). The Shroffs of Western India provide short-term credit to traders who travel great distances to purchase inventory and transfer funds (Ghate et al. 1992, 198–200). Indigenous bankers also may operate as commission agencies or hire-purchase finance companies, basically leasing or financing vehicles and other goods over a fixed term for clients who lack the cash to purchase capital goods up front (Nayar 1992, 199–200). Informal finance in the "Others" category includes indigenous bankers who are not registered as traders or commission agents, unregistered finance corporations, nonprofessional moneylenders (not friends or relatives), various types of leasing, investment, and housing finance companies, chit funds, and Nidhi societies. Whereas chit funds in China are completely informal, in India they can be registered as companies, partnerships, and sole proprietorships (Rutherford and Arora 1997). India regulates them to increase the security of the members' contributions and to reduce defaults. The cost of collecting the pot (i.e., the *de facto* interest rate) is capped at 30 percent of the size of the pot. Chit funds are limited to a maximum of 60 months (Ghate et al. 1992, p. 197). In response to the regulations, many have gone underground and taken their members (who seek higher returns) with them.

Nidhi companies or mutual benefit societies are an important part of the nonbanking world of financial intermediation, especially in south India. They mobilize savings and extend loans collateralized with jewelry or real estate (Nayar 1992, 197–199). When nonmembers wish to make a deposit or borrow from a Nidhi, they take a share of the Nihdi. India has made repeated efforts to regulate these mutual benefit societies (PIB 2002).

V

In China and India, despite an expansion of microfinance programs for poverty alleviation and efforts to eliminate or regulate the curb, informal finance has expanded in both countries. Why?

One reason informal finance continues to play such an important role in rural China and India is that the amount of credit demanded by rural households exceeds that supplied by the formal financial sector. Although official sources of credit have increased and official statistics show the weight of the curb market has declined, the decennial central bank surveys underestimate the true scale of informal finance. Clive Bell notes that the "[moneylender] remained a very important source of finance to rural households, and the expansion of aggregate debt was almost surely so great as to imply that his volume of business grew" (Bell 1990). Despite significant increases in the official supply (over US$15 billion), rural households continue to draw on informal sources of credit due to limited access and continuing high demand (Swain 2002).

In rural China, if people were turning to informal finance only because more institutionalized sources were unavailable, then clients of microfinance programs would rely on subsidized poverty loans rather than high-interest loans from the curb. Yet this turns out not to be so. In fact (Park and Ren 2001), "over 50% of households in program areas had outstanding loans from other sources." It "thus . . . does not appear that microfinance participants lack access to other credit sources, whether formal or informal" (p. 46). Actually, indebtedness is higher among microfinance clients. Only one quarter would have engaged in income-generating activities of the same scale in the absence of the curb. Why is business getting better for moneylenders amidst an expansion in formal sector microfinance institutions?

The increase in the official supply of credit has not translated into a matching decline in informal financial activity because state policies are not implemented properly. This occurs in three main ways: first, state actors may not be distributing targeted credit properly due to insufficient knowledge of how to identify the intended clients of subsidized credit and microfinance institution programs. Second, state actors may intentionally divert credit from the intended recipients. And third, non-state actors may interfere with the proper disbursement of formal and microfinance institution credit. Taken together, all three types of implementation failure could be interpreted as reflecting weaknesses in state capacity (Evans, Reuschemeyer, and Skocpol 1985).

In rural India and China, commercial banks do not have experience lending to the poor who lack both an established credit history and also collateral or a guarantor. But targeting lower-income rural households leads to quota-style lending, where a certain number of loans are disbursed, rather than meeting the needs of worthy borrowers.

Subsidized interest rates in both India and China enhance the likelihood that subsidized loans end up in the hands of local elites who do not feel obligated to repay the loans (Adams, Graham, and von Pischke 1984). While China's political context differs significantly from India's, targeted credit in both is subject to political patronage at the local level.

Beyond top-down weaknesses in state capacity and the distortion of policy implementation by politically important constituents (Migdal, Kohli, and Shue 1994), the curb thrives because informal financiers are determined to evade banking regulations and will do so no matter how much formal credit is available and no matter how stringent the penalties for violating laws. Although it is conceivable that lower-income farmers and rural traders boycott formal and semiformal financial institutions to undermine their legitimacy (Selden and Perry, 2000), there is no evidence for this in India and China. In both countries, intra-state actors (such as local officials and bureaucrats charged with loan disbursal), a privileged slice of the population, are just as likely as non-state actors to distort policy implementation.

There are inherent limits on what a homogeneous policy from a centralized state can achieve. Credit markets are segmented even at the grassroots level. No single type of credit can meet the needs of various potential borrowers; no single type of credit is accessible to everyone (Hoff and Stiglitz 1990). Market segmentation occurs along political and social lines. By definition, directed credit cannot go to the highest economic bidder. The distribution is political. Interest-free lending only occurs among tight-knit groups, typically friends or relatives. Members of rotating savings and credit associations (ROSCAs) usually know one another or the organizer or one other member. Higher rates of interest reflect in part the higher level of risk associated with lending to clients with unconventional forms of collateral (if any). In both India and China local social, political, and economic dynamics mediate both formal and informal finance.

VI

An Indian village studied by J. Howard M. Jones (1994) highlights the nature of the local credit market before and after a village bank was introduced. In 1989, the village was home to over 1,000 people in 200 households. Before a village bank was introduced at the end of 1983, residents relied on informal credit. Six years after the bank opened, the pawnbroker's lending volume in value terms had increased by over

100 percent while the annual volume of loans rose from 290 to 335. Yet the interest rate had remained at 3 percent.[3] The number of pawnshops in the village actually went up from 15 in 1983 to 24 in 1989. Most remarkably, the value of loans extended by pawnbrokers during 1988–1989 was five times that of the village bank (p. 18–4). In addition, mutual finance groups sprung up. By 1991, 50 out of the 200 households in the village participated in these savings and credit groups. By 1992, the loan volume of mutual finance groups was comparable to the pawnshops and exceeded the village bank (pp. 18–8, 18–9). A substantial expansion in curb market activities followed the introduction of the village bank.

Obviously the overall demand for credit increased dramatically such that the village bank could not meet the demand. In 1988–1989 the village bank accounted for less than a quarter of the loans extended in the village (p. 18–3). In addition, the bank was poorly managed and failed to carry out its mandate. Meant to serve a total of 17 villages, over half went to relatively well-off members of one community even though other poorer communities were a specific target group of government policy. It is also worth noting that in 1989, 52 percent of the bank's loan portfolio was in arrears, and 30 percent was past due for over three years, that is, in default. By way of contrast, during the same period 70 percent of the loans extended by the village's main pawnshop were repaid in full.

Furthermore, the bank did not offer the types of services demanded by particular groups. In contrast, pawnbroking and mutual finance groups adapted flexibility to seasonal needs such as housing construction, education, migration, agricultural cultivation, and ceremonial expenditures.

The credit market was also highly segmented along group and occupational lines. Due to their life cycle and consumption needs (e.g., weddings and funerals), a targeted constituency ended up relying on pawnbroking loans. The community of the original pawnbrokers stopped using pawnshops by 1989 and enjoyed privileged access to the village bank while dominating the pawnbroking businesses. Informal credit markets were also segmented along occupational and gender lines. Of 126 villagers participating in mutual finance, 125 were men. Groups were organized by professional occupation but relatively few (8 percent) poor cultivators of a targeted community participated in mutual finance. Most of the bank's loans were monopolized by the local curb market financiers who then expanded the provision of informal financial services at higher interest to other groups in the village.

Consider next a case study from China, a village in a southern coastal province that shows strong internal differentiation even where everyone could be considered a relative. This Chinese village is comparable in size to the Indian one, but 95 percent of the households share a surname and a village temple.[4] Nonetheless, credit was segmented.

The political fault lines were based on the three branches of the single lineage. The first had most of the Communist Party members. Another was the most prosperous one before the communists won power and was subjected to political persecution in the Mao era. Households from the first branch dominate village governance and the allocation of credit. Members in the third branch have a difficult time accessing official sources of credit. Although members of the remaining branch are neither politically privileged nor persecuted, they still suffer disadvantaged access to production inputs relative to the first branch.

In the reform era, the previously disadvantaged two branches found ways to run private businesses without going through official channels. A member of the persecuted branch owns the largest village factory, yet has never borrowed from formal sources of credit. He explained, "It's not worth it to me to apply for a loan from a state bank or rural credit cooperative because the credit officers are dirty and rip me off given my family background." He also noted that households from the privileged branch were more likely to borrow from state banks or credit cooperatives because their relatives work there. Lacking such official connections, the factory owner nonetheless invested 700,000 RMB (US$84,000) in his motorcycle parts factory by using 100,000 RMB (US$12,000) of his own savings, borrowing 200,000 RMB (US$24,000) interest free from his four older siblings, and borrowing 400,000 RMB ($48,000) at 24 percent annual interest through moneylenders (*yinbei*). The latter loans were guaranteed by his sister's good credit.

At the outset of reform, an iron factory, which relied mainly on credit cooperative loans was run by the politically privileged branch. In the early 1980s, about 25 households in the middling branch set up a plastics factory by pooling savings for four years. Clusters of smaller household factories (sugar, lime, paint, auto parts, and textiles) raised their capital in sectorally distinctive ways. The local credit cooperative and county-level agricultural bank could not meet the grassroots demand for capital. Informal financing spread. The businesses of the privileged branch receiving formal sector loans have not performed as well as those financed by the curb. Elites do not view their loans as serious business obligations.

Gender represents another dimension along which credit markets are segmented. In contrast to the male-dominated Indian savings and credit groups, the rotating credit groups in the Chinese village (called *chenghui* or *hui*) are managed by women. In China's southern coastal provinces, women dominate *hui* based on established social networks. A handful of middle-aged women run such groups full time.

Despite the popularity of informal finance in both India and China, the financial landscape differs. While the introduction of formal finance to the Indian village greatly expanded the volume of the curb, in the Chinese village the formal financial institutions have been captured by local political elites who are not adept at business (cf. Adams, Graham, and von Pischke 1984; Otero and Rhyne 1994). The vast majority of commercially successful operations in the Chinese village have relied on the curb. This is typical of China's private sector. As of year-end 2003, less than 1 percent of all loans extended by state banks were going to private entrepreneurs (PBC 2004). Hence, even though there is political and economic segmentation at the local level, the expansion of informal finance in China strongly reflects the limited supply of formal credit going to the non-state sector.

VII

The popularity of informal finance in rural China and rural India can be attributed to a failure of the state in both countries to develop microfinance programs that meet local needs. Merely increasing official credit will not address the problems of cost recovery and reaching the targeted population. Credit officers and other officials face local pressures and incentives for credit distribution that deviate from the poverty alleviation intentions of state authorities. This is especially true for subsidized microfinance programs because microloans are readily turned into political patronage. Meanwhile, the curb at the grassroots has a comparative advantage in knowledge about credit worthiness.

Although it has better social conditions for the creation of successful official microfinance programs, China's state-controlled financial system has so far prevented the country from performing better than India in this realm. In both countries, local state agents often subvert central state objectives. Despite vastly different political systems, the challenge of directing credit to poor rural dwellers remains pressing in both countries. Local state agents may subvert central state objectives in both cases. Neither seems close to achieving the kind of microfinance, which holds the greatest potential for displacing usurious forms of informal finance in the poorest countryside, India mainly for societal reasons, China mainly because of its restrictive financial system.

Notes

The ideas in this chapter were spelled out earlier in an article published in *World Development* 32, 9 (September 2004). Portions of that essay are reprinted here with permission from Elsevier. Earlier versions of this paper were presented at the Workshop on Local Governance in India and China: Rural Development and Social Change, Kolkata, January 6–8, 2003, and the Duke University Comparative Politics Workshop, February 24, 2003. The paper benefited greatly from the constructive input of the workshop participants. I am also grateful for the insights of Richard Baum, Anirudh Krishna, Laura Locker, Eddie Malesky, Mark Selden, Suman Sureshbabu, Sarah Tsien, Fei-ling Wang, Steven Wilkinson, and David Zweig, as well as the editorial assistance of Mary Akchurin.

1. By definition, *informal finance* refers to financial flows that occur beyond the scope of a particular country's formal financial system of banks, nonbanking financial institutions, and officially sanctioned capital markets. Most countries, however, also have a range of financial intermediaries that are best described as *semiformal* because central banking authorities do not regard them as part of the formal financial system, but they may be approved by some government agency or entity. *Informal* and *semi-formal* finance will generally be discussed together because both fall beyond the scope of standard commercial and developmental/policy-oriented financial institutions. In India and China, the definitional boundaries among informal, semiformal, and formal finance have shifted due to changes in their political, macroeconomic, and regulatory environments.
2. Generally speaking, landlord lenders extend credit to tenants; agricultural moneylenders primarily deal with agricultural laborers and small farmers; and professional moneylenders service a wider range of customers and may register themselves as companies, partnerships, and trusts (Ghate 1992, p. 45).
3. The US$ equivalent of the Indian Rupee went from Rs. 9.8 per one US$ in 1982–1983 to Rs. 15.1 in 1988–1989.
4. "Lin Village" is a pseudonym. This case is based on fieldwork in Wenzhou, Zhejiang province, 2000–2001.

References

Adams, D. W. and Fitchett, D. A. (eds.) (1992). *Informal Finance in Low-Income Countries*. Boulder: Westview Press.

Adams, D. W., Graham, D. and von Pischke, J. D. (1984). *Undermining Rural Development with Cheap Credit*. Boulder: Westview Press.

Agricultural Finance Corporation (AFC) (1988). *Agricultural Credit Review: Role and Effectiveness of Lending Institutions*, Vol. V. Bombay: AFC.

Ashe, J. (2002). *Self-Help Groups and Integral Human Development*. Cambridge: Brandeis University & Catholic Relief Services.

Asian Development Bank (ADB) (2000). *The Role of Central Banks in Asia and the Pacific*. Manilla: ADB.

Bagchi, A. K. (1972). *Private Investment in India:1900–1939*. Cambridge: Cambridge University Press.

Bansal, H. (2003). "SHG-Bank Linkage Program in India: An Overview." *Journal of Microfinance* 5(1): 21–49.

Bell, C. (1990). "Interactions between Institutional and Informal Credit Agencies in Rural India." *The World Bank Economic Review* 4 (3): 297–327.

Bhatt, N. and Thorat, Y. S. P. (2001). "India's Regional Rural Banks: The Institutional Dimension of Reforms." *Journal of Microfinance* 3 (1): 65–94.

Bornstein, D. (1997). *The Price of a Dream: The Story of the Grameen Bank*. Chicago: University of Chicago.

Bouman, F. J. A. and Hospes, O. (eds.) (1994). *Financial Landscapes Reconstructed: The Fine Art of Mapping Development*. Boulder: Westview Press.

Bouman, F. J. A. with Bastiaansen, R., Van Den Bogaard, H., Gerner, H., Hospes, O., and Kormelink, J. G. (1989). *Small, Short, and Unsecured: Informal Rural Finance in India*. New York: Oxford University Press.

Chandavarkar, A. (1992). "Of Finance and Development: Neglected and Unsettled Questions," *World Development* 20: 133–142.

Cheng, E. (2003). "Microfinance in Rural China," in C. Findlay, A. Watson, E. Cheng, and G. Zhu (eds.), *Rural Financial Markets in China*. Canberra: Asia Pacific Press at the Australia National University, pp. 120–133.

Cheng, E., Findlay, C. and Watson, A. (1998). " 'We're not Financial Organizations!': Financial Innovation without Regulation in China's Rural Cooperative Funds," *MOCT-MOST: Economic Policy in Transition Economies* 8 (3): 41–55.

China Development Brief (May 1999), 2, 2.

Conroy, J. D. (2000). "People's Republic of China," ADB (ed.), *The Role of Central Banks in Asia and the Pacific*. Manilla: ADB.

Das-Gupta, A., Nayar, C. P. S. and Associates (1989). Urban Informal Credit Markets in India. New Delhi: National Institute of Public Finance and Policy.

Du, X. S. (May 8, 2003). Author's correspondence.

Du, Z. X. (March 1998). The Dynamics and Impact of the Development of Rural Cooperative Funds (RCFs) in China. Working Paper No. 98/2, Chinese Economies Research Centre, The University of Adelaide.

EDA Rural Systems (1996). *India: Micro-finance for the Poor: An Assessment of the Status and Efficacy of Microfinance Institutions and Programmes*. Study prepared for the Asian and Pacific Development Centre, Kuala Lumpur.

Evans, P., Reuschemeyer, D., and Skocpol, T. (eds.) (1985). *Bringing the State Back In*. New York: Cambridge University Press.

Ghate, P. et al. (1992). *Informal Finance: Some Findings from Asia*. Manila: Asian Development Bank, Oxford University Press.

Hannig, A. and Katimbo-Mugwanya, E. (eds.) (1999). How to Regulate and Supervise Microfinance? Key Issues in an International Perspective. Proceedings of the High-Level Policy Workshop, Kampala.

Hoff, K., Braverman, A., and Stiglitz, J. (eds.) (1993). *The Economics of Rural Organization: Theory, Practice, and Policy*. New York: Oxford University Press for The World Bank.

Hoff, K. and Stiglitz, J. (1990). "Imperfect Information and Rural Credit Markets: Puzzles and Policy Perspectives." *The World Bank Economic Review* 4 (3): 235–250.

Holcombe, S. (1995). *Managing to Empower: The Grameen Bank Experience of Poverty Alleviation*. London: Zed Books.

Holz, C. A. (2001). "China's Monetary Reform: The Counterrevolution from the Countryside." *Journal of Contemporary China* 20 (27): 189–217.

Hsiao, K. H. (1971). *Money and Monetary Policy in Communist China*. New York: Columbia University Press.

International Fund for Agricultural Development (IFAD) (2001). *People's Republic of China: Thematic Study on Rural Financial Services in China*. Rome, Italy. Available at http://www.ifad.org/evaluation/public_html/eksyst/doc/thematic/pi/cn/cn_1.htm#2.

Jones, J. H. M. (1994). "A Changing Financial Landscape in India: Macro-Level and Micro-Level Perspectives," in F. J. A. Bouman and O. Hospes (eds.), *Financial Landscapes Reconstructed: The Fine Art of Mapping Development*. Boulder: Westview Press, Ch. 18.

Khandker, S. R., Khalily, B., and Khan, Z. (1995). Grameen Bank: Performance and Sustainability. World Bank Discussion Paper. No. 306, Washington D.C.: The World Bank.

Li, M. Y. (October 2000). "Diandangye: 'jinzi zhaopai' xiexia qianhou" (Pawnshops: Future After Removing the "Gold Store Sign") *Hexun caijing* (Homeway Financial News).

Migdal, J. S., Kohli, A., and Shue, V. (1994). *State Power and Social Forces: Domination and Transformation in the Third World*. New York: Cambridge University Press.

Morduch, J. (2000). "The Microfinance Schism," *World Development* 28 (4): 617–629.

Nagarajan, G. and Meyer, R. L. (2000). *Rural Financial Markets in Asia: Paradigms, Policies, and Performance*. Manilla: ADB.

National Bank for Agriculture and Rural Development (NABARD) (2002). *Ten Years of SHG-Bank Linkage (1992–2002)*. Mumbai: NABARD.

NABARD (2003). Regional Spread of SHGs as on 31 March 2003. Available at http://www.nabard.org/oper/oper.htm.

Nayar, C. P. S. (1992). "Strengths of Informal Financial Institutions: Examples from India," in D. W. Adams and D. A. Fitchett (eds.), *Informal Finance in Low-Income Countries*. Boulder: Westview, pp. 199–200.

Otero, M. and Rhyne, E. (eds.) (1994). *The New World of Microenterprise Finance*. West Hartford, CT: Kumarian Press.

Park, A. (May 1999). "Banking for the Poor," *China Brief* II (2): 9–15.

Park, A., Brandt, L., and Giles, J. (2003). "Competition Under Credit Rationing: Theory and Evidence from Rural China." *Journal of Development Economics* 71 (2): 463–495.

Park, A. and Ren, C. (2001). "Microfinance with Chinese Characteristics." *World Development* 29 (1): 39–62.

Patrick, H. T. (1966). "Financial Development and Economic Growth in Developing Countries." *Economic and Cultural Change* 14 (2): 174–189.

People's Bank of China (PBC) (January 15, 2004). "Financial Industry's Performance was Stable in 2003." Available online at http://www.pbc.gov.cn.

Press Information Bureau (PIB), Government of India (March 22, 2002). "Expert Group on Nihdis Recommends Continuation of Regulatory Measures." Available at http://pib.nic.in/archieve/lreleng/lyr2002/rmar2002/22032002/r220320022.html.

Reserve Bank of India (RBI) (1954). *All-India Credit Survey*. Bombay: RBI.

RBI (February 8, 2000). All-India Debt and Investment Survey (AIDIS). "1991–92—Incidence of Indebtedness of Households, Part I." *RBI Bulletin*. Available at http://www.rbi.org.in.

Rozelle, S., Park, A., Ren, C. and Bezinger, V. (1998). "Targeted Poverty Investments and Economic Growth in China." *World Development* 26 (12): 2137–2151.

Rutherford, S. and Arora, S. S. (1997). *City Savers*. New Delhi: Department for International Development.

Saich, T. (2000). "Negotiating the State: The Development of Social Organizations in China." *The China Quarterly* 161: 124–141.

Satish, P. (2001). "Institutional Alternatives for the Promotion of Microfinance: Self-Help Groups in India." *Journal of Microfinance* 3(2): 49–74.

Schrader, H. (1994). "Moneylenders and Merchant Bankers in India and Indonesia," in F. J. A. Bouman and O. Hospes (eds.), *Financial Landscapes Reconstructed: The Fine Art of Mapping Development*. Boulder: Westview Press, pp. 341–355.

Selden, M. and Perry, E. (eds.) (2000). *Chinese Society: Conflict, Change, and Resistance*. London: Routledge.

Sinha, S. (2000). "India." Asian Development Bank (ed.), *The Role of Central Banks in Microfinance in Asia and the Pacific: Country Studies, Vol.2*. Manilla: ADB, pp. 61–89.

Swain, R. B. (2002). "Credit Rationing in Rural India." *Journal of Economic Development* 27 (2): 1–20.

Tsai, K. S. (2000). "Banquet Banking: Rotating Savings and Credit Associations in South China." *The China Quarterly* 161: 143–170.

Tsai, K. S. (2002). *Back-Alley Banking: Private Entrepreneurs in China*. Ithaca: Cornell University Press.

Tsai, L. L. (2002). "Cadres, Temple and Lineage Institutions." *The China Journal* 48: 1–27.

Tsien, S. (2001). "International Projects Left in the Lurch as Government Weighs In." *China Development Brief* 4: 1.

Unger, J. (2002). *The Transformation of Rural China*. Armonk: M.E. Sharpe.

Walder, A. and Oi, J. (eds.) (1999). *Property Rights and Economic Reform in China*. Stanford: Stanford University Press.

Watson, A. (2003). "Financing Farmers: The Reform of Rural Credit Cooperatives and Provision of Financial Services to Farmers," in C. Findlay, A. Watson,

C. Enjiang, and Z. Gang (eds.), *Rural Financial Markets in China*. Canberra: Asia Pacific Press at The Australia National University, pp. 63–88.

Whiting, S. (2001). *Power and Wealth in Rural China: The Political Economy of Institutional Change*. New York: Cambridge University Press.

Wilson, K. (2002). "The New Microfinance: An Essay on the Self-Help Group Movement in India." *Journal of Microfinance* 4 (2): 217–245.

Wu, J. M. (1998). Local Property Rights Regime in Socialist Reform: A Case Study of China's Informal Privatization. Unpublished doctoral dissertation, Columbia University, New York.

Xin, J. (1993). *Diandang shi* (History of Pawnshops). Shanghai: Shanghai wenyi chubanshe.

Yaron, J., Benjamin, Jr., M. P., and Piprek, G. L. (1997). *Rural Finance: Issues, Design, and Best Practices.* Environmentally and Socially Sustainable Development Studies & Monographs Series 13, Washington D.C.: The World Bank.

Zhongguo yinhang Beijing guoji jinrong yanjiusuo (BOC Beijing Institute of International Finance (1993). *Zhongguo de jinrong jigou jiqi zhuyao jingying* (China's Financial Institutions and their Primary Management), Beijing: Zhongguo jihua chubanshe.

News Sources

Agence France Presse (AFP)
Associated Press (AP)
China Daily
China Internet Information Center (CIIC)
China Online
Jingji ribao (JJRB–Economic Daily)
People's Daily (PD)
Shanghai Information Center (SIC)
Xinhua

8

The Political Basis of Decentralization

Aseema Sinha

I

A pervasive "China Envy" dominates public debates in India; India is mostly compared unfavorably to China. Most comparisons contrast China's double-digit growth and high Foreign Direct Investment (FDI) levels with India's slower growth rate and much lower FDI levels. This contrast is usually attributed to democracy in India, which, it is argued, has negative costs for economic performance.[1] In addition, it is believed that decentralization in China has facilitated its economic success. India's centralized system ("insufficient decentralization") creates obstacles to economic reform. According to Percy Barnevik, a former chairman and chief executive of Asea Brown Boveri (ABB):

> Maybe India would be served well by deeper decentralization. That could make things move faster . . . a lot of economic decisions can be handled locally. And then the Andhra Pradesh guy can talk to the Kerala guy and benchmark—why are they getting more than us? What are they doing that we are not doing? [In China] except certain strategic issues like police, foreign policy etc. the local guys are in charge. And they move. And growth is tremendous. That's not through Beijing but in spite of Beijing.[2]

This chapter explores the impact of decentralization and democratic competition on economic reform. It argues that standard theories of decentralization fail to distinguish between political and economic dimensions of decentralization. In addition, democratic deepening may have some unintended effects on the consolidation of economic reform not accounted for by conventional theories and comparisons. I find that the political dimensions of decentralization are crucial in providing incentives for actors to pursue or support reform-oriented policies, in other words, to the consolidation of economic reforms. Party competition, a product of the ongoing democratic resurgence in India, leads to a more credible political decentralization. In China, intra-party linkages and central-local informal interactions make fiscal decentralization more credible, at least in the short run. Thus, different aspects of *political* decentralization in the two countries have facilitated the consolidation of economic reform in both systems.

The reason is that certain political factors provide *linkage mechanisms* that moderate conflict across levels and enhance *joint* benefits between central and local actors. Whereas political linkage mechanisms facilitate an alignment between national and (some) regional incentives in favor of economic reform, a disproportionate reliance on formal fiscal indicators (subnational revenue and expenditures shares) leads to a zero–sum picture of central-local relations (Chung 2000, 26). The India–China comparison suggests the importance of winner coalitions between gaining provinces and reformist central rulers creating a momentum in favor of economic reform. Intergovernmental (in India) or intra-party (in China) linkages facilitate interactions enabling some regional and central actors to gain from economic reform measures. Where such intra-governmental linkages are missing, zero–sum interactions may result. Contemporary Russia and Brazil lack such linkage mechanisms across levels of governments. China and India, in contrast, both have well-functioning linkage mechanisms that enable interdependence among regional and central rulers' preferences in favor of economic reform.[3]

Seen in this light, India's and China's reform trajectories (post–1991 India and post–1978 China) are more *similar* than is evident by merely looking at their economic features and output indicators. Rather, political linkage mechanisms—of personnel, institutions, and authority—across regional and national governments have created conditions for economic reforms to sustain themselves in both countries. It is this political linkage of the local with the national that holds the key to successful economic reform in the two giants. While the two countries have relied on different political mechanisms—a second democratic revolution in India and policy decentralization in China—the results in terms of protecting local autonomy and consolidating support for economic reforms have been largely similar.

These findings and arguments also suggest a more nuanced treatment of the question of whether democratic or authoritarian systems are better for economic performance. In India, a second democratic revolution embodied in the rise of several regional parties intensified party competition. Coalition governments at the national level allow for more credible decentralization that also commands political legitimacy. Thus, political decentralization and intensification of democratic competition work together to align subnational and national incentives in favor of economic reform. Coalition governments and greater participation by small and regional parties in national and state governments makes economic reform more legitimate and irreversible. This finding runs counter to the arguments that coalition governments are destabilizing for economic reform. These political features of an ongoing democratic revolution provide the indispensable political prerequisites for more formal economic reform steps, even as they also mean that the reform process must be altered to attend to those being left behind.

II

Much work on decentralization and economic policy is informed by the theory of fiscal federalism (Musgrave and Peggy Musgrave 1973; Stigler [1957] 1998; Tiebout 1956). Based on a theory of public goods, it holds that distribution and stabilization are best carried out by central governments, and allocation is most efficient when undertaken by the level of government where benefits are enjoyed. The theory of market-preserving federalism (MPF) states the insights of fiscal federalism in five conditions (chart 8.1).[4] The first (F1) condition is the existence of a hierarchy of governments with a delineated well-defined scope of authority. The second (F2) is that the subnational governments must have primary authority over the economy. The third (F3) is that the national government has the authority to police the market. The fourth (F4) condition is that revenue sharing among governments is limited and borrowing by governments is constrained so that all governments, especially subnational governments, face hard budget constraints. The fifth condition (F5) is that the allocation of authority between federal and subnational governments has institutionalized durability.[5] Together, the five are supposed to preserve markets and produce growth. Translating the theory on a horizontal axis, it is possible to arrange countries by the number of conditions of MPF they satisfy.

Chart 8.1 A comparative theory of market-preserving federalism

(Non-MPF) F1/5	*F2/5*	*F3/5*	*F4/5*	*F5 (MPF)*
Former Soviet Union	India Argentina Brazil Mexico		Contemporary China	Eighteenth-century England Pre-1930s United States

This mapping distinguishes among federal systems and suggests a varying potential for economic performance. However, this account does not differentiate between economic and political realms.[6] Economic "federalism" requires only administrative decentralization, a mere redistribution of economic functions. Political decentralization is distinct. Most economists refer to economic decentralization in terms of factor markets of capital and labor. Autonomy over local economic policy to supply local public goods (condition 2 of the market-preserving arguments) is a key component of economic decentralization.

Political decentralization is decentralization with respect to legislatures, elections, political parties, and patronage systems.[7] Political decentralization calls attention not only to local politics—including their autonomy from local socioeconomic classes and elites—but also to national politics. Regime type and party system affect the extent and nature of political decentralization.

The MPF framework (conditions 2 and 5) assumes meaningful political (as distinct from administrative or economic) decentralization, that is, protections against central government interference (F5). The MPF framework highlights the *policy* autonomy of local governments. It neglects other factors—party system, electoral procedures, legislative authority—which affect local policy autonomy.

Most observers of China find its party system centralized. National organs of the Chinese Communist Party can hire, fire, and transfer party officials.[8] Yet, local governments exercise considerable *policy* autonomy. Decentralization, whether political or economic, does not guarantee liberalization or growth. Political variables shape the preferences of regionally based and centrally located incumbents. Formulaic prescriptions about party system (whether decentralized or not) or fiscal features (whether market-preserving or not) give no clues on the conditions under which politicians with divergent interests may *choose* to act *jointly* in favor of economic reforms. For economic reform to consolidate, some mechanisms must facilitate the *linking* of interests so that contradictory preferences may be made consistent. Linkage institutions can allow the subnational and central actors to collaborate to mitigate conflicts between levels while enhancing cooperative actions.

Linkage mechanisms enhance the prospects for cooperation across levels.[9] Linkage mechanisms may be defined as institutions, networks, and resources that span different levels *allowing* actors located in different spatial arenas to *interact* cooperatively across these arenas. For economic policy in multitiered settings, three types of linkage mechanisms are important. They are linkages of *authority-power, institutions, and personnel.* Authority–power linkage mechanisms refer both to the formal roles conferred on actors as well as the exercise of real or informal power. These linkages refer to legislative and recruitment autonomy.

In China central leaders make recruitment decisions, but organizational norms or informal rules *separate from* the levels of government allow subnational rulers to interact with national level actors. In India, the National Development Council (NDC) and the Interstate Council include the states' and the center's representatives and meet regularly to discuss overlapping issues. Personnel linkages refer to circulation of elites: Do subnational politicians hold central posts? In systems with a high degree of inter-level exchange of elites, economic reforms will be self-enforcing when most actors will have incentives to pursue reform-enhancing policies. Linkage mechanisms affect political and economic incentives of both central and regional (local) incumbents. Successful economic reform in both India and China is explicable with the help of this theory.

III

Comparisons of India and China are widely invoked in current theories and empirical debates (Bhalla 1995; Freidman 1998; Parikh and Weingast 1997; Rose-Ackerman and Rodden 1997; Rosen 1990; Saez 2000). By 2015, these two economies will be among the three largest economies in terms of output (Maddison 1998). The destiny of these two nations will impact the world.

For most analysts it is the *contrast* between India and China's economic performance that forms their starting point. However, correcting for an upward bias exaggerating statistics from China and a significant acceleration in India's growth pattern in the late 1990s leads to a reconsideration of the usual contrast between a supposedly successful China and a low growth India (Krugman and Obstfeld 1997, 268; Maddison 1998; Rawski 2001a; 2001b; 2001c; 2002; Sachs and Woo 1997; Ren 1997). While China's growth in the early

1990s was higher than India's, India grew much faster than China between 1998 and 2003.[10]

A similar revaluation impacts foreign investment performance. Chinese figures overestimate FDI, while India's statistics underestimate FDI.[11] In addition, macroeconomic adjustment has been stable in India since the late 1990s and relatively unstable in China, where inflation has been more of a problem. Yet, economic reforms seem self-enforcing in both countries. In sum, democratic India's and authoritarian China's reform trajectories are actually comparable.

Contrasting India as a centralized federation and China as a market-preserving decentralized state results from an undue focus on administrative and fiscal dimensions. Four of the five conditions outlined by the theory of market-preserving federalism relate to economic or fiscal matters. However, federalism's impact on the success of economic reform is mediated by political institutions and informal political relations. In the post–liberalization phase in India, economic decentralization is evident. In contrast, in 1994, China's national government moved toward fiscal recentralization. Yet, economic reforms continue to be self-enforcing and to generate moderate to high growth in both. Therefore, an explanation centered on fiscal attributes is insufficient.

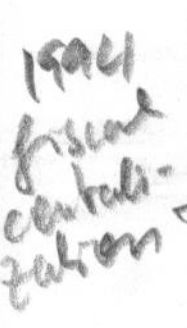

India in the 1990s experienced de facto (unplanned) decentralization, the unintended consequence of liberalization. Economic reforms abolished many central regulations regarding licensing, locational control, and trade. Procedural simplification and a change in location policy followed. Factories could be established beyond 25 km of the major cities. These changes in the regulatory framework contributed to decentralization. First, the abolition of central regulations made the preexisting state-level regulatory machinery more salient for investors (Sinha 2005). Second, reregulation of liberalization by many state-level officials enhanced provincial roles in investment. This process, despite relative fiscal centralism compared to China, generated moderate to high growth in the 1990s. This accelerated growth in the post–1994 period is *not* consistent with the predictions generated by the fiscal or market-preserving literature. That is, a market-federalist system is emerging *despite* disproportionate fiscal power for the central state.

This is because India's federal system subsequent to 1989 is not market-disregarding. Regional states exercise "primary authority" over industrial and economic policies within their jurisdictions (condition 2 of market-preserving arguments). They play an increasing role in attracting FDI and pursuing global integration (as do Chinese provinces).[12] Direct attraction of foreign investment by states has contributed to *de facto* authority to approve foreign investment projects, establish tax rates for foreign investment firms, and establish rules of the game. Thus, state level actors are shaping foreign economic relations (Sinha 2004). This enhancement of regional autonomy has accompanied the introduction of partial hard budget measures (condition 4 of MPF arguments). The 1997–1998 central budget made it more difficult for the central government to borrow from the Reserve Bank of India (RBI), ensuring some central bank independence. Recently, the RBI refused to bankroll state deficits, imposing a hard budget constraint on the states.[13]

Previously in India, president's rule (Article 356), by which the state government is suspended or expelled, gave great power to the center. Recent changes make imposing president's rule very difficult. Since June 1998, soon after the BJP government took office in New Delhi, Jayalalitha, the head of the AIADMK party and a coalition partner in the BJP-led government, urged the central government to dismiss the DMK (a regional party) government in the state of Tamil Nadu. Similarly, the Samata Party, another partner of the BJP based in Bihar, demanded the dismissal of the Rabri Devi government in Bihar. Trinamul Congress's leader, Mamata Banerjee, an ally of the BJP, also demanded the imposition of Article 356 in West Bengal. In July 1998, however, the BJP rebuffed each of these attempts, arguing that Article 356 enshrined only an emergency power and could not be invoked. Also, judicial rulings against invoking Article 356 provide an irreversible institutional remedy.[14] The Supreme Court in 1994 ruled against a misuse of Article 356. A unanimous judgment by the nine-judge constitutional bench delivered on March 11, 1994 further held that any action under Article 356 is subject to judicial review. Consequently, no future government will be able to impose president's rule easily. Federalism is an institutional fact in India. Moreover the resurgence of certain regulatory—for example, the Telecommunication Authority of India (TRAI) and political institutions (judiciary, election commission) strengthen federalism in a credible and institutional way.[15]

In addition, the Indian fiscal system has moved toward giving more fiscal power to regional states. As a result of political reforms, India's federal balance no longer thwarts markets. Other reforms facilitate the persistence of India's liberalization. Beyond reforms that empower the local governments to checkmate the central government's fiscal controls, *linkage mechanisms* generated by party system change in the 1980s and 1990s make local and central preferences for economic liberalization consistent.

While the Congress Party initiated reforms, first tentatively in 1985 and then more thoroughly in 1991, the political consolidation of reforms was facilitated by political decentralization, most notably in the party system and in government formation at the national level. These changes ensure that national and local incentives in favor of reform coincide.[16] The party system in India has changed from a one-party dominant system (the "Congress-system") to a multiparty regionalized system. In the late 1980s the Congress Party declined and backward caste-based and regional parties rose. Minority or coalition governments have ruled since the late 1980s. The role of regional parties in national coalition governments has created *authority-power and personnel linkage mechanisms* across central and regional levels. Regional parties consequently perform national roles as articulated by a regional party member:

Preelectoral alignment between parties seeking a parliamentary majority has changed the political system. In the 1998 and 1999 elections, the BJP was forced to align with regional forces even at the cost of diluting its ideological purism. This "federalized party structure" facilitates credible guarantees against central encroachment even in the absence of adequate fiscal conditions, preventing the center from using president's rule or abusing fiscal powers.[17]

The incorporation of regional elements in the national government is the key. Such political decentralization is almost impossible in China's single-party Leninist system. Being part of the government is seen in India to be important for the regional state. Circulation of regional politicians from regions to the national level ensures *personnel linkages* across spatial levels. Regional incumbents derive patronage advantages from economic liberalization and have a say in the formulation and implementation of nation-wide reform policies. The railway minister, the commerce minister, and the industry minister in the government of 1999, for example, all vied in policy formulation, and in the allocation of reform goodies to their states. Mamata Banerjee (the then railway minister and the head of a regional party in West Bengal) talked of the "Bengal Package."[18] Karunanidhi, the then chief minister of Tamil Nadu, said after being convinced by the prime minister to give up claims to the finance department portfolio in the 1999 government, "We want finances for our state and not finance (portfolio at the center)."[19] Ministerial candidates attempted to reorient reform programs to serve their regional agendas, in the process carrying the reform program forward, although some gains are narrowly particularistic.

Yet, access to regionally specific patronage opportunities facilitates political consolidation of economic reforms, even when it does not further economic rationality. Regional incumbents can compensate losers and ensure their parties' political survival. The potential of participation in the central government—personnel linkages—forces even ideological adversaries, for example, the CPI (M), to channel its political energies toward extracting benefits for their state from the central reform program, rather than oppose the program.[20] A regionalized coalition government ensures positive-sum alignment between national and regional incentives in favor of liberalization and prevents *both* disengagement and opposition to the reform process.[21] This also makes reform more legitimate across India's territory and elites.

In a second stage of reform, vertical authority linkages have been used by the center to ensure some consistency across levels (subnational and central). The center inserted a monitoring mechanism in the Eleventh Finance Commission's award, which benefits states that reduce their fiscal deficit by a stated percentage. Regular consultations with the offending states with the central finance ministry may ensure compliance. The center has played a major role in urging states toward an equivalent sales tax regime, replacing competitive sales competition across the states. The formation of a disinvestment ministry and the appointment of an honest and zealous reformer sped the privatization process in early 2000s. Thus, while personnel linkages—participation of regional parties in the central government—are important for cross-level coalitions in favor of reform, authority linkages and *re-assertion of vertical linkages*—in the form of finance ministry consultations and central reformers—ensure some (not total) consistency of reform goals in India. As a result, India's reform program has more legitimacy and wider support.

IV

China, in contrast to India, has a very centralized party system. Yet linkage mechanisms *across* levels of the party-state created a dynamic in favor of reform. China's reforms, begun in 1978, involved a more formal fiscal realignment in revenue structures than subsequently in India. The major fiscal reform of 1980 ("eating in separate kitchens") made each subnational level responsible for its own revenues and expenditure. Fiscal revenues were shared upward, each level sending a share of its revenues to the upper level while each level of government could keep a share of the revenues it collected based on a multiyear contract negotiated with the higher level. Moreover each could, through extra-budgetary revenue collection, bypass the center and enhance local revenue capacity. Thus, local governments acquired strong incentives for tax collection and self-financing. Local government's expenditure responsibilities rendered the revenue imperative acute, leading to an "investment hunger" (Huang 1996). This unleashed rapid economic growth.[22] Rural industrial output grew at an average annual rate of nearly 25 percent after 1978 (Whiting 2001, 2).

In short, fiscal autonomy enhanced the power of the local government, providing "considerable political protection for China's reforms, including limits on the central government" (Montinola et al. 1995, 52, 68–73). The fiscal reforms of the 1980s created local incentives facilitating crucial partnerships, "local state corporatism" between local party leaders and entrepreneurs.[23] This fusion of local government-firms linkages accelerated a *cross*-regional competition to attract FDI. This dynamic stimulated horizontal "competitive liberalization" among local units (Yang 1997).

While horizontal competition explains the onset of local reform policies, it does not explain their persistence in the face of economic crisis (inflation, for example) or counterchallenges. Despite attempts at enhancing central revenue capacity,[24] China's economic reforms endured because of a political factor, the overlapping informal mechanisms linking some local and central reform-oriented party officials.[25] These linkage mechanisms facilitate interaction across coastal provinces and central levels rendering key local and central preferences over reforms consistent. Political linkage is the key to China's self-enforcing reform process.

The consolidation of reform can only be explained by the vertical linkages and the formation of new reform coalitions between coastal party secretaries with pro-reform leaders at the center as well as by the interests and choices of aspiring provincial party secretaries who want inclusion in the process. Overlapping preferences (between central and some local elites) and the formation of cross-level reform coalitions were evident in the evolution of a coastal development strategy. The center has gained from the rapid growth of the coastal regions, which provide economic resources to service China's foreign debt and pay for imports. "The CDS [coastal development strategy] could potentially purchase political support [for central leaders] from representatives of the coastal provinces, while also delivering a considerable economic benefit to the country as a whole."[26] Wan Li, a party leader in Anhui, used his links with the reformist coalition (of Deng Xiaoping and

Zhao Ziyang) at the center to get support for his experiments at the local level (Chung 2000, Chapter Four). In addition, the continued success of economic liberalization gave political legitimacy to the reformist factions in Beijing against conservatives.[27] Deng and the reformist coalition at the center used Wan Li's "successful household responsibility system" to counter the "conservative" groups at the central level. The self-enforcing (although yet not institutionalized) character of the Chinese reform process rests on the creation and revival of inter-level interactions and converging interests between some central level party actors and local (largely coastal) party leaders.

Interactions across levels in China reveal dense communication links and interchange of resources, people, and ideas about reform through a two-way process. Most economic reform declarations by the central leaders as well as local initiatives have been preceded by tours by central leaders to the provinces, by Deng Xiaoping, Zhao Ziyang, and Zhu Rongji (Lee 2000, 1013; Yang 1991, 50). These visits not only bring recalcitrant provincial leaders into line, they also activate cross-level network and communication linkages allowing greater interaction and bargaining between central and local leaders.[28] In January 1994, Shanghai sent its mayor to Beijing twice to protest a 1993 tax. Reform is a two-way process. These multiple cross-level interactions facilitate consistency of central and local preferences over reform that would be impossible without the *modus operandi* of bargaining, interaction, and dialogue about partially conflicting interests.

More strongly, an intra-party flow of party and state personnel—personnel linkages—sustains consistency between potentially contradictory central and (some) local preferences over economic reforms and holds the key to the self-enforcing reform dynamic. Careers of party leaders at the local and central levels are linked to each other. Key reformist leaders in China began their political careers in the regions. Reforming provinces have a major presence in the politburo or are benefactors at the center.[29] Of the 15th congress politburo 83 percent has had administrative experience at the provincial level; 58 percent served as provincial chiefs. Only four members of the politburo had no provincial experience (Li 2002). Of the 16th congress (concluded in November 2002) politburo 88 percent have had significant provincial experience.[30] While 65 percent of the politburo had served as provincial chiefs, only three members of the politburo had no provincial experience. All members of the Standing Committee of the Politburo (nine) have had some provincial experience.[31] This upward orientation of local party leaders' career trajectories (a central feature of the Chinese party system creating cross-level linkage mechanisms) ensures convergence between central and local incentives in favor of reform.

An analysis of subnational variation in reform trajectories within China highlights the role of personnel linkage mechanisms. Crucial economic and locational factors (proximity to foreign markets, access to FDI, market infrastructure, etc.) played a major role in strengthening reform in the coastal provinces. But these economic advantages were complemented by informal political linkages. Provinces with regular cross-level personnel linkage have been supporters of the reform process and effective bargainers; the laggard inland provinces lack such linkages. In China, as in India, personnel circulation accompanies linkages across levels. To be sure, the central organs of the Communist Party of China (CPC) retain control of personnel policies (Huang 1996; Shirk 1993, 150). Conventionally, this should have adverse effects on regionally based reform prospects (Montinola, Qian, and Weingast 1995; Garman, Haggard, and Willis 2001). However, informal political mechanisms facilitate linkage between central and local elites, changing the incentives even in China's centralized party system. Top-down authority linkage mechanisms in China have facilitated compliance with central reform agendas, ensuring macroeconomic stabilization at crucial times but for the purpose of maintaining the dynamism of reform. In October 1993, the party secretary of Jiangsu was sacked for defying tax reform (Lee 2000). The central government recentralized some fiscal powers first during 1988–1989 and later in 1993–1994 to remove dysfunctional fiscal effects, modifying the agendas of provincial leaders at crucial times but ensuring consistency with the reform program across levels.[32]

What was significant about the Chinese reform trajectory was not whether recentralization was successful or whether the center had lost vis-à-vis the localities, but that vertical intra-party linkages and institutions spanning levels of government continue to function in favor of reform. The center ensured compliance with reform. Rather than a zero–sum game in which local governments must check the arbitrary power of the central government, informal linkages within the party-state made consistent local and central interests and preferences. Effective control from the top and local career incentives to be upwardly mobile were compatible in the pursuit of economic reforms. In India, regional participation in national government, institutionalization of political federalism and reassertion of central authority in key policy domains, similarly, make economic reform self-enforcing.

Nevertheless, several difficulties confront China's future developmental trajectory, implied by the earlier analysis. China's market friendly decentralization is not as credible, legitimate, or institutionalized as India's. It relies on mutual exchange within a hierarchical party and informal networks across levels. In a hypothetical counterfactual scenario, a China moving toward competitive parties and democratic elections—a democratizing China—might very well face serious challenges to its national policy of economic reform, or at the very least, require serious modifications of its key components. Losing provinces, or excluded elites, in such a transitional system might very well challenge and create much greater conflict around economic policy. Moreover, a non-legitimate and top-heavy system substantially increases the difficulty of the "second generation" institutional changes necessary for future economic reforms.[33] This is true for financial sector reforms and for ensuring that workers, peasants, as well as backward regions acquire a stake in future reform measures. Rising inequalities and poverty levels will need to be addressed to make economic reform fully sustainable in the future. Thus, while the informal compact between regional and central elites outlined earlier explains the success of the "first generation" economic reforms in China, this compact may yet prove insufficient for the tasks of the "second generation" reform agenda. In contrast, the underlying legitimacy and credibility generated by party competition in India's political system is likely to make sustaining economic reform less painful and easier in the future. Despite rising inequality in India, political protests around reform have been nonexistent; in contrast, in China peasant revolts have risen sharply in the last five years.[34] China will have to expend a lot of political and economic capital to ensure a more institutionalized and legitimate pathway to reform in the future.

V

Fiscal decentralization and economic changes attendant to economic liberalization alter the economic incentives of provincial and central leaders making conflict over economic policy more likely. In such contexts, institutions of local fiscal autonomy, and hard budget constraints are important to ensure growth-enhancing policies. Yet, political linkage mechanisms are indispensable in making sure that potentially conflictual central-local interactions do not degenerate into zero–sum conflict. Political linkage mechanisms generated by regionalized party competition in India and intra-party linkages in China make consistent local and central preferences and incentives over policy changes. Rather than, the "de-politicization of economic decisions," (Montinola, Qian, and Weingast 1995, 57) linkages across central-local arenas, a deeply political process involving circulating personnel, overlapping institutions, and authority mechanisms, facilitate pro-reform policies.

Moreover, democratization embodied in resurgent party competition and openness of the political system revealed by participation of regional elites in national coalition governments speeds the process of economic reform in India. In China, recentralization allows better intra-party overlap and congruent economic and fiscal policies. The trajectory of economic reform in large and diverse countries such as China and India shows that the ends of development cannot only be economic growth rates; development must be legitimate, stable, and involve diverse actors (elites at the subnational level, for example) in a participatory way. Economic reform consolidation and nonconflictual process of development should be one end of development. Reconciling political continuity and economic development requires the activation of political linkages across different levels of government.

A theory of linkage politics is better able to explain the variation in the consolidation of economic reform than the prevailing theories of fiscal federalism. First, it incorporates political-institutional and informal variables explicitly contributing to the literature on institutionalism and economic development. Second, it goes beyond a zero–sum view of central-subnational relations found in much of the economic federalism literature. Third, by analyzing a democratic state (India) and a nondemocratic state (China), it challenges the usual dichotomy between democratic and authoritarian states and explains their reform prospects by a general theory of policy change in multitiered states.

Notes

The theoretical part of the argument given here was first published as "Political Foundations of Market-Enhancing Federalism: Theoretical Lessons from India and China," *Comparative Politics*, Volume 37, Number 3, April 2005. This chapter is revised and expanded version of that article.

1. Authors that subscribe to the usual contrast between India and China are: Rosen (1990), Bhalla (1995) and Chhibber and Eldersveld (2000).
2. "Interview," *Economic Times (India)*, December 12, 1997, New Delhi Edition.
3. In contemporary Russia, for example, parties lack personnel and institutional mechanisms that *link* local and national politicians denying the expression and mediation of center-periphery interests. Peter Ordershook and Olga Shvetsova (1997) find that ". . . the electoral system [in contemporary Russia] . . . fails to encourage regionally based political parties that are integrated with a national organization" or are integrated in national campaigns. In Brazil, the constitutional rules (role and representation in the senate) and electoral system (open list PR), encourages regional representatives to veto any policies that affect their region adversely. Regionally inflected individualism and weak parties prevent the formation of electoral (as in India) or intra-party (as in China) linkages and coalitions among regional and central actors in both Russia and Brazil.
4. Weingast (1995). The theory of market-preserving federalism is simultaneously a "comparative theory of federalism." In the prevailing accounts of MPF, the non-market-preserving federal cases are India, Mexico, Argentina, and Brazil while the MPF cases are contemporary China, eighteenth-century England, and pre-1930s United States. For an extension of the analysis to India, see Parikh and Weingast (1997).
5. While departure from even one condition is enough to characterize a country as a non-market-preserving federal country, it is an open question if some conditions are more important than others. Despite China's inability to meet condition three (the common market condition), Montinola et. al. characterize China as market-preserving federal. Tsai (2004) argues that China satisfies only three out of the five conditions. Some contend that without constitutional constraints, China's authoritarian decentralization is not institutionalized and can be changed by a mere policy decision of rulers.
6. Hutchcroft (2001, 23–53) in a similar vein differentiates between administrative and political aspects of decentralization.
7. Ibid., pp. 32–37. Also see Stepan (2001) for attempts to analyze political aspects of decentralization.
8. Huang (1996) especially notes the combination of political centralization and subnational policy autonomy.
9. Lohmann (1997). For nested games, see Tsebelis (1990) and Putnam (1988).
10. Thomas Rawski (E-mail communication). Rawski also contends that while there may be overestimation of industrial output in China, there may well be an underestimation of service sector growth in China. Also, in 2004 China seems to have grown more rapidly than India. In a recent paper Lester Thurow, Nong Zhou and Yunshi Wang (2003), find that "growth rate in the 1990s was not the official rate of 9.7 percent but an adjusted rate of around 5 percent." Thus, while scholars differ about the extent of overestimation, it is clear that China's growth figures at least for the period 1998–2003 and most probably for the 1990s may be lower than supposed.
11. See Priya Ganapati (2002, 32, 36), which cites an ongoing study to remeasure FDI figures in India and China being done by the International Finance

Corporation. According to this study China's FDI figures for 2001 may be around 20 billion rather than $40 billion (official data), while India's may be $8 billion and not $3 billion (official Indian data). This study finds that FDI accounts for 2 percent of China's GDP while it accounts for 1.7 percent of that of India. See also Bajpai and Dasgupta (2004).

12. Jenkins (1999); L. Rudolph and S. Rudolph (2001); and Saez (2002).
13. Rao (2000, 195) and McCarten (2003, 333) confirm that states in India face a relatively hard budget constraint.
14. J. Bednar, W. Eskridge, and J. Ferejohn (2001) highlight the role of the Supreme Court in making U.S. federalism self-enforcing.
15. The revival of these intermediate institutions has been noted by many analysts. See Echeverri-Gent (2002) for how the revival of the election commission contributes to a significant "decentering" in India's system.
16. Ordershook (1996, 205) suggests that the *relationship* between local and national politicians is the key to understanding the preconditions for federal consolidation. I thank Barry Weingast for pointing me toward this reference.
17. This "federalized" party competition sustains the independence of the judiciary and its rulings over the president's rule in India. This is consistent with theoretical expectations: recent positive political theory arguments suggest that courts exert political independence under conditions of increased party competition. See Weingast (2002, 678–679 and 667–669) for a review of this literature.
18. *The Telegraph*, December–January 1999.
19. *The Hindu*, February 23, 2000.
20. Some reformers use their power at the center to slow reforms—most notably, privatization—in their regions. This has been true of Chandrababu Naidu who sought to delay disinvestment in Rashtriya Ispat Nigam Ltd., a government steel company, and of Karunanidhi, the erstwhile provincial leader of Tamil Nadu who fought the privatization of Salem Steel, and A. Jogi, the chief minister of Jharkhand, who fought the privatization of BALCO.
21. In Brazil and Russia, by contrast, regional incumbents refused to even seek patronage advantages from liberalization and engaged in explicit confrontational behavior by either refusing to pay taxes to the central government (Russia) or refusing to honor their central debts (Brazil); this hurt the reform process. In India, while many regional politicians sought to fulfill self-interested agendas, they did not engage in such confrontational behavior. They hoped to derive benefits from their participation in the central government in the near future. Since the decentralized power of regional politicians can deepen conflict over economic policy, the key to reform sustainability is the linkage mechanism.
22. Other scholars have noted that economic growth was accompanied by problems of "persistent overinvestment, duplication, regional blockages, and continuing bureaucratic management of industry" (C. Wong [1992, 198]).
23. The term is from Jean Oi (1999). Also see Solnick (1996) and Shirk (1993).
24. In 1988 and again in 1994 the central government attempted to recalibrate fiscal relations. The 1994 fiscal reform was aimed toward enhancing central

revenues: the central government would automatically take 50% of shared revenues and calculate the remittance quota on the remaining revenues on a set formula. Also, all provinces were to receive net transfers based on retained revenues in 1993.

25. Not all provinces have benefited from the reform process or even been at the forefront of new initiatives; inland provinces have been losers (Shaoguang and Angang 1999). My arguments do not imply that the reform experience of all provinces has been uniform; in fact, these cross-level linkages are strongest in the reforming coastal provinces.
26. Barry Naughton, cited in Mary Gallager (2002, 349).
27. The conflict over reforms between reformist and conservative groups has been a pervasive feature of intra-party interactions in China. For example, Zhao Ziyang's initiation of a new policy, "coastal developmental strategy" in 1988 was a direct attempt to deal with pressures posed by Li Peng who was attempting to take over economic management (Dali L. Yang [1991, 45]).
28. Yet, they rely on informal networks; the informality of cross-level linkages also creates corruption, and exclusion of a wider set of political actors or institutions.
29. Major central reformers started their careers in local government—Zhao Ziyang, Jiang Zemin, Zhu Rongji, and Hu Jintao. The 1982 politburo was an exception. Not all provinces have equal power at the central level: Shanghai gained in status after the rise of the "Shanghai gang." Beijing, and to a lesser extent, Guandong, enjoyed special power at the central level in the 1980s and 1990s. This means that *particular* reform alliances between reformist central leaders and some provincial regions, which benefit some regions at the cost of others, hold the key to the stability of China's reform path.
30. I define significant as, provincial experience (administrative and party) in the last 10 years at higher than the deputy secretary level.
31. My calculations of the careers of the 16th congress' politburo. See http://www.china.org.cn/english/features/45340.htm for career descriptions that were used to make these calculations.
32. Evidence is mixed on the effectiveness of recentralization attempts by the center in 1987–1988 and 1994; it was successful across some policy arenas (large-scale investment) and some regions but a failure in other respects (non-budgetary revenues).
33. These include pensions reform, anticorruption reforms and the reform of the financial system. In addition integration with the WTO (World Trade Organization) will demand more institutional changes.
34. A report in the *International Herald Tribune* notes: "Recent official police statistics are striking. The number of demonstrations increased from 8,700 to 32,000 from 1993 to 1999—an increase of 268 percent. The number probably swelled past 40,000 in 2000. In no year during this period did protests increase by less than 9 percent, and in the financial crisis years of 1997 and 1998 they spiked by 25 and 67 percent, respectively." Murray Tanner, "Protests Now Flourish in China," *International Herald Tribune* June 02, 2004 (Accessed on March 4, 2005 from http://www.iht.com/bin/print.php?file=522966.html).

References

Primary Sources

The Hindu, April 2, 1999.
The Hindu, February 23, 2000.
The Telegraph, December–January 1999.

Secondary Sources

Bajpai, Nirupam and Nandita Dasgupta (2004). What Constitutes Foreign Direct Investment? Comparison of India and China. CGSD Working Paper, No. 1, January, Center on Globalization and Sustainable Development, The Earth Institute at Columbia University.

Bednar, J., W. Eskridge, and J. Ferejohn (2001). "A Political Theory of Federalism," in John Ferejohn, Jack N. Rakove, and Jonathan Riley (eds.), *Constitutional Culture and Democratic Rule*. Cambridge, New York: Cambridge University Press.

Bhalla, A. S. (1995). "Recent Economic Reforms in China and India." *Asian Survey* 35(6) (June): 555–572.

Bramall, Chris (2000). *The Sources of Chinese Economic Growth, 1978–1996*. Oxford: Oxford University Press.

Chhibber, Pradeep and Samuel Eldersveld (2000). "Local Elites and Popular Support for Economic Reform in India and China." *Comparative Political Studies* 33(2): 350–373.

Chung, Jae Ho (2000). *Central Control and Local Discretion in China: Leadership and Implementation During Post-Mao Decollectivization*. Oxford, New York: Oxford University Press.

Editorial. 1998. "Who's Afraid of Art. 356." *Frontline* 15(14) July 4–17.

Echeverri-Gent, John (2002). "Politics in India's Decentered Polity," in Alyssa Ayres and Philip Oldenburg (eds.), *India Briefing: Quickening the Pace of Change*. Armonk, New York: M.E. Sharpe.

Freidman, Edward (1998). "Development, Revolution, Democracy, and Dictatorship: China Versus India?" in T. Skapol (ed.), *Democracy, Revolution and History*. Ithaca: Cornell University Press.

Gallager, Mary (2002). " 'Reform and Openness': Why China's Economic Reforms have Delayed Democracy." *World Politics* 54(3) (April): 338–372.

Ganapati, Priya (2002). "India's FDI Flow almost at Par with China." *India Abroad*, June 21.

Garman, C., S. Haggard, and E. Willis (2001). "Fiscal Decentralization: A Political Theory with Latin American Cases." *World Politics* 53 (January): 205–236.

Huang, Yasheng (1996). *Inflation and Investment Controls in China: The Political Economy of Central-Local Relations during the Reform Era*. Cambridge: Cambridge University Press.

Hutchcroft, Paul (2001). "Centralization and Decentralization in Administration and Politics: Assessing Territorial Dimensions of Authority and Power." *Governance* 14(1) (January): 23–53.

"Interview." *Economic Times (India)*, December 12, 1997, New Delhi Edition.

Jenkins, Rob (1999). *Democratic Politics and Economic Reform in India.* Cambridge: Cambridge University Press.

Krugman, Paul and M. Obstfeld (1997). *International Economics: Theory and Policy.* Reading, MA: Addison-Wesley.

Lee, Pak K. (2000). "Into the Trap of Strengthening State Capacity: China's Tax-Assignment Reform." *The China Quarterly* 164 (December): 1007–1024.

Li, Cheng (2002). "After Hu, Who?—China's Provincial Leaders Await Promotion." *China Leadership Monitor* 1 (Winter): 1–14.

Lohmann, Susanne (1997). "Linkage Politics." *Journal of Conflict Resolution* 41(1) (February): 38–67.

Maddison, Angus (1998). *Chinese Economic Performance in the Long Run.* Paris: Development Centre of the OECD.

McCarten, W. J. (2003). "The Challenge of Fiscal Discipline in the Indian States," in Jonathan Rodden, Gunnar S. Eskeland, and Jennie Litvack (eds.), *Fiscal Decentralization and the Challenge of Hard Budget Constraints.* Cambridge, MA: MIT Press.

Musgrave, Richard A. and Peggy Musgrave (1973). *Public Finance in Theory and Practice.* Cambridge: MIT Press.

Oi, Jean (1999). *Rural China Takes Off: The Institutional Foundations of Economic Reform.* Berkeley: University of California Press.

Ordershook, Peter C. and Olga Shvetsova (1997). "Federalism and Constitutional Design." *Journal of Democracy* 8(1) (January): 27–44.

Ordershook, Peter (1996). "Russia's Party System: Is Russia Federalism Viable?" *Post-Soviet Affairs* 12(3) (July–September): 195–217.

Parikh, Sunita and Barry R. Weingast (1997). "A Comparative Theory of Federalism: India." *Virginia Law Review* 83(7) (October): 1593–1615.

Putnam, Robert (1988). "Diplomacy and Domestic Politics: The Logic of Two-Level Games," *International Organization* 42 (Summer): 427–460.

Rao, M. Govinda (2000). "Fiscal Adjustment and the Role of State Governments in India," in S. Kahkonen and A. Lanyi (eds.), *Institutions, Incentives and Economic Reforms in India.* New Delhi: Sage.

Rawski, Thomas (2001a). "What's Happening to China's GDP Statistics?" *China Economic Review* 12(4) (December): 347–354.

Rawski, Thomas (2001b). "China's Reform Watch: Turning Point Looming." *China Perspectives* 38: 28–35.

Rawski, Thomas (2001c). "China's GDP Statistics—A Case of Caveat Lector?" available at: http://www.pitt.edu/~tgrawski/

Rawski, Thomas (2002). "Measuring China's Recent GDP growth: Where Do We Stand?" *China Economic Quarterly* 2(1) (October).

Ren, R. E. (1997). *China's Economic Performance in an International Perspective.* Paris: OECD.

Rose-Ackerman, Susan and Jonathan Rodden (1997). "Does Federalism Preserve Markets." *Virginia Law Review* 83(7) (October): 1521–1572.

Rosen, George (1990). "India and China: Perspectives on Contrasting Styles of Economics Reform." *Journal of Asian Economics* 1(2) (Autumn): 273–290.

Rudolph, L. and S. Rudolph (2001). "The Iconisation of Chandrababu: Sharing Sovereignty in India Federal Market Economy." *Economic and Political Weekly* (May 5): 1541–1567.

Saez, Lawrence (2000). Globalization and Market-Preserving Federalism: Evidence from China and India. Conference paper presented at the 2000 Annual Meeting of the APSA, Washington, D.C., August 31–September 4.
Saez, Lawrence (2002). *Federalism Without a Center: The Impact of Political and Economic Reform on India's Federal System.* New Delhi: Sage.
Sachs, J. and W. T. Woo (1997). "Chinese Economic Growth," in Joint Economic Committee (1997): *China's Economic Future*. Washington, D.C.: U.S. Congress.
Shirk, Susan L. (1993). *The Political Logic of Economic Reform in China.* Berkeley: University of California Press.
Shaoguang, Wang and Hu Angang (1999). *The Political Economy of Uneven Development: The Case of China.* Armonk, New York: M.E. Sharpe.
Sinha, Aseema (2004). "The Changing Political Economy of Federalism in India: A Historical Institutionalist Approach." *India Review* 3(1) (January): 25–63.
Sinha, Aseema (2005). *The Regional Roots of Developmental Politics in India: A Leviathan Divided.* Indiana: Indiana University Press.
Solnick, Steven (1996). "The Breakdown of Hierarchies in the Soviet Union and China: A Neo-Institutionalist Perspective." *World Politics* 48 (January): 209–238.
Stepan, Al (2001). *Arguing Comparative Politics.* Oxford: Oxford University Press.
Stigler, G. (1957 [1998]). "The Tenable Range of Functions of Local Government." Reprinted in Wallace Oates (ed.), *The Economics of Fiscal Federalism and Local Finance.* Northampton, MA: Edward Elgard.
Tiebout, Charles (1956). "A Pure Theory of Local Expenditures." *Journal of Political Economy* 64(5) (October): 416–424.
Tsai, Kellee S. (2004). "Off Balance: The Unintended Consequences of Fiscal Federalism in China." *Journal of Chinese Political Science* 9(2) (Fall): 7–26.
Tsebelis, George (1990). *Nested Games: Rational Choice in Comparative Politics.* Berkeley: University of California Press.
Weingast, Barry (1995). "The Economic Role of Political Institutions: Market-Preserving Federalism and Economic Development." *Journal of Law, Economics and Organization* 11(1) (April): 1–31.
Weingast, Barry R. (2002). "Rational Choice Institutionalism," in Ira Katznelson and Helen U. Milner (eds.), *Political Science: The State of the Discipline.* New York: W. W. Norton & Co.
Whiting, Susan H. (2001). *Power and Wealth in Rural China: The Political Economy of Institutional Change.* Cambridge: Cambridge University Press.
Wong, C. (1992). "Fiscal Reform and Local Industrialization: the Problematic Sequencing of Reform in Post-Mao China." *Modern China* 18(2) (April): 197–227.
Yang, Dali L. (1991). "China Adjusts to the World Economy: The Political Economy of China's Coastal Development Strategy." *Pacific Affairs* 64(1) (Spring): 42–64.
Yang, Dali. Y. (1997). *Beyond Beijing: Liberalization and the Regions in China.* London: Routledge.

9

Indigenous versus Foreign Business Models

Yasheng Huang and Tarun Khanna

I

Although there are broad similarities between China and India—two large, populous, physically contiguous, ancient, Asian civilizations that formed nation-states roughly contemporaneously—there are stark differences in their development trajectories. Equally important, there are pros and cons to the models chosen by the two countries even if one restricts the comparison to the economic domain.[1]

According to China and most policy experts, the fastest route to economic development is to welcome foreign direct investment (FDI). But a comparison with India suggests that FDI is not the only path to prosperity. Indeed, India's homegrown entrepreneurs may give it a long-term advantage over a China hamstrung by inefficient banks and capital markets.

India is not outperforming China overall, but it is doing better in certain key areas. That success may enable it to catch up with and perhaps even overtake China. If so, it will not only demonstrate the importance of homegrown entrepreneurship to long-term economic development; it will also show the limits of the FDI-dependent approach China is pursuing.

Our conjecture is that a strategy that promotes both FDI and domestic entrepreneurship is superior to a strategy than promotes only FDI (China in the 1990s) or one that promotes only domestic entrepreneurship (India in the 1970s). So far China has grown faster but the gap in growth rates between the two is narrowing and it is possible that China's growth can be more volatile. India has some underappreciated strengths and these strengths—better protection of property rights and a relatively better allocation of financial resources—constitute a long-term advantage. As the new century begins, India's business strengths compared to China are already showing up in its higher growth rates and technology boom.

II

Both China and India are far more "FDI-led" than other developing countries were in the past. In the 1970s, FDI accounted for an average of only 1.2 percent of annual capital formation in Taiwan, for example. By contrast, FDI accounted for nearly 15 percent in China during the 1990s and reached 2.3 percent in India in 2000. Taiwan's growth was led by domestic entrepreneurs.

However in the China–India comparison, China is far more FDI-led. Of course, China began the reform effort much earlier than did India. If one were forced to pick dates, one would pick 1978 for China and 1991 for India. In particular, China embraced FDI earlier but, more importantly, far more extensively, whereas India remained, at best, indifferent to such a prospect and, at worst, hostile to multinationals (Encarnation 1989).

Walk into any Wal-Mart and you won't be surprised to see the shelves sagging with Chinese-made goods—everything from shoes and garments to toys and electronics. But the ubiquitous "Made in China" label obscures an important point: few of these products are made by indigenous Chinese companies. In fact, you would be hard-pressed to find a single homegrown Chinese firm that operates on a global scale and markets its own products abroad.

That is because China's export-led manufacturing boom is largely a creation of FDI, which effectively serves as a substitute for domestic entrepreneurship. During the 1980s and 1990s, the Chinese economy took off, but few local firms followed, leaving the country's private sector with no world-class companies to rival the big multinationals. As Huang (2003) shows, the 1990s FDI flows into China surged in part because the government (motivated to protect state-owned enterprises) curtailed the investment potential of the domestic private sector. This was done both directly as well as indirectly through the inefficiencies of China's financial institutions. Efficient private entrepreneurs could not get financing from Chinese banks, which forced them to access financing from foreign firms—mainly based in Hong

Kong and Taiwan. Financing from foreign firms became FDI. That means that as China's financial institutions improve, FDI's role in China's economy should decline. In 1995, FDI accounted for about 6 percent of China's GDP; in 2002, it came down to 4 percent due to the financial and some legal reforms.

Foreign investors were among the biggest beneficiaries of the constraints on private business in China. One indication of the large payoff they have reaped on the back of China's phenomenal growth: in 1992, the income accruing to foreign investors with equity stakes in Chinese firms was only $5.3 billion; by 2002 it had reached more than $22 billion. (This money does not necessarily leave the country; it is often reinvested in China.)

Some argue that the positive "spillover" effects of FDI in China have outweighed the negative impacts of the constraints on domestic business. Chief among these is alleged to be the transfer of management skills and technology. But the consensus among economists who study this issue is that FDI has negligible or negative impacts on such transfers. In one recent research article (Aitken and Harrison, 1999), a team of economists found that the costs of attracting FDI more than offset any positive spillover effects. More recently, researchers have shown that positive contributions of FDI are conditional on efficient domestic financial institutions, something not true in China.

III

India has not attracted anywhere near the amount of FDI that China has. In part, this disparity reflects the confidence international investors have in China's prospects and their skepticism about India's commitment to free-market reforms. It also reflects politics. For democratic, postcolonial India, allowing foreign investors huge profits at the expense of indigenous firms is simply unfeasible. Recall, for instance, the controversy that erupted a decade ago when the Enron Corporation made a deal with the state of Maharashtra to build a $2.9 billion power plant there. The project proceeded, but only after several years of acrimonious debate over foreign investment and its role in India's development.

The FDI gap is also partly a tale of two diasporas. China has a large and wealthy diaspora that has long invested its money. During the 1990s, more than half of China's FDI came from overseas Chinese sources. The money appears to have had at least one unintended consequence: the billions of dollars that came from Hong Kong,

Macao, and Taiwan may have inadvertently helped Beijing postpone politically difficult internal reforms. For instance, because foreign investors were acquiring assets from loss-making State-owned enterprises (SOEs), the government was able to drag its feet on privatization.

By contrast, the Indian diaspora was, at least until recently, resented for its success and much less willing to invest back home. New Delhi took a dim view of Indians who had gone abroad, and of foreign investment generally, and instead provided a more nurturing environment for domestic entrepreneurs.

The main reason for the FDI gap however concerns their relative treatments of private enterprise. China has been far bolder with external reforms but has imposed substantial legal and regulatory constraints on indigenous, private firms. In fact, only in 1998 were domestic companies granted the same constitutional protections that foreign businesses have enjoyed since the early 1980s. As of the late 1990s, according to the International Finance Corporation, more than two dozen industries, including some of the most important and lucrative sectors of the economy—banking, telecommunications, highways, and railroads—were still off-limits to private local companies.

These restrictions were designed not to keep Chinese entrepreneurs from competing with foreigners but to prevent private domestic businesses from challenging China's SOEs.

China's Communist Party came to power in 1949 intent on eradicating private ownership, which it quickly did. Although the country is now in its third decade of free-market reforms, it continues to struggle with the legacy of that period—witness the controversy surrounding the recent decision to officially allow capitalists to join the Communist Party.

Some progress has been made in reforming the bloated, inefficient SOEs during the last 20 years, but Beijing is still not willing to relinquish its control over the largest ones, such as China Telecom. Instead, the government has ferociously protected them from competition. In the 1990s, numerous Chinese entrepreneurs tried, and failed, to circumvent the restrictions placed on their activities. Some registered their firms as nominal SOEs (all the capital came from private sources, and the companies were privately managed), only to find themselves ensnared in title disputes when financially strapped government agencies sought to seize their assets. More than a few promising businesses have been destroyed this way.

Most Chinese entrepreneurs who succeed do so in places where local officials—ignoring central government prohibitions—have privatized state firms and financed private entrepreneurs. Attempts to pick and build up state-owned "winners," if fully implemented, would kill off even the limited private entrepreneurial successes in China.

This bias against homegrown firms is widely acknowledged. A report issued in 2000 by the Chinese Academy of Social Sciences concluded that, "Because of long-standing prejudices and mistaken beliefs, private and individual enterprises have a lower political status and are discriminated against in numerous policies and regulations. The legal, policy, and market environment is unfair and inconsistent." Many Chinese officials agree. In 2002, a top Chinese legislator, Tian Jiyun, criticized the government's policies to impose more restrictions on domestic private firms than on foreign ones. In 2004, a constitutional amendment was passed to protect private property rights.

India, on the other hand, developed a softer brand of socialism. Fabian socialism aimed not to destroy capitalism but merely to mitigate the social ills it caused. It was considered essential that the public sector occupy the economy's "commanding heights," to use a phrase coined by Russian revolutionary Vladimir Lenin but popularized by India's first prime minister, Jawaharlal Nehru. However, that did not prevent entrepreneurship from flourishing where the long arm of the state could not reach.

While China created obstacles for its entrepreneurs, India made life easier for them. In the 1990s, New Delhi backed away from micro-managing the economy. Government involvement at all levels remains far more pervasive in China than in India. The Indian government has, gradually from the mid-1980s and in accelerated fashion since the early 1990s, retreated from its earlier explicitly interventionist position to occupying the intellectual terrain of an enabler of private sector enterprise (even if the reality of intervention continues to be a daily one in many areas).

True, privatization is proceeding at a glacial pace in India, but the government has ceded its monopoly over long-distance phone service; some tariffs have been cut; bureaucracy has been trimmed a bit; and a number of industries have been opened to private investment, including investment from abroad.

Indian policy-makers never explicitly set out to nurture indigenous entrepreneurs (Khanna and Palepu 2004). Indeed, for quite a few decades under the License Raj, they explicitly discriminated against big business (Hazari 1986). The flowering of Indian entrepreneurs occurred in a situation where multinationals were (relatively) absent. The exact reason why this occurred remains a subject of ongoing debate.

India has also developed much stronger institutional infrastructure to support private enterprise. Its capital markets operate with greater efficiency and transparency than do China's. Its legal system, while not without substantial flaws, is considerably more advanced.

IV

In the process of lifting restrictions on private firms, India has managed to spawn a number of companies that now compete internationally with the best that Europe and the United States have to offer. Moreover, many of these firms are in the most cutting-edge, knowledge-based industries—software giants Infosys and Wipro and pharmaceutical and biotechnology powerhouses Ranbaxy and Dr. Reddy's Labs, to name just a few. Last year, the Forbes 200, an annual ranking of the world's best small companies, included 13 Indian firms but just 4 from mainland China.

As a consequence, entrepreneurship and free enterprise are flourishing. A measure of the progress: in a recent survey of leading Asian companies by the Far Eastern Economic Review, India registered a higher average score than any other country in the region, including China (the survey polled over 2,500 executives and professionals in a dozen countries; respondents were asked to rate companies on a scale of 1 to 7 for overall leadership performance). Indeed, only two Chinese firms had scores high enough to qualify for India's top 10 list. Tellingly, all of the Indian firms were wholly private initiatives, while most of the Chinese companies had significant state involvement. Some of the leading Indian firms are true start-ups, notably Infosys, which topped the review's survey. Others are offshoots of old-line companies. Sundaram Motors, for instance, a leading manufacturer of automotive components and a principal supplier to General Motors, is part of the T.V. Sundaram group, a century-old south Indian business group. Not only is entrepreneurship thriving in India; entrepreneurs there have become folk heroes. For instance, Narayana Murthy, the 56-year-old founder of Infosys, is often compared to Microsoft's Bill Gates and has become a revered figure.

The difference in diasporas has also begun to shift in India's favor. Until now, the Indian diaspora has accounted for less than 10 percent of the foreign money flowing to India. With the welcome mat now laid out, direct investment from non-resident Indians is likely to increase. And while the Indian diaspora may not be able to match the Chinese diaspora as "hard" capital goes, Indians abroad have substantially more intellectual capital to contribute, which could prove even more valuable.

The Indian diaspora has famously distinguished itself in knowledge-based industries, nowhere more so than in Silicon Valley. Now, India's brightening prospects, as well as the changing attitude vis-à-vis those who have gone abroad, are luring many non-resident Indian engineers and scientists home and are enticing many expatriate business people to open their wallets.

With the help of its diaspora, China has won the race to be the world's factory. With the help of its diaspora, India could become the world's technology lab. India may soon have the best of both worlds: it looks poised to reap significantly more FDI in the coming years than it has attracted to date. After decades of keeping the Indian diaspora at arm's length, New Delhi is now embracing it. In some circles, it used to be jokingly said that NRI, an acronym applied to members of the diaspora, stood for "not required Indians." Now, the term is back to meaning just "non-resident Indian." These success stories never would have happened if India lacked the institutional infrastructure needed to support Murthy and other would-be moguls. But democracy, a tradition of entrepreneurship, and a decent legal system have given India the underpinnings necessary for enterprise to flourish. Although India's courts are notoriously inefficient, they at least comprise a functioning independent judiciary. Property rights are not fully secure, but the protection of private ownership is certainly far stronger than in China. The rule of law, a legacy of British rule, generally prevails.

These traditions and institutions have proved an excellent springboard for the emergence and evolution of India's capital markets. Distortions are still commonplace, but the stock and bond markets generally allow firms with solid prospects and reputations to obtain the capital they need to grow. In a World Bank study published last year, only 52 percent of the Indian firms surveyed reported problems obtaining capital, versus 80 percent of the Chinese companies polled. As a result, the Indian firms relied much less on internally generated finances: only 27 percent of their funding came through operating profits, versus 57 percent for the Chinese firms.

Corporate governance has improved dramatically, thanks in no small part to Murthy, who has made Infosys a paragon of honest accounting and an example for other firms. In a survey of 25 emerging market economies conducted in 2000 by Credit Lyonnais Securities Asia, India ranked sixth in corporate governance, China nineteenth. The advent of an investor class, coupled with the fact that capital providers, such as development banks, are themselves increasingly subject to market forces, has only bolstered the efficiency and credibility of India's markets. Apart from providing the regulatory framework, the Indian government has taken a back seat to the private sector.

In China, by contrast, bureaucrats remain the gatekeepers, tightly controlling capital allocation and severely restricting the ability of private companies to obtain stock market listings and access the money they need to grow. Indeed, Beijing has used the financial markets mainly as a way of keeping the SOEs afloat. These policies have produced enormous distortions while preventing China's markets from gaining depth and maturity. (It is widely claimed that China's stock markets have a total capitalization in excess of $400 billion, but factoring out non-tradable shares owned by the government or by government-owned companies reduces the valuation to just around $150 billion.) Compounding the problem are poor corporate governance and the absence of an independent judiciary. The corporate heroes we celebrate today succeed by their capabilities, not by policy protection.

Consider the question, "Which country has a better business environment?" Any attempt to "add up" different dimensions of strengths of the two countries in an unweighted fashion will point to China. But this is a dubious exercise at best. Academics will concur that it lacks theoretical justification; practicing managers doubt its operational utility.[2]

As a first-cut analysis, we rely on the World Business Environment Survey (WBES) designed by the World Bank. The survey was designed to capture firms' views on the aspects of the business environment that affect their operations. An important feature of WBES is its emphasis on entrepreneurial firms. The vast majority of surveyed firms are owned privately. Only 12 percent of the firms reported having some government ownership. Thus this survey can be read as reflecting not the business environment for all the firms but for privately owned firms specifically. This is an important feature for our analysis because so much of our argument rests on the differential treatments of domestic privately owned and entrepreneurial firms between China and India. The survey was implemented in 1999–2000 and it covered 81 countries and some 10,000 firms. A huge advantage of this survey is that for the first time both China and India are included in a single survey. This enables us to compare the two countries directly.

Table 9.1 presents a number of WBES responses in three main areas—efficiency of government service, general business constraints, and a tax compliance measure. The detailed explanations of the

Table 9.1 Business environment in China and India: evidence from WBES

	Efficiency of government service (% of firms responding "mostly" to "very" inefficient)	General business constraints (% of firms responding "moderate" to "major"obstacle)						Tax compliance (% of firms estimating a reporting of 80% or more of income for tax purposes
		Corruption	Judiciary	Financing	Policy instability	Taxes and regulations	Economic and social constraints (average of responses to inflation, exchange rate, street crime, and organized crime)	
China	21	31	14	80	41	29	26	28
India	55	60	29	52	63	39	39	69
United States	49	24	21	39	29	43	25	75

questions that generated these responses are attached to the table. For the efficiency of government measure and the general business constraint measure, higher values indicate greater obstacles facing the firms. For the tax compliance measure, a lower value indicates less compliance.

Out of these eight measures, China is ranked better than India in six areas—efficiency of government, corruption, judiciary, policy instability, taxes and regulations, and economic/social constraints. On the government efficiency measure, only some 21 percent of Chinese firms rate the performance poorly (defined as "mostly inefficient" or "very inefficient). By contrast, 55 percent of Indian firms rate their government performance poorly. On the six general business constraint measures, the Chinese scores are lower than the Indian scores in all but financing. In financing, Indian firms hold a considerable edge. Only 52 percent of Indian firms were substantially constrained by financing, compared with 80 percent of Chinese firms. On the tax compliance measure, Indian firms also did much better than Chinese firms. Only 28 percent of Chinese firms believed that a typical firm in their industries reported 80 percent or more of its income for tax purposes. In India, this figure is 69 percent.

One is tempted to sum up the scores across all these measures and conclude that China offers a superior business environment than India. This conclusion would strike an intuitive chord with the prevailing image of India as a lumbering, inefficient, and unwieldy giant. In particular, the fact that India is ranked unfavorably on policy instability, corruption, and taxes and regulations would resonate with executives of many multinationals who have been subjected to the rough-and-tumble of competition, and of regulatory uncertainty, in India.

As intuitive and as seemingly rooted in "numbers" as such a view is, it will be wrong. For one thing, not all surveys point in the same direction. Heritage Foundation surveys rank China and India quite similarly. According to Guy Pfefferman of International Finance Corporation (IFC), internal IFC surveys have slightly favored India in their assessments of the overall quality of business environments in the two countries.

Drawing conclusions on the basis of survey data is an art, not a science. We have to know how the data were generated in the first place to be sure of the quality of the data and we have to be aware of any potential biases in the data. There are known measurement errors in the WBES. In the draft version of the report based on the WBES data, Voices of Firms, on p. 28, footnote 13, the World Bank authors provided the following disclaimer on corruption data regarding China (a disclaimer that was omitted from the published version of the same report):

> The reader should note that this general constraint question was the only question on corruption that could be posed in China. The consultant carrying out the survey reported that surveys are subject to rigorous censorship by the State statistics agency and that posing detailed questions on corruption would not only invoke censorship, but might also derail the entire survey and even threaten the license of the consultant to carry further survey work.

It is entirely possible that China looks better in comparison with India simply because entrepreneurs in India can afford to be honest. In this regard, it is actually remarkable that 30 percent of firms surveyed in China report corruption as a major constraint facing their operations and that 20 percent of firms rating government service as very inefficient. To amplify this point that firms in a democracy can be more forthcoming, we impose a plausibility check by including the survey data on the United States in the table. If it is the case that different levels of honesty explain some of the differences between China and India, we should expect that the United States also compares unfavorably with China.

Indeed, this is the case, at least for some of the measures reported in the table. Chinese firms rate their government service, judiciary, and taxes and regulations better than their American counterparts of the same areas in their home business environments. On economic/social constraints, the two countries are similarly ranked. It is possible that the business environment in China is objectively better than that in the United States; for example, the finding on the judiciary may very well reflect the long-standing opinion of the business community in the United States that the American system is too litigious. But some of the findings, taken at their face, would appear to be implausible. It is hard to believe that the government in China is more efficient than the government in the United States.

An alternative interpretation is that the patterns presented in this table identify those areas of the business environment that most constrain a firm and those that least constrain it. Different countries can impose different types of constraints on their firms; simply averaging all the constraints into a single number masks reality. WBES, thus, is more useful in intra-country comparisons of specific features of the business environment. It is less useful when it comes to a judgment about the overall quality of business environments across different countries. This approach, we believe, is the most productive way of interpreting the WBES data.

This methodology would produce conclusions at variance with these data. For example, the judiciary is ranked as the least constraining on business in China, but this may reflect the fact that China's judiciary has no teeth. An efficient and business-friendly judiciary can produce a low score on this measure but so can an irrelevant judiciary. Understanding the meaning of the responses to this and other questions in China is critical for rendering a judgment about the comparative quality of the business environments in India and China.

Applying the aforementioned methodology, we can conclude that the most problematic areas of the Chinese business environment are financing and income reporting. If we put aside the two questions that directly required Chinese firms to assess government performance—government efficiency and corruption because of the potential for biases in the Chinese data—then the most problematic areas of the Indian business environment are policy instability, financing, and taxes and regulations. To compare the two countries within categories, we can conclude that Indian firms do better in financing and tax compliance than the Chinese firms but they suffer more from policy instability and the tax and regulatory system.

V

The lessons of India's local enterprise-based development strategy can be seen within China itself (see Huang and Di 2003). Consider the contrasting strategies of Jiangsu and Zhejiang, two coastal provinces that were at similar levels of economic development when China's reforms began. Both are coastal, indeed, both neighbor Shanghai. Both have a deep industrial and entrepreneurial history. Both have been open to foreign trade and FDI to a similar degree. The difference—and one that for a long time did not strike outside analysts as significant—is that ownership biases against the indigenous private sector in Zhejiang were less onerous than those in Jiangsu.[3]

Jiangsu relied largely on FDI to fuel its growth. Zhejiang, by contrast, placed heavier emphasis on indigenous entrepreneurs and organic development. Zhejiang did not restrict FDI. Rather it welcomed both FDI and domestic entrepreneurship. During the two decades to 2000, Zhejiang's economy grew at an annual rate of about 1 percentage point faster than Jiangsu's. Twenty years ago, Zhejiang was the poorer of the two provinces; now it is unquestionably more prosperous.

Zhejiang today has some of the best indigenous firms in the country. In per capita income terms, Zhejiang was ranked seventh in the country in the late 1970s but today it is ranked first (without counting the three province-level cities, Beijing, Shanghai, and Tianjin, which do not have agricultural sectors). Jiangsu, by contrast, was already third richest in the country in the late 1970s and it stayed that way in 2003 (again not counting the three cities). The within-country evidence about the contrast between an FDI-biased model and a model supportive of indigenous entrepreneurship (while being open to FDI) is compelling.

VI

China and India are the world's next major powers. It has long been an article of faith that China is on the faster track, and the economic data bear this out. The "Hindu rate of growth"—a pejorative phrase referring to India's inability to match its economic growth with its population growth—may be a thing of the past, but when it comes to gross domestic product (GDP) figures and other headline numbers, India is still no match for China.

If India has so clearly surpassed China at the grassroots level, why isn't India's superiority reflected in the numbers? Why is the gap in GDP and other benchmarks still so wide? It is worth recalling that India's economic reforms only began in earnest in 1991, more than a decade after China began liberalizing. In addition to the late start, India has had to make do with a national savings rate half that of

China's and 90 percent less FDI. Moreover, India is a sprawling, messy democracy riven by ethnic and religious tensions, and it has also had a long-standing, volatile dispute with Pakistan over Kashmir. China, on the other hand, has enjoyed two decades of relative tranquility; apart from Tiananmen Square, it has been able to focus almost exclusively on economic development.

That India's annual growth rate is only around 20 percent lower than China's is, then, a remarkable achievement. And, of course, whether the data for China are accurate is an open question. The speed with which India is catching up is due to its own efficient deployment of capital and China's inefficiency, symbolized by all the money that has been frittered away on SOEs. And China's misallocation of resources is likely to become a big drag on the economy in the years ahead.

In the early 1990s, when China was registering double-digit growth rates, Beijing invested massively in the state sector. Most of the investments were not commercially viable, leaving the banking sector with a huge number of nonperforming loans—possibly totaling as much as 50 percent of bank assets. At some point, the capitalization costs of these loans will have to be absorbed, either through write-downs (which means depositors bear the cost) or recapitalization of the banks by the government, which diverts money from other, more productive uses. This could well limit China's future growth trajectory.

India's banks may not be models of financial probity, but they have not made mistakes on nearly the same scale. According to a recent study by the management consulting firm Ernst & Young, about 15 percent of banking assets in India were nonperforming as of 2001. India's economy is thus anchored on more solid footing.

China has greater economic potential than India, but that is precisely our point: despite its weaknesses, India's growth is approaching 80 percent of China's growth, with a substantially lower ratio of nonperforming loans. Furthermore, India has more efficient domestic firms.

By the early 2000s, India's annual economic growth rates were approximating those of China. Leaving aside the complicated issue of whether Chinese statistics are accurate, this one-on-one comparison between China and India always casts China in a better light but we should keep in mind a number of parameters when judging and comparing economic performance of these two countries.

First, China invested more than twice as much as India. The investment/ GDP ratio in 2003 was a just a notch below the 50 percent mark in China. This is extraordinary. China had started in the early 1980s with a high investment/GDP ratio typical of many centrally planned economies. This ratio declined continuously throughout the 1980s and in the early 1990s as microeconomic reforms raised enterprise-level productivity, enabling China to enjoy a growth spurt while devoting more resources to consumption. The investment/GDP ratio achieved in 2003 is a huge throwback to history—in the late 1950s and 1960s the ratio climbed to a high level on the back of huge investment programs organized by the government. To be sure, the mechanisms that led to the investment surge in 2003 were different from the ones during the centrally planned era but at least according to one economic study, China's investment planning process, even as of the late 1990s, had an uncanny resemblance to its central planning progenitor (Rawski 2001).

Second, China is faced with some unrelenting inflationary pressures in a way that India, despite its huge budgetary deficit, is not. This is not just a question of economic policy, as it turns out; it is an issue of the kind of transparency discrepancies we highlighted in this chapter. India's budgetary deficit is large, to be sure, but it is transparently large. We actually do not know the true extent of China's budget deficit because the Chinese government finances many of its investment and infrastructural projects through its banking system, not via its budget. The current inflationary pressures in China have to be viewed from this perspective. The Chinese government's assumption of the debts of the country's banking system, to a degree similar in a number of Southeast Asian countries before the 1997 financial crisis, is an issue of monumental concern.

In the past, when India was growing at its leisurely "Hindu rate of growth," one could make an intellectually passable argument that the merit of the two growth models would depend purely on one's risk profile: a risk-averse person might think that India's model is better and vice versa for a person with a greater tolerance for risk. As growth rates begin to converge between the two countries, India's model begins to look unambiguously more attractive.

An implicit contention is that if China had adopted a growth model more conducive to indigenous entrepreneurship, it would have grown even faster. But one of the challenges in comparing China and India, two giant and complex countries, is that there are, naturally, other dimensions of differences between them that might account for some of the phenomena we observe regarding the variations in competitiveness of indigenous enterprise.

VII

The reactions to an earlier article we wrote about the comparative development models (Huang and Khanna 2003) were different in China and India. These reactions offer clues of likely developments in the two countries. Indian reactions were instantaneous. Groups of Indian entrepreneurs reported to us, via e-mail, that they had set up reading groups to discuss the article. Audiences of policy-makers, businesspeople, trade associations, and universities in India and among the Indian diaspora, asked for one or the other of us to present the paper. Clearly, ideas, especially those ideas with an edge, traveled quickly, far and wide in a society with the benefit of a free press.

The initial Chinese reactions were hesitant and even hostile. At least one major Chinese university was exceedingly cautious about allowing a discussion of the argument on campus, pleading reasons of sensitivity. But once Chinese censors decided to publish the piece, on November 11, 2003, on Chinanews.com, an official website run by the Xinhua News Agency, the initially hesitant reactions became a torrent. The university, which had objected to the piece, immediately dropped its complaint. There were four or five translations of the article appearing in publications ranging from current events journals to serious scholarly outlets. These different reactions are emblematic of the untrammeled flow of information in India and the relatively constrained availability of information in China.

Another reaction to the piece, however, reflects China in a far better light than India. The Chinese reactions, so far, have been more reflective and methodical than those that we have seen in India. A number of Chinese bureaucrats, armed with data and fact sheets of both countries, discussed the paper in scholarly detail with one of us in Boston; clearly they were prepared to learn something from the exercise. The Chinese media discussions of the major points raised in our paper are serious in tone and more reflective. It could be a matter of sheer coincidence but the number of official study delegations from China to India, reported in the Chinese press, increased dramatically. Former Chinese ambassadors to India were sought out by the Chinese media for their impressions of the country. Some of the most prominent Chinese intellectuals, while reserving judgment on the conclusion of our article, all pointed out that there is a need to understand more about China's southern neighboring giant.

In contrast, the Indian reactions verged on self-indulgence. The Indian counterparts in government and media, we can only surmise, were far too blasé about the prospect of learning from engagement, or too self-congratulatory to let their rare moment in the sun be possibly eclipsed by academic scrutiny. The stars of the Indian political and bureaucratic firmament did not analyze the article to nearly the same depth as their Chinese counterparts.

Interest also extended across Southeast Asia reflecting the challenges that the economic rise of China and India pose for the business models of these two countries (Huang, Yeung and Morck 2004). Indonesia, Malaysia, and Singapore have courted FDI as assiduously in the recent past as does China today, but the latter threatens the former with its more compelling economics. There are also indications that the institutional quality of ASEAN has declined in recent years amidst a single-minded trade and FDI liberalization agenda.[4] The rise of India's service sector and the emergence of Indian multinationals (Khanna and Palepu 2002) has caught the attention of Southeast Asia's indigenous entrepreneurs and policy-makers.

In the United States, interest was directed mainly at India, since China is "well known" whereas India is not.[5] The familiarly of U.S. audiences with China, and the relative fog through which India has been viewed, is long-standing and was a point we used to motivate our prior work (see Isaacs 1958).

VIII

The real issue, of course, isn't where China and India are today but where they will be tomorrow. The answer will be determined in large measure by how well both countries utilize their resources, and on this score, India is doing a superior job. Is it pursuing a better road to development than China? We won't know the answer for many years. However, some evidence indicates that India's ground-up approach may indeed be wiser.

Focusing on whether or not China and India can learn from each other is better than focusing on which of China or India will win some imprecisely defined "race." That is, there are pros and cons to each of the Chinese and Indian models. With China–India trade at unprecedented (if still small) levels, and a partial thawing of the political relationship, attention has shifted to the question of whether or not China and India can learn from each other. Surely, people surmise, if the benefits of China's hard infrastructure have resulted in voluminous FDI, India should get its act together and build roads and power plants, and, if India's intellectual property laws have nurtured its "knowledge based industries," China should hasten its adoption of (intellectual) property rights.

From our vantage point, such imitation as will occur will be partial at best. For China to embrace intellectual property laws, for example, will require deep-seated changes to the fabric of several aspects of its society.[6] For India to build highways and power plants with ruthless efficiency and breathtaking speed, it would need a greater element of a fiat mechanism, which is inconceivable under its democratic structure. That is, the extent to which each country is able to adopt institutional features of the other's system depends on deep-seated political changes that are hard to predict.[7]

So far, India's institutional infrastructure and flexible democratic politics have been better at nurturing a dynamic business sector than China's hard infrastructure and centralized authoritarianism. Politics will determine which country advances faster in the new century.

Notes

1. Sen (2000), and his coauthors in related work, have pointed out numerous social pros and cons of the models chosen by the two countries. For example, costs of the Chinese model are the constraints that it puts on free choice, an integral element of a developed society. A cost of the Indian model is its neglect of primary education and primary health care. In some sense our domain of comparison is more constrained. While the above have long-run economic consequences, we have a more immediate economic context in mind—having to do primarily with the ease with which entrepreneurs, indigenous or foreign, can engage in day-to-day economic activity.
2. As one way in which such a question could be posed more usefully, note Farrell's (2004) more nuanced approach that focuses on industry-level realities and concludes that one can array industries along a spectrum ranging from those where China trumps India, through those where it is a "toss-up," to those where India comes out ahead.
3. The work draws from Yasheng Huang's ongoing book-length project on these two provinces. For a sampling of finished papers, see Huang and Wen (2003) and Huang (2004). Huang and Wen (2003) show that credit-constrained private firms ceded more control rights and equity to foreign firms when forming joint ventures. Huang (2004) shows, via survey data, that private firms more restricted in financing and in access to property rights protection prefer to move their assets to the better-protected foreign sector. Thus, in a biased business environment FDI and domestic entrepreneurship are substitutes, rather than complements.
4. Huang and Yeung (2004) have highlighted this phenomenon.
5. The idea that China is "well known" must draw a simultaneously bemused and frustrated smile from Western investors, many of whom have not found the

investment terrain easy going. See, e.g., the recent book by Mann (1997); also Clissold (2005).

6. Alford (1995) claims that there are deep-seated historical roots of China's very different attitudes to intellectual property than those that prevail in "the West."
7. This should not be confused for opining that trade is not possible. Trade has little or nothing to do with similarity in microeconomic fundamentals.

References

Aitken, Brian and Ann Harrison (1999). Do Domestic Firms Benefit from Direct Foreign Instrument? Evidence from Venezuela," *American Economic Review* 89(3) (June): 605–618.

Alford, William (1995). *To Steal a Book is an Elegant Offense: Intellectual Property Law in Chinese Civilization*. Stanford, CA: Stanford University Press.

Clissold (2005). *Mr. China: A Memoir*. New York: Harpercollins Publishers, Inc.

Encarnation, Dennis (1989). *Dislodging Multinationals: India's Comparative Perspective*. Ithaca, NY: Cornell University Press.

Farrell, Diana (2004). "Sector by Sector," in "China and India: A Race to Growth," *McKinsey Quarterly*, Special Edition, China Today.

Hazari, R. K. (1986). "Industrial Policy in Perspective," in *Essays on Industrial Policy*. New Delhi: Naurang Rai Concept Publishing Company.

Huang, Yasheng (2003). *Selling China: Foreign Direct Investment during the Reform Era*. New York: Cambridge University Press.

Huang, Y. (2004). *Ownership Biases and FDI in China: Evidence from Two Provinces*. Cambridge: MIT Sloan School.

Huang, Y. and H. Wen (2003). *A Tale of Two Provinces: Foreign Ownership and Domestic Private Sector in Jiangsu and Zhejiang*. Cambridge: MIT Sloan School of Management.

Huang, Yasheng and Tarun Khanna (2003). "Can India Overtake China?" *Foreign Policy* 137 (August 31): 74–81.

Huang, Yasheng and Wenhua Di (2003). *A Tale of Two Provinces: The Institutional Environment and Foreign Ownership in China*. Available at http://www.yale.edu/leitner/huang.pdf.

Huang, Y. and B. Yeung (2004). "Asean's Institutions are Still in Poor Shape." *Financial Times*. September 2.

Huang, Y., B. Yeung, and R. Morck (2004). "ASEAN and FTAA: External Threats and Internal Institutional Weaknesses." *Business and Politics* 6(1).

Isaacs, Harold. (1958). *Scratches on Our Mind: American Views of China and India*. White Plains, NY: M. E. Sharpe Inc.

Khanna, Tarun (2004). "India's Entrepreneurial Advantage," in "China and India: A Race to Growth," *McKinsey Quarterly*, Special Edition, China Today.

Khanna, Tarun and Krishna Palepu (2002). "Emerging Giants: Building World-Class Companies in Emerging Markets," Harvard Business School Publishing Case #9–703–431.

Khanna, Tarun and Krishna Palepu (2005). "The Evolution of Concentrated Ownership in India: Broad Patterns and a History of the Indian Software

Industry," in Randall Morck (ed.), *The History of Corporate Governance around the World: Family Business Groups to Professional Managers*. Chicago: University of Chicago Press.

Mann, James (1997). *Beijing Jeep: A Case Study of Western Business in China*. New York: HarperCollins Publishers.

Rawski, T. G. (2001). "Will Investment Behavior Constrain China's Growth?" *China Perspectives* 38: 28–35.

Sen, Amartya (2000). *Development as Freedom*. New York: Anchor Books/Doubleday.

IV

New Perspectives

10

Why Democracy Matters

Edward Friedman

I

From a global perspective, reform in both China and India is a success in terms of poverty alleviation, a most important dimension of regime performance. Poverty was reduced by one-third in India in the first decade or so of reform. The World Bank found that "China, along with India, was also responsible for the fall in the share of the world's population living in extreme poverty—from just over 40 percent in 1981 [when the socialist command economy was just beginning to be rejected by China's rulers] to just over 20 percent by 2001" (Balls 2004). Economic reform pays off, even for the poor. Raising the question of how India and China have been able "to take advantage of globalization . . ." (Fukuyama 2004), both seemed successes. "China is going places, but so is India" (Pesek 2003).

The contention that China was a success and India a failure, however, long dominated comparative studies of the world's two most populous nations. In opting for Leninist socialism, people often legitimated their choice by the proclaimed achievements of Mao's market-disregarding policies. Analysts as diverse as the traditionalist Sam Huntington (1968) and the iconoclast Barrington Moore, Jr. (1966) agreed in the 1960s that it was doubtful if Indian democracy would even survive.

Whatever the reality then, authoritarian China seems way ahead entering the twenty-first century. Looking at the awesome Shanghai skyline in 2002, an Indian business reporter worried "that maybe the 21st century really does belong to China" (Kripaleni 2002). From the beginning of China's economic reforms out of Leninist command economy trammels in 1978–1979 until democratic India in 1991 launched itself firmly on a similar course, China's economy grew to more than double India's. How can India catch up?

Or are observers again being misled into a false polarized binary of a successful China and a failed India, with authoritarianism superior to democracy? Informed analysts of China who see behind the glitz of a skyline imagine China's future as a more "somber reality," including a "crisis of governance," "the pathologies of both the political stagnation of . . . Brezhnev's Soviet Union and the crony capitalism of Suharto's Indonesia" (Pei 2002, 97, 99). It has been referred to in China as "Sudan-ization" or "Sicily-ization." Dictatorship may actually be destabilizing Chinese society, putting achievements at risk.

It is worth probing unexamined presuppositions to clarify the dynamics driving the two Asian giants, India and China. In comparing their civilization to India, many Chinese pit their Confucianism against Hinduism or, at least, prejudiced stereotypes thereof. The Chinese assumption is that Confucianism is sober, rational, and practical, while Hinduism is mystical, irrational, and otherworldly. That is why China must succeed and India invariably fails. Chineseness is superior to Indianness. It is this assumption, that China just has to be the success and India has to fail, that this chapter will explore.

II

A Chinese stereotype of India was "overpopulation, poverty . . . and train accidents" (Li 2003). Chinese tend to learn that Buddhism, the popular religion pervading China, came from India, to China's west. But Chinese reject the notion that their Buddhist popular culture is Indian. A strong Chinese tree cannot grow from a weak Indian seed. Chinese tend to learn that Indian Buddhism, imagined as soft, was transformed by Chinese culture into something hard, such that a this-worldly Chinese Buddhism has little in common with an otherworldly Indian Buddhism, a pre-Hindu source of failure, rooted deep in India's civilizational essence.

However, civilizational binaries that ignore multiple differences and potentials within a society and instead homogenize a multistranded culture into a single strand in order to oppose it to an alleged homogeneous "other" are projections of prejudices, not explanations of rates of growth or of gender inequalities or almost any other dimension that one might compare (Morgan 2004). The polarizing binary even hides similarities. While "India and China are competitors for power and influence in Asia," they share a nationalistic narrative. "At the beginning of the 21st century, India and China see themselves as great powers fallen on bad times centuries ago, but well on their way back to reclaiming their rightful places as Asia's pre-eminent nations" (Malik 2004).

Yet, some Indians accept the notion of Confucians as uniquely capable of disciplined frugality. Actually, Japanese, seen in the twentieth century as a nation of disciplined savers, imagined themselves as a land of status-conscious wastrels before they began to rise in the Meiji era. They then copied European banking systems and savings incentives. Any people can do it. What is decisive are policies and institutions and also national identities that could otherwise permit political mobilizations to block the adoption of suitable policies and institutions. It is misleading to essentialize rich and mutable cultures as successes or failures.

A binary privileging China over India, however, has been the presupposition of much error. The *Journal of Asian Studies*, the prestigious organ of the Association for Asian Studies, ran a special issue during Mao Zedong's Great Leap Forward of 1958 to 1961 to explain how China had overcome rural misery while Indian villagers were still mired in it. Actually, Mao's Leap brought the most murderous manmade famine ever, causing at least 30 million premature deaths, mostly villagers.

Yet the binary of authoritarian Chinese success and democratic Indian failure is usually treated as a fact. A typical conservative Chinese superpatriot, knowing better than to praise Mao for policies that helped villagers, writing, instead, in defense of Mao's squeezing of the peasantry, contended in a 1994 book that because Mao sacrificed the peasantry in order to build heavy industry, "Mao was able to pursue industrialization for three decades and was able to turn China into a nuclear power. Had he not done so . . .'today China would look like India' " (Fewsmith 2001, 149). In other words, although China had not done well for its rural poor, it was still a success. It built the science and industry that made China a nuclear power, creating a military that could conquer the buffer region of Tibet, humiliate India in a war in 1962, and help India's South Asian rival, Pakistan, to get nuclear weapons and missiles. China was a success, despite rural misery. India was a failure, despite becoming self-sufficient in food production. The unexamined presupposition of China as a success and India a failure obscures the continuously changing dimensions of the comparison so as to "prove" the presumed conclusion.

China, despite Mao's monstrous famine, began to win votes for inclusion in the UN once it exploded nuclear weapons in the 1960s. In the amoral interstate world, military stature matters for a nation's standing. "When President Richard Nixon first went to China it was widely assumed that he was ignoring India and courting China because China had nuclear weapons and could help balance the Soviet Union. But since 1998 India has possessed nuclear weapons and can balance China" (Power 2004). IT software success is not the only reason India's standing rose in the late 1990s. It is worth being clear about the dimensions on which one judges success and failure.

India's standing has suffered from the application of double standards. Visitors to India see beggars who have fled rural poverty panhandling all over city streets. In China in the Mao era visitors were kept from seeing the rural misery. In the post–Mao era of reform in which over a hundred million have run from rural stagnation, foreign visitors need locals to direct them to see the rural poor who have fled without legal documents to cities, with street kids sent out to beg. China's Calcutta-like poverty is hidden. In India, it is manifest. To accurately compare India and China therefore requires penetrating Chinese facades.

India is transparent. China "stir-fries its books." Even the most able of journalists will proclaim that while only three-quarters of Indian children finish primary school, "In China, virtually all children complete primary school" (Kristof 2004, 56), a claim which is patently absurd, as any researcher in China's poor countryside quickly learns. Actually, Chinese school attendance "is consistently inflated" (Shih 2004, 209). In 2003 I was in a poor area where almost no one above the age of 20 could read. Rachel Murphy urges "caution" "interpreting the rates published" in Chinese government statistics, often the percentage of final year students who graduate. Those numbers ignore those who have dropped out. Murphy reports on a village where one-third of primary school students do not graduate (p. 9). In poverty areas, "the literacy rate is 50 per cent, as opposed to a national average of 80 per cent" (Pocha), just a bit better than India, maybe close enough, given statistical errors, to be judged in the same league. That is, poor villagers suffer in both of Asia's giants.

III

Many once praised Mao–era China for equalizing and raising health care and schooling, especially for the rural poor. Yet, as shameful as the Indian record was, supposed Mao era achievements were, Peking University Center for Economic Research Director Justin Lin has pointed out, both artificial and unsustainable. The rural poor in Mao's China were hidden away from the eyes of outsiders as were the almost 2 of 22 million who died from famine in North Korea at the end of the twentieth century. Foreign observers can readily be kept from comprehending the inhumanity of authoritarian state socialism.

Mao locked up villagers in the countryside, blocking urbanization and modernization that could create higher value production. Starting in 1957–1958, the poor had to self-fund. During the Cultural Revolution of his last decade, Mao destroyed education, turning teachers into targets for degradation. A Chinese junior middle school graduate in the countryside actually received less education than an elementary school student had received in but six years in the prior era. Chinese figures on education in the Mao era, bad as they are, hide how much worse it really was, especially for the rural poor, females, and minorities, the most vulnerable of people.

While the Mao era educational disaster is now well known, a similar disaster in health care is obscured by a discourse about gains to longevity and equal state-subsidized access to medical treatment. That longevity gain was real. It was the achievement of the era before Mao's fundamentalist communism rose in 1957–1958. The health delivery system put in place between 1949 and 1956 saw that virtually everyone was vaccinated and inoculated, producing great gains in life expectancy.

Once Mao took control in 1957–1958, however, he insisted on self-reliance, meaning self-financing. The poor were not subsidized by the state. Unfunded clinics decayed and declined. They were staffed by untrained people incapable of medical diagnoses. They had no medicines or surgeries to offer. The rural poor were abandoned. The urban party-state-military monopolized benefits.

Mao era villagers knew that higher officials with serious medical problems did not use the primitive rural facilities that villagers were consigned to. Those officials could go instead to specialized urban, especially military, hospitals, which provided international level care for China's power elite. Even if villagers found a way into one of those urban facilities, they were relegated to a section that was crowded, lacked medicines, was noisy, understaffed, and harried, while the elite monopolized a special and separate section hidden from the hoi polloi. It was spacious, tranquil, and staffed with more medical personnel per patient than in most hospitals in the industrialized democracies.

Once reform began, villagers sought real medical care. Traditional herbal medicines—whose growth was barred in the Mao era because growing a profitable economic crop would lead tillers to abandon socialist collectives—suddenly became available. No one would pay for seeing the untrained Mao era personnel at the village clinic. I was in rural China interviewing clinic workers and villagers soon after Mao died. Villagers abandoned the useless clinics of the Mao era. It is a myth that under Mao Chinese villagers had medical coverage, which was lost in the age of reform.

In the reform era, the health situation actually is much better. Demographer Judith Banister concludes, "The public health situation in China has improved dramatically . . . since the beginning of the economic reforms." According to UNESCO figures, life expectancy has risen greatly and infant deaths have plummeted. Villagers see a "significant reduction in malnutrition," "cleaner water," "access to tap water," and "increased utilization of health facilities" (Huang 2004, 369, 379). New roads allow the ill to get medical help.

Despite rising incomes that permit better nutrition in the reform era, villagers note that a new and growing middle stratum now have the money to buy quality service. Poor villagers without money, on the other hand, cannot afford health care since health care workers, in contrast to the Mao era, cannot be coerced to work for virtually nothing. Such poorest people have gone from very bad Mao era care to unaffordable reform era medicine. In either case, China was not and is not a model. China does not even have hospitals for the indigent or charities for the poor as India does, however feeble. In fact, the Indian government spends more on health care than does China.

Illness in the Mao era, however, did not drive people under or produce great income disparities, as is tragically the case in the reform era whose priorities have not included social safety nets. In the Mao era, in contrast, misery was shared. No one could go out and earn money. Everyone had to live on collectively distributed relatively equal survival minimums. No one got ahead while an ill person lay untreated. There was an artificial and unsustainable equality of shared stagnation, a point stressed by Justin Lin. No villager today would accept living at such a primitive level with no hope for a better material life for the next generation, as was the cruel reality of the Mao era.

Social expectations have risen. The poor hate the corrupt gains of the coddled rich. Violent incidents are on the rise. Chinese grow nostalgic about the past and misremember and romanticize it in order to criticize the polarizing priorities of today's brutally corrupt and greedy officials. Nostalgia, however understandable, should not be confused with facts.

To be open to a realistic comparison, one should remember that there were two other Mao era famines after the Great Leap disaster. Picture each of the many millions of victims of China's three deadly Mao era famines.

> An inhabitant of a Xinyang village reported at that time, "I just came back from our native village. . . . Everyone in my family has starved to death. . . . Only my aunt remains. Her son died too. . . . How can she go on living? . . . . In the middle of one night, a pig so starved that it was nothing but skin and bones rushed into her courtyard. She shut the door at once. Then she beat the hunger dazed pig to death. She skinned the pig during the night and buried it. She got up in the middle of the night, dug up the pig and cooked a piece of it to eat. She did not give any of it to her five-year-old son to eat for fear that he would talk about it. Once they found out, those who were still alive in the village would come rushing in and threaten to kill her. They would beat her to bring out the pig. She looked at her son crying that he was hungry. Mama, I'm hungry. Mama! This went on until he died. ("Bai Hua," p. 9)

Even as Chinese died from Mao's utopian socialist dictatorial project, Indians trekked to China to seek the secret of its developmental success. The presupposition was that (bourgeois) democracy had to be bad for the poor. Yet, India only escaped mass famine for the vulnerable poor, as India's Nobel Prize-winning economist Amartya Sen long ago established, because it was a democracy. As Barrington Moore Jr. argued, however bad a particular democracy may be for the weak, it tends to be worse under authoritarianism (Moore 1970).

IV

In a brilliant rumination on empire, a leading historian concludes that, in contrast to the overseas empire of England, which was intentionally multiethnic, the continental empires of India and China, even as nation-states, are similarly oppressive of minorities. "India . . . treats its Sikh and Kashmiri separatist freedom fighters with a ferocity that the [British] Raj would scarcely have exceeded." Likewise, "The Chinese [People's] Republic rules over provinces that . . . were conquered . . . long after the Spanish . . . conquest of the New World, and—again [i.e., as India]—does not always do so with the conspicuous consent of the governed" (Colley 2002, 378).

While India, as virtually all nation-states, does indeed resist secessionists, at times, brutally, still its Sikhs and other religious, language, and ethnic minorities are free. Often they get their own state and enjoy democratic autonomy. They form political parties, make alliances, publish, run schools, and are totally free in their religious practices. Sikhs even become prime ministers.

None of this is true for a Communist Party dictatorship. China's party state is not about to be headed by a Uighur Muslim or Tibetan Buddhist. The party is atheistic. Han chauvinists have treated Uighur Muslims and Tibetan Buddhists with extreme inhumanity. Consent of the governed in China by minorities is not merely not "conspicuous," it does not exist. China is not India "again." India is a universe better. It is extraordinary to have Han Chinese authoritarian repression equated with India's vibrant democratic civil society of diverse communities.

While our historian praises India as an "extraordinary experiment in democracy," India actually is no more a democratic experiment than are Germany, Italy, Spain, Portugal, and Austria. In fact, India has been a stable democracy longer than all of these European countries.

Samuel Huntington (1991), a world famous Harvard political scientist, in order to find a unique third wave of democracy between 1974 and 1991 counts India, home to almost one-fifth of the human race, as a new democracy in the 1970s, ignoring that India won its freedom after World War II. His trick is to treat Prime Minister Indira Gandhi's moment of emergency rule as ending India's democracy, while ignoring France's "suspension of democracy in 1958" when a "military uprising . . . ended the Fourth Republic" (O'Kane 38, 242).

In fact, a great wave of democratization came with the defeat of the fascist racist powers in World War II, and, with it, the discrediting of rule over people deemed inferior and incapable of self-government. (Although inside authoritarian China, minorities are still mistreated in a colonial way.) With democracy in Japan, Italy, West Germany, Austria, and India (as well as the two dozen island republics of the Pacific and the Caribbean, which our political scientist also does not count), far more people and nations came to enjoy the blessings of freedom after World War II than in the 1974–1991 period. In either case, it is India's achievement that is weightiest and deserves emphasis. Indian democracy, despite our historian and our political scientist, is not a fragile tottering experiment but a great and well-established advance for humanity. Yet, in America, "of college-bound high school students" "80 per cent do not know that India is the world's largest democracy" (Platt).

In the standard academic discourse, Indians are not even given credit for their robust democracy. Instead it is said to be the consequence of British colonialism (Chirot 2004, 322). It is a strange claim. After all, the great majority of British colonies became authoritarian. This failure of democracy is usually ascribed to divide-and-rule British colonial tactics, which were also applied in India. But Indians, nonetheless, democratized India. Its Congress Party, founded in 1885, took on a mass base in the Gandhi era of nonviolent mass resistance to colonialism and won election after election after independence as the party that led the liberation struggle against British colonialism. The Congress Party's quarter century as the head of a one-party dominant democracy, similar to Sweden, Japan, South Africa, and Israel, is not a British creation. Yet Indian democracy, in the conventional wisdom, is not even comprehended as the work of Indian democrats.

Since its major achievements are presumed not even to exist, studies of Indian performance tend to focus on negatives, on its low rankings on development indexes. Indeed, our famous political scientist, in his major study of modernization (Huntington 1968) touted Pakistan's military dictatorship as the future, while India was dismissed as too "westernized," as run by alien liberal democratic elites, supposedly bound to fail and be rejected by a non-Western people.

In the conventional wisdom, India has political freedom, albeit barely and undeservedly. Meanwhile China does well on the dimensions measured by quality of life or human development indicators. On literacy (where Chinese numbers are inflated), life expectancy and mother's survival at birth, China scores much higher than India. The conventional wisdom finds a trade-off. A people can be politically free or they can enjoy the basic material prerequisites of a tolerable life.

With India's material failures ascribed to its democratic political system and with China's performance exaggerated, India's democracy is dismissed as a hoax. Little attention is given to how India scores much higher than China on all the freedom indices compiled by Freedom House. A freedom to starve is ridiculed as no freedom at all. India is dismissed as Karl Marx ridiculed free labor. It is actually (wage) slavery. "Freedom" is stigmatized as a fraud to protect a narrow elite. Democracy then is dismissed or marginalized.

Every step in the above logic is erroneous. Freedom-loving people in democracies do not sufficiently appreciate the long-term benefits of liberties, not seeing how wage slaves can, over time and with struggle, become middle-class citizens who are members of strong unions, which are part of a progressive party coalition that maintains high social welfare benefits. There never was a factual basis for the two standard pieces of conventional wisdom for comparing India unfavorably with China, (1) that India was a failure and China a success and (2) that there is a trade-off between political and economic success.

In the Mao era, ruling groups in both China and India ill-served their people by entrenching economically self-wounding institutions borrowed from Stalin's Soviet Union, including a policy of economic autarky, which denied their people the benefits of exporting to the world market. "In 1970, when inward-looking policies reigned supreme, the [Indian] ratio of trade in goods and services to GDP was a mere eight percent, the lowest in the world, but for China" (Survey, 2). That is, while India was bad, China was worse. Per capita income in China at the end of the Mao era was lower than in India. Such facts explode the conventional wisdom that democracy made growth slower in India than in China. Democratic India was not a failure in comparison to authoritarian China.

V

Learning the truth about China's dictatorship, its treatment of minorities, Mao's famine, etcetera, however, did not end misleading binaries of a good socialism (China) and a bad capitalism (India). Since the Chinese dictatorship tends to present itself as a model of success, it does not highlight its own catastrophic experiences. With the dictatorship fostering fear and complicity, truth is a scarce commodity. In the 1960s, belief that Leninist socialism was superior to market-oriented democracies was shaped by the Soviet Sputnik's winning of the space rocket race and by America's defeat by Fidel Castro at the Bay of Pigs, followed by America's bloody involvement in an unwinnable war in Vietnam. Although American aid to India was "aimed at helping democratic India prevail over China in a 'development contest' and thus prove the superiority of the democratic model to a watchful Third World," few believed it (Kochaxi, 101).

People "knew" that Stalinist big push industrialization worked. North Korea was a success, South Korea a basket case. Thailand was going nowhere, while Socialist Vietnam was rising. Castro's Cuba's turn to Leninism did better for the nation than people in class-polarized Latin America could hope for. While these erroneous binaries are now clear, amazingly, many progressive Indians, even in the twenty-first century, imagine Mao's or Fidel's way as somehow a success worthy of emulation.

Outsiders could not readily see how polarized and unequal was Mao era China. They even imagined reform-era China as a turn for the worse. In the prior Mao era, however, the life expectancy gap in China between its countryside and its city was larger than the gap between China and India. Leninism created extreme inequality. A Chinese villager was constrained by the state even from leaving the village for the city, locked on to land one was not allowed to own, and forced to grow crops decided by the state at below market prices imposed by the state. Such a limit on life choices did not exist in India, as Cambridge University economist Suzie Paine long ago pointed out.

Freedom, both in the sense of knowledge as the basis for rational choice and of physical mobility as a capacity to get away from what is awful are central to well-being (there are, after all, plenty of awful things in India). The Chinese hinterland villager in the Mao era, limited in information by a single political line, either believed, wrongly, that all Chinese were equal in condition and living better than the exploited of Taiwan (imagined as living on banana skins), or helplessly raged at being locked in to the equivalent of an apartheid caste society. In contrast, the marginalized Indian villager, joining an opposition political party, a protest movement or an exodus to the city, had capabilities forcibly denied to the virtually enserfed Chinese villager. In ways that matter to human dignity, the Indian villager was much better off.

While all societies are wasteful, it may be that Leninist statistics uniquely obscure how extraordinarily much of production never usefully reaches an end-user or consumer, how stupendously much is wasted on the courtly lifestyle of the parasitic and very large official stratum of feudal-like rulers, how much goes to the military and especially to the many secret police. Maoism imposed an abysmally low condition of life.

Yet, despite the suffering of marginalized groups in authoritarian China, people kept saying that India's relatively slow growth was the price of democracy. "Mrs. Gandhi's supporters" believed that "brutality and repressive discipline" made possible "development in China and the Soviet Union . . ." China purportedly advanced faster than "democratic India precisely because China was totalitarian" (Tharoor, 290 and 303). Since Mao era China in fact grew more slowly than democratic India, blaming democracy for slow growth is patent nonsense.

By the 1970s, as Brezhnev's Russia stagnated and the truth about Mao's China and Pol Pot's Cambodia became known, state socialism increasingly seemed a dead end for the rural poor. Japan-led East and Southeast Asia, with a policy of export-oriented industrialization (EOI) combined with import substitution industrialization (ISI) showed how to rise out of poverty. But proud, anti-imperialist Indian patriots dismissed Japan and the newly industrialized economies of East Asia, of South Korea, Taiwan, Hong Kong, and Singapore for having lost their independence, for becoming Americanized, and called it a sad Coca Cola-ization and an absolute loss of dignity. Back in 1919 Gandhi had declared, "Japan has been Westernized; one can no longer even speak of China." Despite Indian myopia, Japan or South Korea was as Japanese or Korean as ever (Watson). India's nationalistic political mobilization, however, blocked a path that could lift the rural poor out of misery.

VI

Reform-era China abandoned the self-wounding policies of stagnant Mao era socialist anti-imperialism and lifted hundreds of millions out of poverty. It abandoned revolutionary tourism, where China paid to fool foreigners into thinking socialism was paradise, for money-earning tourism, in which the splendors of ancient China earn tens of billions in hard currency from delighted visitors. (India has, in comparison, invested little to make ancient glories accessible to international visitors.)

After Mao died, but before reform gains kicked in, some Chinese realized that "even" India was doing better than China. That reality hurt Chinese pride. It was inconceivable to Chinese that India should do better. To argue even for a higher sports budget, one said "even India" spent more (Brownell 1991, 296). India was conceived of as the bottom of the barrel.

In fact, Mao had devastated Chinese higher education. Female illiteracy had risen to the same rate as Indonesia. "Even" India spent more on education than did China, which brought up the rear in the world rankings of per capita spending on education. With an unreported famine ravaging its southwest when Mao died, China imported grain to feed its people, while India had moved to grain self-sufficiency.

Yet, by the early 1980s, soon after Mao died, a reforming rural China was booming. It happened so fast. Few paused to ponder why state socialism in the Mao era had been a devastating failure. Instead, by the mid-1980s, the question once again was how to explain unreformed India's failure and reform China's success. Ignoring that, depending on policy, the very same political system could do well or poorly in economics, as manifested in China's sudden turnaround, once again the false assumption was that the India–China gap proved that democracy was inferior to authoritarianism. This discourse legitimates a brutal dictatorship.

Rural workers in export factories in the reform era whose foreign exchange earnings have been central to China's post–Mao rise were said to be prepared for that work by good Mao era education. Such education, however, did not exist. It was family socialization that continued in the Mao era despite attempts to destroy the culture which produced young people who were hard-working on behalf of family enrichment, with family enrichment a value that was the antithesis of Maoism. But, of course, given an opportunity, the poor work hard everywhere.

The hard-working poor in reform era China complain about greedy power-holders, an indication of how China has become more unequal than India or Russia, perhaps as unequal as Brazil. The causes lie in the continuation of certain Mao era institutions and priorities. The biggest source of the rural–urban gap remains the locking up of villagers in the countryside in state-imposed forced production of low-priced basic crops. At the end of the Mao era, over 80 percent of Chinese lived in the countryside where there was little work and less money. In addition, as in the Mao era, investment still privileges the central cities. State workers get unemployment insurance, not villagers. Also, as in the Mao era, there is still no health care or pension provision from the central government for the rural poor.

The unaccountable ruling party cares for itself. When property is privatized, right down to county towns and villages, officials (as in Russia) grab the lion's share, as in the Mao era they grabbed the food so that their family members did not die in the three famines. But Stalin concentrated wealth in centralized vertical hierarchies. Mao decentralized Stalinism. Consequently, in the reform era, China's corrupt property-seizing oligarchs can grab wealth right down to local levels. Economic inequality in China is a reflection of the entrenched inequality of the party dictatorship, which denies voice and self-representation to the village poor and the well over 100 million migrant workers. Analysts of transitions out of command economy Leninism conclude that democracy should be the first priority so that there can be a debate, with decisions publicly taken, on how fairly to share the pain of the economic reforms (Linz and Stepan). That would legitimize and stabilize the system. China lacks such political stability. It therefore promotes a war-prone chauvinism.

In short, the growing polarization and increasingly visible poverty of reform era China reflect some unchanged priorities, institutions, and policies of the Mao era that have deepened, intensifying social tensions. The tendencies were manifest in the pre-reform era when poor villagers, three times, were allowed to starve to death. Continuity with the Mao era is seen in the suffering in populous, rural, poor Henan province. It had the most famine deaths in the Mao era. It has the most HIV AIDS deaths in the reform era. China, in contrast to democratic India, lacks a vibrant civil society to help the suffering. In the popular consciousness of the newly prospering and grossly uncaring of China, the wounded of Henan are ridiculed. The level of uncaring inhumanity in an authoritarian China, which does not welcome organized, independent religious charity is extraordinary. By UN standards, China's poverty reduction is quite ordinary for its level of development, while its inequality is extreme. Does that make China a success?

Yet, even in 1997 the Indian prime minister held to this shibboleth that India has "to pay the economic price for political democracy" (Gujral). Authoritarians could, in this Indian view, grow faster than could free societies whose slow proceduralism combines with vested private groups tied to corrupt bureaucratic and political interests to block rapid development. Without denying the weight of such negative forces in democratic India, they were worse in the Leninist world. It was the entrenched interests of Soviet Russia's corrupt Brezhnevian era that blocked Gorbachev's reform project, leading to Russia's tragic decline. Those interests had reversed Khrushchev's reforms.

China was, ironically, lucky that Mao's vigilante war on his party kept it from similar entrenchment. Authoritarian vested interests are more difficult to overcome than are democratic ones. Communist Vietnam is confronted by "the unwillingness of the Party to follow its [reformist] words with actions . . . If an entrenched and resistant bureaucracy, driven by vested interests, is able to frustrate a meaningful reallocation of scarce natural resources, it may prove difficult for the state to sustain economic progress" (St. John). The consensus of numerous studies is that democracy is not, in comparative perspective, an obstacle to growth. India's problem was the political will of leaders. What mattered for growth was leaders willing to implement helpful policies and build good institutions, not the political system.

Of course, as with Brezhnev's Soviet Union, the socioeconomic base of a ruling elite could turn the politically powerful against economic reform, as Barrington Moore, Jr.'s classic study of the *Social Origins of Dictatorship and Democracy* makes clear. All the so-called East Asian miracle economies enjoyed the advantage of beginning with land reform providing land to market-oriented farmers. India did not. Moore (1966) found that China's advantage in having destroyed landlord power in Mao's anti-landlord revolution would allow China to develop much faster than India, where rural lords oppressed poor villagers. In India marginalized rural dwellers, the most miserable of the worst off, would, Moore predicted, eventually abandon democracy and, to win the blessings of modernity, support an authoritarian alternative to reactionary, landlord-based power. Democracy was irrelevant.

Moore was wrong (Friedman 1998), at least until 1978. Mao's socialist state actually locked China's villagers into stagnant misery. Collectivization in 1955–1956 reversed the gains of the initial land reform that was merely a tactic to win peasant support in China's revolutionary civil war (Friedman, Pickowicz and Selden 1991). But in 1978, economic reformer Deng Xiaoping became China's paramount leader. He abandoned Leninist socialism and launched an era of high growth. Households tilled the land. Growth soared (Friedman, Pickowicz and Selden 2005).

Market-oriented reform began in India only in 1991 and remains quite constrained. Even if India's growth rate since 1991 is almost as high as China's, since China, by 1991, had an economy more than twice the size of India's because of high growth in the early post–Mao era before India began to reform, the absolute gap between the two countries just keeps growing. Indeed, there is reason to believe that Chinese growth is actually faster than its government reports (Kynge). Patriotic Indians anxiously imagine a future where Chinese might laud it over India. Once again, the issue of national strength, something not captured by measures of freedom or growth, weighs heavily for patriots. In an age of nationalistic peoples, success or failure can be comprehended on many different dimensions.

Perhaps Moore's analysis of China's advantage in having destroyed landlord power by violent means was merely premature. Hasn't Moore been proven correct since 1978 when China abandoned inhuman Soviet-style collectivities and allowed household farming? Isn't such a path still blocked for many in India by entrenched rural elites? Even the poorest of the poor in an extraordinarily unequal rural China will now sacrifice to take advantage of the new opportunities of reform, no matter how much they curse the corrupt, self-serving, and unaccountable dictatorship. In contrast, democratically committed observers found India's poor beaten down and defeated. "Even though there is little obvious sign of the hunger or deprivation that can be found in any city, say, in neighboring India, the fatalistic acceptance of one's lot that is pervasive among India's poor is also lacking in China" (Miles 1996, 136). India's poor supposedly would suffer in silence, just as the presuppositional binary of fatalistic Hinduism and pragmatic Confucianism implies.

Yet by the early 1990s lower caste parties of the poor rose in the various states of India. They built coalitions and sought a share of national power. India's democracy was their democracy. In contrast to Moore, who believed that India's alienated rural poor would prove the Achilles' heel of its democracy, actually, India, uniquely, is a democracy where the poor believe that constitutional liberties serve the interests of people such as themselves. India is a success on many political dimensions. Free people make India a uniquely stable polity.

Not so with China (Zweig). The urban–rural gap keeps widening. Poverty worsened in 2003 (Watts). Villagers in non-coastal provinces tend to see the system as corrupt and serving only entrenched elites who care not a fig about people like them. As a result, violent incidents keep growing. The dimension on which comparisons are usually made in which freedom and material factors are separated does not understand how they interact over the long haul. Could it be that in political freedom lie some sources of long-term Indian success (and of dignity for the rural poor) that are missed by conventional measures?

Rural oppression is more deadly in authoritarian China. Not only do far more women commit suicide in rural China than in India but also more than in all the other nations of the world combined. In both India and China, the gender ratio is hideously anti-woman. In both there are regions that are so bad that they seem to have institutionalized a war against women.

But one advantage Indian women have is that democracy engenders a robust civil society where caring people can join to help those who are in pain and need. Authoritarian China, in contrast, fears that autonomous popular societal groups would undermine the Communist Party's monopoly of power. Therefore, however sad the plight of rural women in India, it can be far worse in China (Xue) where victims are left totally isolated. In rural China, a hellish life experience of dashed dreams makes death frequently seem a better option than life for women, and, increasingly, elder men. People in pain in China have no place to turn for succor precisely because China is an authoritarian system.

Surely comparing the fate of the least of them is an important dimension on which to judge success and failure. Usually, the worst off are young, poor females from minorities living in the peripheries. Rather than comparing China versus India in the abstract, one should ask how similar sectors are doing on diverse dimensions, such as kidnapping, prostitution, HIV AIDS. Based on qualitative ethnographic studies, a comparison of sectoral inhumanities does not seem to show China as singularly superior to India, although India surely is not doing well.

One should not romanticize India. The burning of brides by dissatisfied families of husbands is a public scandal. It should be. In China, however, the kidnapping and sale of women into prostitution and forced marriage, a large-scale venture with police complicity is kept quiet. Communal strife is headline news in India. Little of analytic value is published in China to help Chinese understand and deal humanely with regional and communalist strife. They would not know that more Muslims can be executed in one year in but one province of China, Xinjiang, than are executed in a year in any country other than China.

VII

Evaluating China versus India in terms of the life prospects of the weak and vulnerable requires exploring the fate of minorities, especially religious communities. India's vicissitudes in trying to build a certain kind of secular society are well known. The victims of communalist atrocities and the impact of fundamentalist forces from Gujarat to Delhi on religious minorities are ugly. But rulers in the PRC keep outsiders from knowing just how bad things are for Tibetan Buddhists and Uighur Muslims. All international human rights groups find evidence of pervasive and continuing crimes against humanity in China, from forced abortion to the harassment, arrest, torture, and murder of diverse believers. Yet Chinese in the post–Mao era have joined in an extraordinary revival of faith-based commitment. The Chinese Communist Party (CCP) is trying to constrain, control, co-opt, or crush this popular spiritualism. How does one measure the superiority of life in India from the enjoyment of religious freedom, from embracing "the heart of a heartless world," as Karl Marx long ago put it?

The rulers in Beijing, looking on religion as would a half-educated village atheist proud of his narrow materialism, are anxious about China's explosion of spiritualism. There is in China "a widening gap between the inability of the political leadership to appreciate religion and the growing fascination with religion." Even Christianity and underground house churches are spreading. This contrasts with India, Tu Weiming, America's leading philosopher of neo-Confucianism, finds. India is a vibrant democracy, a civilization where religious vitality and societal dynamism flourish together, while China "suffers from an inability to understand religion as an integral part of the complex modernizing process," such that China should "take from" India, understood as one of China's "reference societies" (Tu 2002, 85–87).

Another measure of how the least of them are treated is capital punishment. Better-off Chinese tend to see the poor and unemployed as dangerous classes. They applaud China's huge number of executions of "criminals." A south China defense attorney, who has struggled against capital punishment for minor crimes, finds India a society, which cares about the dignity of the weak, that is, in comparison to China, which executes more people in a year than the whole rest of the world put together, at least twice as many. Better-off urban Chinese, seeing rural migrants as spreaders of crime, drugs, disease, and filth, welcome the large number of hasty, often mass, executions of members of the "dangerous classes," the rural uprooted. But, the Chinese defense attorney campaigning against these arbitrary abuses that target the poor and vulnerable comments, "When [Chinese] people say, 'What does it matter if a few die, there are over a billion of us,' I say, what about India? They have only executed five or six people, and there are nearly a billion of them" (Becker). It is said that "India has the highest number of torture and custodial deaths in the world" (Mishra 2004, 17), but, as with literacy, Chinese numbers are suspect.

The worst off in China are undoubtedly worse off than Chinese statistics allow. The statistics are unreliable. "Official figures during the 1990s became less reliable as the rural economy stagnated and village cadres come under pressure to inflate their achievements . . . reported per capita income in 1997 was 2,700 Yuan [$US 330], a figure that even the village cadres openly admitted was false. The real per capital income in the late 1990s . . . stood at about 1,000–1,100 Yuan [$US 135]" (Yan 2002, 31). While Chinese rural incomes stagnated in the four years from 1997 to 2000, the PRC's National Bureau of Statistics touted a 17 percent rise. The rich–poor gap in China, which is wider than India's even according to official numbers, is actually far worse than the statistics suggest.

VIII

Ignoring China's abysmal failures, paranoid Chinese patriots drive themselves mad worrying they may be Coca Cola-ized if they remain open to the world's best practices. Victory for antireform forces is possible. Former president Jiang Zemin was widely seen as traitorously selling out to Americans for doing what was necessary to maintain access to the American consumer in order to earn the foreign exchange that helps drive Chinese growth.

China's reform could be threatened by chauvinistic, corrupt, conservative, entrenched Brezhnevian political interests. Chinese are still being taught that they are the victim of an unfair world, even though China actually is the world's leading beneficiary from globalization. An expansionist chauvinism toward democratic Taiwan could produce military action against Taiwan that would alienate China's leading markets and investors.

Xenophobia blinds. Chinese, their creativity limited by a repressive political system, whine that the "racist" and politicized Nobel Prize Committee for Literature refuses to recognize Chinese greatness. These chauvinists ignore the fact the Nobel laureate Gao Xingjian had to flee Communist Party repression in the PRC to write in Chinese and publish in Taiwan and Hong Kong. China's premier referred to Gao as a Frenchman and complained that communist-sponsored Chinese novelists were overlooked.

In contrast, Indian authors regularly produce numerous masterpieces of world excellence, enriching all humanity. The Academy Award-nominated Indian film Lagaan, about a tax revolt against the British Raj, did not caricature the British as did the Chinese box-office flop about the Opium War. On numerous global cultural debates, Indian voices must be heeded while repression makes brilliant Chinese seem stupid. It is mind-boggling that people could consider this abnormal China, which represses its people's capacities, a success, and a vibrant and democratic India a failure.

But not only does India's superiority on freedom indexes have implications for a better quality of life for the marginalized that are usually missed in the conventional comparisons of the political versus the economic, but many now wonder if authoritarian China even does better in the economic sphere. India has done brilliantly in IT software. China has sent missions to find out why. IT may prove a weighty factor in the post–Fordist world economy. Indian political freedom may be a major advantage in the information age. Given authoritarian China's fear of its own people, the regime tightly controls Internet cafes and web access. This could constrain IT growth. A democratic India may come to enjoy economic opportunities denied to the Chinese people by the Communist Party's dictatorial system. Democracy could actually be an asset for growth.

Fascinated by India's amazing IT software success, increasingly analysts find that "Slowly but steadily, India will overtake China" (Power). India's capital markets are more efficient and transparent. They serve local firms better. Consequently, India has far more world-class companies. Their employees are far more competent in English, the language of international business. Competitive firms in India include cutting-edge sectors such as pharmaceuticals and biotechnology. "India's unique approach to development is preparing it to overtake China in the economic-growth race." "India is developing more efficient corporations, healthier banks, more robust service industries and a bigger consumption base. China has won the sprint. But India is training for the marathon" (Fireman).

World-class research and development is required for continuous global success. But intellectual property piracy pervades China (Marsh), with economic crime high and the legal protections of multinational business low. Consequently, "Over 199 transnational companies set up research and development centers in India. At the same time, only 33 transnational companies that rank in the top 1,000 companies . . . opened such centers in China." The future therefore could belong to India (Xiao, 44).

India's GDP growth in the fourth quarter of 2003, a strong 10.4 percent, exceeded China's growth. Compared to China, democratic India provides foreign investors a level playing field, stability, and enforceable contracts (Bradsher, June 12). If democracy were an obstacle to economic success, then the democracies in Taiwan, South Korea, Australia, New Zealand, Finland, and Botswana would not be enjoying their stellar performance in wealth expansion. Authoritarian regimes that perform pitifully are legion.

China's banking system could even collapse. It is bankrupt. The non-state sector in India, with the largest firms capitalized at U.S. $7 billion or so, contrasts with China's largest private firms, which, despite a quarter century of reform, are still only 10 percent of the size of India's behemoths. India can build on many advantages if it completes the project of economic reform.

"If"! The obstacles to more rapid growth seem to me much weightier in India, despite a recent switch by many in judging the future. India is not rushing to reform finance, privatize money-losing parastatals, end rigid labor restrictions, or free up food markets. Far more people are locked into miserable subsistence labor in the countryside, where caste, gender, and landlord oppression continue in many regions. The bloated state budgets that support the bureaucracy and debt and keep villagers tethered to subsistence minimums provided by the state block the freeing of agricultural production and freeze out investment in basic health, education, and welfare. That is, self-serving people in India still favor economic policies and institutions that lock Indians into poverty. The lack of health, education, property rights, and power for so many Indian villagers seems deeply entrenched. No doubt the treatment of China's rural poor has been corrupt and brutal, but industrialization, a rural exodus, a successful competition for foreign investment and huge infrastructural transformations make China's continuing rapid rise, albeit at a heavy price in human suffering, far more likely than India's. Indeed, it is quite possible that China's performance is on a Kuznets curve and China's deepening inequality is about to turn around and move in the direction of equity. While it is not true that China is a success and India is a failure, it is not obvious that China must do worse than India.

While China is amazingly open to the world, Indian chauvinism hinders India's reform project. China continues to do far better in export promotion, wooing foreign investment, attracting expatriates to return home to invest, promoting tourism, and in absorbing the best practices of the world in science, technology, and business administration (Baipei et al. 1997). A nationalistic fear of alien pollution keeps India from acting in the interest of the nation's economic rise.

In Indian nationalism, India must be "wary of opening the economy to foreign business for fear of repeating the experience of the [British] East India Company, whose merchants had become rulers of India" and obstructed India's continuous upgrading to standards of global excellence. Fearful that market openness means dependency on imperialism, India wounds itself, subsidizing waste and producing shoddy goods, rejecting the export-oriented industrialization that rapidly expanded wealth in East and Southeast Asia (Tharoor 1999, 162, 172–173). Indians have far too much clung to the "Nehruvian developmental model . . . based on import substituting industrialization leading to self-reliance," while damning export-oriented industrialization as an American "imperial" conspiracy to keep developing nations as "client and protégé states" who are forced to "follow the footsteps" of an exploitative America (Karirag 1996, 132, 181). For India, "Nehru held most of the countries which later . . . formed ASEAN in contempt because of their alignment with either Britain or the U.S. He maintained that they had 'Coca-Cola governments' and shared none of India's lofty vision. Today, more than 30 years later, India as a full dialogue partner, is looking eastward to ASEAN, most of whose economies have left India's recently liberalized economy decades behind" (Sidhva). India is only gradually abandoning the bad lessons of the past. Gradualness is no advantage in economic reform. If it were, India would already be way ahead of China, which has reformed so much more swiftly and thoroughly than has India, or Russia for that matter.

Indian anticolonialism, as in historian K. M. Pannikar's view that the "Portuguese of the 16th and 17th centuries had nothing to teach the people of India except improved methods of killing and bigotry in religion," slows reform. Indians would do better if their national mythos insisted that when European ships reached India in the sixteenth century, "India was enormously productive, wealthy and densely populated. . . ." "Indian ports and shipping had for centuries been tied into the Arabian Sea, Red Sea, and Mediterranean system on one side and into the Bay of Bengal, Straits of Malaka, and China Sea on the other." A decentralized and open India absorbed advanced technologies, while "Indian diamonds, pepper, hand-woven cotton and silk textiles, and other commodities kept their old markets and found new ones . . . Dutch purchases of textiles in Bengal in the late seventeenth century likely generated 100,000 new jobs for the region." India was a beneficiary of the expansion of the world market "earlier and more than . . . Europe . . ." (Richards 1997, 205, 206, 208). The mobilizational power of one's national mythos, democratic polity or not, impacts growth. Indian nationalism, facilitating political mobilizations against global opportunities, restricts openness and keeps India far poorer than it has to be. It wounds the weak.

IX

However one chooses to measure the economic performance of Asia's two giants, the causes are seldom Hinduism versus Confucianism or democracy versus dictatorship, but matters of political institutions, policy, leadership, identity, and will. The two nations have very different military traditions, different notions of civilian-military relations. They approach federalism and decentralization differently. Their ruling parties work differently. They handle issues of diversity in language, religion, and ethnicity or regional identity very differently.

Here democracy again is an advantage. The Indian political system seems more legitimate and flexible. In contrast, Chinese are far more worried about their nation falling apart. Riven by persistent Leninist creations of regional polarization, ruled by a corrupt, brutal, and self-serving Brezhnevite party, Chinese are anxious that their reform path will lead to national disintegration as in Yugoslavia, the Soviet Union, Czechoslovakia, and Ethiopia.

But that is not how leaders of poor nations elsewhere see it. They still see Indian beggars in India's urban streets and see China's magnificent urban sky lines. They therefore ask, what is the secret of China's success? They tend to be unaware of invisible factors—path dependent inheritances, geographic region, timing. They do find China's rulers preaching about their policy wisdom, an extraordinary openness to the global and a brilliant managing of the currency. Visitors are told that China's dramatic rise results from what the ruling CCP dubs stability and party leadership, that is, a continuation of the CCP dictatorship. Until democratic Indian outperforms China economically, authoritarian rulers elsewhere are likely, as in the Mao era, to self-servingly echo CCP propaganda that China is a success precisely because it is authoritarian. The headline in the May 28, 2004 *Financial Times* describing the reaction of representatives from poor countries attending a World Bank conference on poverty alleviation was "China's success inspires envy and awe."

By 1996, China's GDP was almost three times India's. India's chauvinist obstacles to foreign investment in power and in other infrastructural projects still combined (along with environmental activism of a dogmatic left that will not see the importance of globalized growth to alleviating poverty) to constrict growth in India's energy sector, which is needed to power new wealth and more jobs. India does not seem even close to carrying out the reforms that would permit its wealth to catch up to Chinese levels.

Writings in the official newspaper of the Central Committee of China's ruling Communist Party acknowledge that India was world class in IT software exports and that China was not, that Indian banks were far less exposed by nonperforming loans, that capital was used far more efficiently in India and that India had many more world-class firms. But China was so far ahead. And India was a mess. "Delhi's urban infrastructure level—no expressway in its real sense, only a second grade highway linking the airport and Delhi, vehicles of all kinds were running in a disorderly way with herds of livestock wandering about. . . ." Projecting into the future, the Chinese ruling party's organ saw China catching up with the advanced while India merely would hold its own. In sum, "India should learn from China's experience . . ." ("Is Will"). Despite certain sectoral achievements, India is not competitive with China.

In comparison to rural Chinese, the two-thirds of Indians who live in villages produce less than a fourth of India's wealth; they lack water, electricity, and good roads to markets. In both countries, huge numbers die of water-borne diseases and of water pollution. In both, cell phones are allowing farmers to respond to their own advantage to market signals. But the pollution is so much worse in India and the cell phone use so much more widespread in China. In "2001 the number of people earning less than $1 a day accounted for 18.8 percent of the total in China, while in India the figure was 44.2 percent" (Luce). "In 2001, there were 15.9 computers for every 1,000 Chinese people, but only 4.5" for India. "China had 150 million mobile phone subscribers while India had just over 6 million" (Fu). With Indian state governments doing so little to help villagers escape their misery, China, for all the brutal greed of its local CCP pashas, seems far more likely to reduce rural poverty faster than India.

At least now most analysts understand that the difference in economic performance is not explainable in terms of authoritarianism versus democracy. "India and China have followed similar economic policy arcs over the last half-century: decades of pervasive state intervention, with mostly dismal results, and then a shift . . . toward deregulation and free markets, with spectacular results" (Bradsher, May 19). Actually, neither India nor China is a free market, whatever that phrase could possibly mean since all markets are embedded in rules. Property is not legally secure in China. Subsidies are huge in both countries. And neither, in order to protect their currencies, allows free entry and exit for short-term capital. In both, the state nurtures growth through tough bargaining on agriculture, apparel, and intellectual property rights with OECD nations in WTO fora. Neoliberal rosy colored glasses, which see a free market producing growth (as if U.S. growth in the industrial era was not aided by a high tariff policy), and growth producing a middle class that, in turn, leads on to democracy distort reality. The authoritarian rulers of China have no intention of relinquishing power.

Yet the absurd notion that democracy is "a handicap" hindering growth will not die. After the 2004 elections brought Congress back to parliamentary power allied with more dogmatically left parties, a policy analyst in New Delhi averred that "Democracy in some respects is quite a burden for . . . India" "China can . . . plan for the long run. They're not looking at short-term results on major issues. Here we don't even know what we're doing next week" (Waldman). Actually, local leaders in reform era China always have had ways to evade and avoid central directives. A dictatorship understood as greased lightening effectiveness is silly. Chinese "decision-making . . . is . . . far more ponderous, far more erratic and far more prone to profiteering by rent-seeking officials than it appears to some envious Indians" ("Two").

Democracies as far apart as France and Japan do much more long-range planning than does China. "In India, Economic Growth and Democracy Do Mix" (Waldman), just not enough. But an authoritarian elite can also build institutions and implement policies that deliver growth, as authoritarian Germany and Japan did starting in the nineteenth century. Growth is not a dimension on which the issue of democracy versus nondemocracy is salient. Workers in China are far more productive. Infrastructure is so much better. "China's market is three or four times the size of India's." It has a "cheaper, more reliable power supply . . . more rapid turn-around at its ports." "India is coming late to the party, and . . . is still taking too long" (Luce and Kynge).

Yet numerous analysts insist that China's market Leninism cannot last. Either the market will create a middle class that will force an opening in the direction of democratization or corrupt Brezhnevite party interests (perhaps allying with fascist type security forces) that are ever more entrenched will block further reform or things will fall apart. While any of these changes, of course, might occur in China, none is inevitable. The regime could well muddle through.

In sum, democratic and authoritarian regimes are equally able to do what is needed to reform and sustain growth. There is no trade-off of growth for freedom. But liberty remains a treasure that citizens of democratic India enjoy and Chinese subjects are denied. This dimension of difference matters very much for the quality of life available to a people, especially for the weakest.

X

Democracy, a political system, is not a solution, however, to economic problems. That requires proper economic policies and institutions. "Democracy is not in itself a solution to poverty and inequality. . . . The act of voting cannot change the harsher rules of economics." But in 2004, "India's latest election defies such false distinctions. It celebrates the freedom of ordinary citizens to check the arrogance of those in power, to assert the rights of minorities . . ." (Stephens). The alienated powerless overwhelming majority of Chinese lack any similar way to express their sentiments legally and meaningfully. They must instead lie and fawn and complain in private. Authoritarianism wounds human dignity. Authoritarian China is not a success. Democratic India is not a failure. In fact, democracy is a weapon of the weak.

References

"Bai Hua Speaks His Mind," *Don fang* (Hong Kong), nos. 40 and 46, December 1987 and January 1988, translated in JPRS–CAR–88–009, March 4, 1988.

Baipei, Nirupam, Tianjun Jian, and Jeffrey Sacks (April 1997). *Economic Reforms in China and India*. Cambridge: Harvard Institute for International Development.

Balls, Andrew (2004). "Focus Now on Logistics of Poverty Reduction." *Financial Times*, May 25.

Becker, Jasper (2002). *The Christian Science Monitor*. July 3, p. 6.

Bradsher, Keith (2004). "Made in India vs. Made in China." *New York Times*, June 12.

Bradsher, Keith (2004). "Old Reflexes Hurting 2 Asian Economic Giants." *New York Times*, May 19.

Brownell, Susan (1991). "The Changing Relationship Between Sports and the State in the PRC," in Fernand Landez et al. (eds.), *Sports . . . The Third Millenia*. Saintes-Foy: Les Presses de l'universite Leval.

Chirot, Daniel (2004). *Modern Tyrants*. Princeton: Princeton University Press.

Colley, Linda (2002). *Captives: Britain, Empire and the World, 1600—1850*. New York: Random House.

Fewsmith, Joseph (2001). *China Since Tienanmen*. Cambridge: Cambridge University Press.

Fireman, Dan (2004). "Growth Model." *Far Eastern Economic Review*, April 15, 2004, p. 41.

Friedman, Edward, Paul Pickowicz, and Mark Selden (1991). *Chinese Village, Socialist State*. New Haven: Yale University Press.

Friedman, Edward (1998). "Development, Revolution, Democracy and Dictatorship: China Versus India," in Theda Skocpol (ed.), *Democracy, Revolution and History*. Ithaca: Cornell University Press, pp. 102–123.

Friedman, Edward, Paul Pickowicz, and Mark Selden (2005). *Revolution, Resistance and Reform in Village China*. New Haven: Yale University Press.

Fu Xiaoqiang and Kuang Ji (2003). "Avoiding the Clash: Paving the Way for Sino-Indian Cooperation." *Beijing Review*, November 13, pp. 44–45.

Fukuyama, Francis (2004). "An Antidote to Empire." *New York Times Book Review*, July 25, p. 12.

Gujral, Inder K. (1997). "Democracy is the Key." *Far Eastern Economic Review*, August 21, p. 40.

Huang Yanzhong (2004). "Bringing the local State Back In: The Political Economy of Public Health in Rural China." *Journal of Contemporary China*, 13 (39) (May): 367–390.

Huntington, Samuel (1968). *Political Order in Changing Societies*. New Haven: Yale University Press.

Huntington, Samuel (1991). *The Third Wave*. Norman: University of Oklahoma Press.

"Is India China's Imaginative Rival?" *People's Daily*, February 23, 2004.

Karirag, Sudipta (1996). "Dilemmas of Democratic Development in India," in Adrian Leffwich (ed.), *Democracy and Development*. Cambridge: Blackwell.

Kochaxi, Noam (2002). "Limited Accommodation, Perpetual Conflict." *Diplomatic History*, 26.1 (Winter).

Kripalani, Manjeet (2002). "An Indian's Epiphany in China." *Business Week Online*, February 14.

Kristof, Nicholas (2004). "A Little Leap Forward." *The New York Review*, June 24, 2004, pp. 56–59.

Kynge James (2004). "China's Economic Growth." *Notes* (National Committee on US–China Relations), pp. 10–12.

Li Haibo (2003). "China and India in a Win-Win Race." *Beijing Review*, January 30, 2003, p. 48.

Linz, Juan and Alfred Stepan (1996). *Problems of Democratic Transition and Consolidation*. Baltimore: The Johns Hopkins University Press.

Luce, Edward (2004). "From India's Forgotten Fields, a Call for Economic Reform to Lift the Poor." *Financial Times*, May 18.

Luce, Edward and James Kynge (2003). "India Starts to See China as a Land of Business Opportunity." *Financial Times*, September 23.

Malik, Mohan (2004). "Chinese Conundrum," I and II, *Force* (New Delhi), February and March 2004.

Marsh, Peter (2004). "Fear of High-Tech Piracy Makes some Microchip Companies Cool about China." *Financial Times*, July 15.

Miles, James (1996). *The Legacy of Tienanmen*. Ann Arbor: University of Michigan Press, p. 136.

Mishra, Pankaj (2004). "Bombay: The Lower Depths." *The New York Review*, November 18, pp. 17–20.

Moore, Barrington, Jr. (1966). *Social Origins of Dictatorship and Democracy*. Boston: Beacon Press.

Moore, Barrington, Jr. (1970, 1972). *Reflections on the Causes of Human Misery and Upon Certain Proposals to Eliminate Them*. Boston: Beacon Press.

Morgan, Jamie (2004). "Distinguishing Truth, Knowledge, and Belief. A Philosophical Contribution to the Problem of Images in China." *Modern China*, 30.3 (July): 398–427.

Murphy, Rachel (2004). "Turning Peasants into Modern Chinese Citizens." *The China Quarterly*, pp. 1–20.

O'Kane, Rosemare (2004). *Paths to Democracy: Revolution and Totalitarianism*. London: Routledge.

Pei, Minxin (2002). "China's Governance Crisis." *Foreign Affairs*, September/October.

Pesek, William, Jr. (2003). "It's All China, China, China. India Anyone?" *Bloomberg*, October 13.

Platt, Nicholas (2004). "Make Global Skills a Top Priority." *Financial Times*, July 2, 2004.

Pocha, Jehangir (2003). "Day of the Dragon," "Who's Afraid of China?" *India Today* (International), June 20.

Power, Jonathan (2004). "Slowly but Steadily, India Will Overtake China." *International Herald Tribune*, May 6.

Richards, John (1997). "Early Modern India and World History." *Journal of World History*, 8.2.

St. John, Ronald Bruce (1996). "Reviews." *Bulletin of Concerned Asian Scholars* 28.3–4: 117.

Shih Chih-yu (2004). "3 + 3 + 1 = 1, *Issues and Studies*, 40.1 (March): 203–223.

Sidhua, Shiraz (1997). "Trading Positions." *Far Eastern Economic Review*, August 21, p. 96.

Stephans, Philip (2004). "India's Triumph of Democracy." *Financial Times*, May 21.

Survey on India, *Financial Times*, June 24, 1997.

Tharoor, Shashi (1999). *India: From Midnight to Millennium*. New York: Arcade.

Tu Weiming (2002). "Whither China?" *Bulletin*, American Academy of Arts and Sciences, Spring.

"Two Systems, One Grand Rivalry—India and China—India's Fear of China." *The Economist*, June 21, 2003.

Waldman, Amy (2004). "In India, Economic Growth and Democracy Do Mix." *New York Times*, May 23.

Watson, James (ed.) (1997). *Golden Arches East*. Stanford: Stanford University Press.

Watts, Jonathan (2004). "China Admits First Rise in Poverty Since 1978." *The Guardian*, July 20.

"Will China be Replaced by India?" *People's Daily*, March 12, 2004.

Xiao Zhou (2003). "India's Great Economic Potential." *Beijing Review*, November 13, pp. 44–45.

Xue Xinran (2002). *The Good Women of China*. New York: Pantheon.

Yan Yun Xiang (2002). "Courtship, Lore and Premarital Sex in a North China Village." *The China Journal*, No. 48, July.

Zweig, David (2002). *Democratic Values, Political Structures, and Alternative Politics in Greater China*. Washington, D.C.: United States Institute of Peace.

11

China Rethinks India

Huang Jinxin

I

China has a self-image that is filled with contradictions. (Wang 1999, 21) Such contradictions are particularly reflected in the evolving perceptions of "the other," that is, countries against which Chinese measure themselves. The rise of the Internet has provided new space for discussion of other nations, among them India in particular. This chapter sheds light on this changing discourse through a survey of postings about India on two prominent websites in China. The views are varied. But few Chinese netizens appear to believe any longer that China is an unalloyed success and India a plain failure.

Today, Chinese continually compare India with China. As Dreze and Sen note, "China [is) the only country in the world comparable with India in terms of population size, and it [has) similar levels of impoverishment and distress" (Dreze and Sen 2002, 113). One is a democracy and the other is not. Both are populous, diverse, and heirs to glorious ancient civilizations that their citizens take pride in. India gained its independence from British colonial rule in 1947. It has remained a parliamentary democracy ever since despite bitter ethnic and religious cleavages. In 1949, the Chinese Communist Party (CCP) took control of the mainland of China and established the People's Republic of China (PRC), an authoritarian regime. In 1978, China embarked on economic reform. Thirteen years later, India began implementing market-oriented reforms. India grew rapidly. As a result, the prior assumption of comparisons, that authoritarian China is an economic success and democratic India is not, is being reexamined in China.

Over the years, comparisons of India and China have been filled with as much myth as reality. Each has striven to maintain an advantage over the other. Intense competition filled the nastier passions after their 1962 war. The rivalry between China and India was often seen as a contest between two political systems—democratic versus authoritarian. Conventional wisdom in China has held that India's democracy led to entrenched poverty with religious intolerance, while China's economic reforms without political freedom provided the *only* correct path to development with stability.

These conclusions were important in shaping China's self-image. Depictions of India as poor and unstable as a result of democracy long served as a stark contrast with a prosperous and orderly authoritarian China. Because of the similarities in demographics and history, the CCP would legitimate its dictatorial rule by portraying India as the failed "other." In a standard Chinese elementary school geography textbook, India and China are juxtaposed side-by-side on population, literacy, GDP per capita, exports, and industrial output.[1] India is shown to lag in almost every category. Such a presentation usually ends with plaudits to Chinese socialism (i.e., the CCP dictatorship) and economic reform policies. Based on India's comparative experience, Chinese concluded that development and democracy were a trade-off.[2] China's successful economic liberalization programs and its entry into international trade were hailed as a model of success, for which Chinese were willing to give up personal freedom. Afraid of chaos and ethnic conflicts as supposedly suffered by India, even Chinese who were not Communist Party loyalists dismissed democracy as an option.

A backward India copied an advanced China. In early 2000, seeing how China benefited from ethnic Chinese investors from all over the world, the Indian government tried to attract non-resident Indians (NRIs, Indians who have taken citizenship in other countries) to invest in their home country. Laggard should learn from leader.

Yet by the early twenty-first century, the political discourse in India comparing the two Asian giants had changed. Considering how the prior Chinese discourse had attributed Indian stagnation to Indian democracy, a change in Chinese thinking about India may well reflect changing thinking about the alleged virtues of China's authoritarian policy.

The abysmal living conditions of many among the lower castes in India, the prospect of India surpassing China as the most populous country in the world, and India's crushing defeat in their 1962 war are what most Chinese used to know of India. But international travel and India's global success in information technology (IT) have shaken the Chinese consensus about India as a negative model. Front-page news articles in China describe India as the second largest exporter of computer software and highlight Bill Gates (an idol to many aspiring Chinese) praising India as the next IT giant.[3] The success of Indian computer engineers overseas and a surging Indian domestic software industry have impressed many Chinese.

II

Chinese awareness of economic and societal changes in India came very slowly, long after Indian technicians and entrepreneurs were at the very top of world rankings in innovating and running advanced Internet companies. Almost 40 percent of Internet start-up companies during the 1990s in California's Silicon Valley were founded by Indian entrepreneurs (Warner 2000). Marcus Franda argues that "India has developed a superior [compared to China) software industry, resulting largely from the creativity and language capabilities of a dynamic core of homegrown software engineers working primarily out of southern India and the Silicon Valley in California" (Franda 2002, 170).

The shift in perceptions can be seen in the post–2001 web postings on two prominent Chinese websites: www.creaders.net and www.cc.org.cn. Both are leading sites for online postings, with the former appealing to a general audience and the latter to scholars. Half of all articles pertaining to India, particularly those relating to the discussion of political systems, were posted either by anonymous writers or by Chinese using pseudonyms.

Previously, the discourse on India among Chinese treated India as a monolithic whole. Parliamentary federal democracy was blamed for economic stagnation and poverty across India. Recent postings, however, show Chinese discovering regional diversity in India. Scholars and visitors from China agree that South India has exhibited more economic vitality than the north.[4] Such economic dynamism and social progress, according to the Chinese, is primarily a result of liberalization and international commerce due to historical locational advantages. Cities in India tend to be located along the shore of the Indian Ocean, the key route for international commerce in India for some 2,500 years. India was a world leader in science and technology in premodern times. Openness and social mobility continued afterward. A one-dimensional view of an impoverished India from time immemorial disappeared. The recent Indian technology boom has also centered in South India due to incentives created by local states to attract foreign direct investment (FDI) (see Sinha's chapter in this volume). Personal accounts posted on the web suggest that in the south of India, there is more household agriculture instead of landed elites, less dominance by Brahmans, and more gender equality.

With Chinese anxious over challenges from secession movements and religious revivalism, a federal, democratic India suddenly seemed better capable of building national cohesion despite its regional diversity than did an over-centralized authoritarian regime in China. An anonymous netizen found that it was India's decentralized democracy that allowed India to hold together a poor, populous, and linguistically and religiously diverse society.[5] According to this netizen, "democracy has created a shared commitment for all those who live in India regardless of religious and ethnic backgrounds."[6] In short, for the first time ever, some Chinese find India's democracy to be an advantage.

Commenting on India's caste system, an anonymous writer compared "the untouchables" in India with marginalized villagers in China who lack the right to move to cities and send their children to urban government schools. This netizen argued that "even though a discriminatory attitude [not a government policy] in Indian society towards the lower caste is entrenched, the Chinese government adopts the most systemic legal discrimination again the peasants."[7] That is, the Chinese caste system is actually worse than India's since rural Chinese are legally barred from living in the cities and thereby barred from state welfare and education, as well as being underrepresented in circles of power, and burdened by disproportionately heavy miscellaneous taxes.[8] Acute awareness of the rich–poor gap in authoritarian China undermined the prior conventional wisdom where democracy was the polarizing force. While lower-caste Indians could elect representatives to promote their interests in parliament, Chinese villagers were treated as a threat to stability, a group to be kept from rebellion. Democracy was stabilizing.

Reflection on the pre-1991 economic stagnation in India constituted much of the debate among Chinese who suddenly needed new answers to an old question. Instead of blaming the earlier failure on democracy in India and attributing China's very recent fast economic growth to social stability resulting from a continuation of communist authoritarian rule, recent analyses focus on historical, institutional, and economic particulars.[9] Given the new complexities, Indian democracy is no longer presented as a negative, a singular source of economic stagnation and social instability.

Evaluations of India's economic development by international analysts are mixed. Rone Tempest, a journalist at *Los Angeles Times* whose article was fully translated into Chinese and posted on the web, suggested that "from 1990 to 1994, the average annual GDP growth rate was 3.8% in India, while in China, it was 12.9%. Further, by year 1994, the GDP per capita was $320, around 60% of that of China ($530)."[10] However, mass famine was avoided in democratic India for 50 years despite natural disasters and dire poverty. An anonymous netizen argued that, in contrast, "both the former Soviet Union and China, now North Korea, have experienced the worst famines in human history. More than 30 million people died between 1958 and 1961 in China alone. India suffered mass famines under British colonial rule, with the last one occurring in 1943. Despite natural disasters in 1973, an accountable democratic government made sure that no widespread famine took place. It was unthinkable to have a prolonged famine in India as we have seen in China."[11] Nobel Laureate economist Amartya Sen's "famine theory" is very popular among Chinese scholars, who pay less attention to Sen's observation that endemic deprivations in India killed as many. He asserts that "no [mass] famine has ever taken place in the history of the world in a functioning democracy" (Sen 1999).

Among the Chinese who have engaged in the debates on the two websites, most consider income disparity as an impediment to economic development in India, particularly in the north. The dominant view in China is that land reform in North India was never implemented. The landed elites combined with the traditional Indian caste system to trap the lower caste and landless peasants in poverty.[12] In contrast, CCP's sweeping land reform in the early 1950s not only redistributed the land but also eliminated the entire landed elite, though ruthlessly. The collectivization that followed delayed the benefit of the land reform until the late 1970s, when a reformist China de-collectivized its rural agriculture, finally reaping the benefits of its earlier land reform, which facilitated market-regarding household agriculture. Chinese showed no awareness of the mainstream proposition that land reform and a lack of powerful traditional landed elites was a facilitator of growth all over East Asia.

India is now portrayed as having societal advantages as well as political ones. One prominent Chinese economist, Zhang Wuchang, had warned in the early 1980s that the privatization of pension, health care, and education in a reforming China could result in worse income disparity than even in India, as it indeed has. Zhou Qiren argued that recent evidence has confirmed Professor Zhang's predictions. Various government regulations have resulted in rampant corruption that the current system is not capable of dealing with. That is, China does not have a free market but one that is embedded in the unaccountable and hierarchical networks of a corrupt and self-serving CCP. The gaps in China between rich and poor, urban and rural, southeast coast and central hinterland have grown.

Furthermore, without active religious groups or a vibrant civil society, poor Chinese may feel even more marginalized.[13] At least democratic India had societal mutual aid groups even if the Indian central government's distributional functions have been minimal. A large part of the social welfare is performed by Hindu temples or through charitable contributions to civic organizations, organizational advantages not available in an authoritarian China that feared nation-wide religious organizations serving the basic needs of a hurting populace.[14]

III

It was India's extraordinary IT successes that triggered the recent debates in China. Though China is a great success in exports of labor-intensive manufactured products, the debate focused on China's lag in IT, because IT seemed to symbolize the future whereas apparel exports did not seem a way China could catch up with America. Chinese researchers ask why India has become so competitive in the international software market when India has so many unattractive features. The development of IT is presented as the cornerstone for the twenty-first century economy (Wong and Ling 2001; Bhatnagar and Schware 2000; Franda 2002).

The Chinese see how inadequate Indian infrastructure combines with a strong xenophobia to weaken India's attraction to Foreign Direct Investment (FDI). Despite the lure of cheap labor, labor-intensive industries have been hesitant to go into India. Such industries require an extensive network of transportation, communication, service, and complementary production facilities that India lacked. Chinese visitors to India were dismayed by the dilapidated roads, congestion, and lack of clean water.[15] Also, an antiforeign Indian nationalism, despite reform changes since 1991, still keeps India from going all out to attract FDI.

The IT industry, in contrast to labor intensive light industry, requires only an educated work force and telecommunications, in both of which the Indian government has invested heavily, particularly in India's more progressive south. English language, a legacy of the British colonial rule, is still taught and used. This has worked to the advantage of the Indians in exporting information software, which is English language based.[16] Some believe that India's emphasis on higher education, particularly on science education since independence, started to pay off in the early 1990s, while China still suffered from the disasters of Mao's wounding of education during anti-intellectual vigilante campaigns. In the 1950s, Nehru championed and set up six Indian Institutes of Technology to train engineers.[17] Complementary training was also introduced in the secondary education curriculum. Learning from the success of the Indian Institutes of Technology, local state governments set up Indian Institutes of Information Technology at the state level, with America's Intel Corporation helping by training nearly 200,000 IT teachers in India as of spring 2003.[18]

China lagged behind in public education, something that angered most Chinese. A Chinese scholar under the pseudonym of "Megaplay" criticizes the Chinese government's "commercialization of education (*jiaoyu chanye hua*)" policies, which have been adopted since 1997 and which make it difficult for the poor to get educated.[19] "Megaplay" argued that privatizing public education, especially elementary and secondary education in rural China is reversing the advantage of high literacy that China enjoyed in the prior three decades. Katarina Tomasevski, the UN special rapporteur on the right to education, reported that the "Chinese government covers only 53 percent of school funding, with parents paying the rest in fees—a much lower percentage of government funding than in almost all other countries that have compulsory education policies" (Pan 2003). It is an error to assume that China is successful on every dimension where India is unsuccessful—in this case the funding of rural schools.

India's 1991 economic reform was a turning point for economic development. Even though India had never fully adopted the Soviet-style command economy (India did not collectivize agriculture), the state-owned sector still constituted 26 percent of the Indian economy in 1991.[20] India's trade barriers protected industries that were not internationally competitive. The suffocating statist system was mocked as a "license raj." The 1991 reforms simplified administrative procedures, changing the government's role from planner to regulator. The IT boom then led the Indian federal government to begin to improve basic infrastructure—electricity, transportation, and telecommunication—to complement the country's strong institutional infrastructure. Not so China where, an anonymous netizen complained about the failures to protect both private property and intellectual property rights in innovation and economic development.[21] In comparative perspective, Chinese participants in the recent website debates are very much focused on these and other Indian political advantages.

Growing nationalism and antiglobalization in India, however, will hurt India's ability to take advantage of global market opportunities. Such nationalism, however, has not impeded the development of the IT industry in southern India. IT industries take advantage of high-speed Internet connections, jumping over traditional Indian trade barriers.[22] Indian IT engineers' experience of living in an open, mobile, multicultural, multilingual society also allows them to more readily cooperate with engineers across the globe.[23] In IT, China seemed relatively slow and closed.

An anonymous posting argued that "India's IT success is also attributed to the large cohort of educated overseas Indians who have good connections and invested heavily in their home country in recent years as a result of favorable government policies. The dynamism brought by the overseas Indians was comparable to the boost brought by the overseas China since the 1978 economic reform in China."[24] India and China seemed more alike, not a contrast between failure and success.

Market-regarding success was facilitated by helpful government nurturing. Beijing University Professor Zhou Qiren made the point in a vivid metaphor about "government's role in providing grassland so that cattle can settle and prosper."[25] The Indian government was still democratic but its policies were now helpful to wealth expansion. Competitive IT companies, such as Infosys, were set up by Indian entrepreneurs with overseas experience. "After decades of keeping the Indian Diaspora at arm's length, New Delhi is now embracing the 'Nonresident Indians.' "[26] Good reform did not mean authoritarianism instead of democracy or replacing the state by the market. Good reform was a matter of the state being helpful rather than hindering to market-regarding wealth expansion.

IV

The online journal *Century China* dedicated an entire issue to the People's Science Movement (KSSP) in Kerala, a southwestern state in

India known for societal equality.[27] Chinese scholars are fascinated by the vibrant civil society, high adult literacy rate, and easy access to health care and public education in Kerala. In China, these are all pressing problems. According to Liu Jianzhi, "by the year 2001, the national average adult literacy rate in India is 65%, with the lowest state only 48%."[28] Kerala's adult literacy rate, however, is close to 95 percent, with women's literacy rate near 80 percent. There are more than 5,000 public libraries and 3,000 local publications.[29] A high adult literacy rate combined with open public discussion on population problems to lower Kerala's birth rate to 1.7, lower even than China's 1.9.[30] And, in contrast to China, Kerala does not use coercion against women for population control. Authoritarianism was not needed to achieve social goals, another point long since made by Professor Amartya Sen.

In May 2001, prominent Chinese scholars convened at *Reform* magazine publishing house to discuss lessons that could be learnt from India's KSSP movement in Kerala.[31] Chinese scholars' fascination with the KSSP is facilitated by the fact that the Indian Communist Party is the state's ruling party. Interested in legitimating the Kerala experience for China, the Chinese new left, committed to more equity and abjuring growth at any price, is eager to show that Kerala can be emulated without challenging Communist Party rule.

One scholar, Liu Jianzhi, argued that the "science movement in Kerala made democratic governance and participation possible." Another, Dai Jinhua, suggested that the "Kerala experience makes us reconsider the form of democracy and the content of democracy. Election is only the form of democracy. Universal health care, education, equity and political participation are the contents of democracy, which cannot be guaranteed by elections alone. What we see in Kerala is part of a worldwide 'democratizing democracies' movement." He concluded that China could learn from the Kerala experience by "consolidating local governance and encouraging local initiatives." Arguing in the same magazine, one scholar, Wen Tiejun, argued that highly centralized systems—meaning the CCP state in China—are "too costly and too corrupt to be enforced through the village level." Some kinds of democracy were superior to some kinds of authoritarian systems. Another scholar, Huang Ping, concurred that "past social movements in China were generated through government decrees, while [according to the success in Kerala] a 'bottom-up' reform would be an empowering experience for the people."

Grassroots movements—precluded by China's authoritarianism—are lauded as the most efficient means of governance, the most empowering experience in the rural area. Any Chinese reader could follow the logic and draw the conclusion that China would be doing better both in material achievement and societal equality if it were a decentralized, federal democracy. It was India's political system that was superior.

The virtues and vices of openness to globalization were also debated. Discussants weighed the antiglobalization policies adopted by the Communist Kerala government. Huang Ping argued that "globalization is harmful to democracy. Management and investment of multinational corporations are mobile, which in turn, have no stake in building democratic government. Self-sufficiency in Kerala has worked into an environmentally sustainable model." Liu Jianzhi proposed that "the United States is the key force behind globalization to promote its own national interests. Kerala state is too weak to fight against the globalization trend. India and China should join together."[32] For China's new left nationalists, globalization was Americanization and therefore bad; popular "Chinese nationalism appears to be . . . much stronger than just a reaction to specific foreign pressures. It has a great deal to do with an identity crisis in the post–Mao China" (Christiansen 1999, 249–250). Depending on how political clashes played out in Beijing, Chinese nationalism could become an obstacle to China's future economic rise.

While its high literacy rate, widely available public health facilities and libraries contrast Kerala sharply with other Indian states, they have not ensured Kerala rapid economic development. Lu Aiguo, who was not present at the roundtable, cautioned elsewhere that stagnation and a high unemployment rate (more than 10 percent) plagued Kerala, with the export of cheap educated Kerala labor overseas and to other states in India that were open to the forces of globalization actually earning Kerala the cash and foreign exchange its people wanted. More than 40 percent of local labor fled the region looking for job opportunities in other Indian states and in the Middle East.[33] Close to 90 percent of nurses in India are educated in Kerala state.[34]

Another scholar, Zhao Menghu, argued that "even for those who are employed, the average number of working days [in Kerala] is between fifteen to eighteen days a month. Latent unemployment is prevalent."[35] He concluded that "the current equity in Kerala is based on the assumption of 'minimum guarantee under dire poverty'," a popular way in China to describe Mao–era stagnation.[36] That is, Kerala suffers from Mao era style evils, is not a model for emulation, and is not doing worse only because its people plug in to opportunities offered by a domestic market outside of Kerala and by globalization.

Continued import substitution policies and complex investment procedures (a legacy of the pre-1991 "permit Raj") choke off economic dynamism in Kerala. Foreign exchange comes from Kerala migrants in the oil-rich Middle East. While not embracing Kerala's stagnation, new left netizens tried to differentiate "social development (*shehui fazhan*)" from "economic development (*jingji fazhan*)," privileging the former, a reflection of Chinese discontent with festering societal problems and inequality in China, a destabilizing polarization that is the source of the rage that gives currency to new left analyses in China.

Some pointed out differences between China and India that have made Kerala politics a possibility. Feng Keli argued that "what we should learn from the Kerala experience is *equal opportunity*, meaning each individual resident, rural or urban, has equal access to health, education, and decision-making in Kerala politics." The "current situation in rural China is a result of a lack of protection of equal rights under the Chinese Constitution. Not only were peasants' equal rights not assured, many new regulations are discriminatory, particularly in health, education, and other social welfare issues."[37] Therefore, only a constitutional government where officeholders could be held accountable by an independent judiciary would be a solution to China's most pressing social problems. In sum, if you care about growth with equity, you should choose, in addition to global openness and market-regarding economic policies, a decentralized, federal democratic polity facilitating a robust civil society.

V

The recent revived interest about India among politically conscious Chinese is important. The new discourse challenges the conventional wisdom that China is a success while India is a failure. It also reflects a Chinese reassessment of China's own economic reforms. Debates have been centered around three issues.

First, there is a revisiting of India's colonial past. In Chinese communist rhetoric, India's colonial experience under British rule had symbolized a demise of Eastern glories and a rise of Western imperialism. It was a history of shame, exploitation, and strife that Indians were not capable of handling until after independence in 1947. Without glorifying colonialism, Chinese netizens, in contrast, found that in the vicinity of coastal cities, people tied to trading routes benefited, that there are legacies from ancient and early modern achievements that post–independence India can build upon. Further, English serves as a national language for a multilingual India. In an information age, mastery of such an international language gives enormous advantages to the Indians in international competition.

Second, instead of attributing Indian's economic stagnation to democracy and China's growth to socialism (economic reform with socialist characteristics, that is, single-party dictatorship), growing attention has been given to particular policies. Chinese land reform gave China households land ownership and equity. Several postings warned that at the current rate of growing income disparity in China, without political reform, Chinese villagers would suffer a similar or even a worse fate than that of an impoverished North India. In China's countryside, an economic slowdown could be accompanied by popular uprisings. Thus, the immiserated Indian masses, instead of being seen as the evil consequence of democracy, are now understood more as the result of failed government policies, especially the failure to provide public education and health care, a failure also pervading rural areas of authoritarian China.

Chinese divided over import substitution development policies. They worried about the impact of globalization on national industries and on labor's status. Some researchers called for coordinated government policies to protect national industries by ensuring them a sizable domestic market share. On the other hand, import substitution obviously has failed in India. Even in antiglobalization KSSP, with the highest literacy rate in India, economic development was not guaranteed. Zhou Qiren acknowledged that a "gradual lifting of foreign investment barriers such as 'permits' since 1991 allowed India to succeed in the software industry."[38] Not taking advantage of global opportunities was self-wounding.

Third, Indian democracy was seen as a positive factor that provided a basis for unifying a multiethnic, multireligious, and multilingual society. In contrast, Chinese are experiencing growing regional alienation and violence that could threaten national unity. The fascination over KSSP is as much about a robust civil society, something that China lacks, as it is about the movement itself. Chinese authors cite the Buddhist tradition as a vital source of philanthropy in India and lament a moral decay in China linked to the authoritarian regime's obstruction of freedom for religions.

This is an extraordinary rejection of the prior conventional wisdom that a thisworldly Confucianism is practical and Indian Buddhism is otherworldly. In recent years, the rise of religion and the growth of spirituality in China are a direct response to gross material crassness.

Chinese political culture has changed such that Chinese are weighing good and bad in new ways. Chinese netizens' multifaceted evaluation of China's own economic development is reflected in their growing respect for India. The call for social progress and equity by these Chinese writers offers a sharp contrast to the government's suppression of any autonomous social groups and to an "economic development at any price" dogma whose side effects are so bad and worrisome as not actually to serve the long-term interests of the Chinese nation. Postings were diverse and complex. The simple tale of Chinese success and Indian failure so long drummed into the national conscience by state propaganda was challenged in many ways. As a mirror for national reflection, China's rethink of India offers many insights into how a country is rethinking itself.

Notes

An earlier version of this paper appeared in the Journal of Contemporary China, 14:45, 2005. I wish to thank Professors Edward Friedman, Aseema Sinha, Bruce Gilley, and Edward Reed.

1. All the textbooks use official Chinese governmental numbers that are criticized by economists elsewhere. See, e.g., Frederick Wu, "Chinese Economic Statistics—Caveat Emptor!" *Post Communist Economies*, Vol. 15, No. 1 (2003): 127–145.
2. In several articles published in *People's Daily* (Renmin Ribao) after June 4, 1989, editorials warned Chinese readers that China would have slipped into chaos as India and some East European countries if democracy was allowed in China.
3. Anonymous, "The Next Two Decades Belong to India"(cited August 8, 2003). Available at http://www.cc.org.cn/wencui/010102200/0101022002. htm.
4. Megaplay, "Real India" (cited September 5, 2003), available at http://www.creaders.org/articleReader.php?idx=38660.
5. Anonymous, "India's Democracy" (cited August 8, 2003), available at http://www.cc.org.cn/wencui/010102200/0101022007.htm.
6. Anonymous, "India's Democracy" (cited August 8, 2003), available at http://www.cc.org.cn/wencui/010102200/0101022007.htm.
7. Anonymous, "Indian's Untouchables and Chinese Peasants," (cited August 18, 2003), available at http://www.creaders.org/articleReader. php?idx=25115.
8. Wen Tiejun, participant at the roundtable discussion "Lessons from Kerala—India through Chinese Intellectuals' Eyes" (cited August 7, 2003), available at http://www.cc.org.cn/wencui/030728200/0307282000.htm.
9. For instance, in the roundtable discussion "Lessons from Kerala—India through Chinese Intellectuals' Eyes" participants discussed pre-reform (before 1991) policies in India that have resulted in poverty and stagnation. (Cited August 7, 2003), available at http://www.cc.org.cn/wencui/030728200/0307282000.htm.

10. Chinese version (cited August 8, 2003), available at http://www.cc.org.cn/wencui/010102200/0101022005.html.
11. Anonymous, "Discussions of Indian Democracy" (cited August 8, 2003), available at http://www.cc.org.cn/wencui/010102200/0101022007.htm.
12. Zhao Menhu, "Travel Through Southern India" (cited August 7, 2003), available at http://www.cc.org.cn/wencui/030728200/0307282009.htm.
13. Zhou Qiren, "An Alternative Indian Path" (cited August 8, 2003), available at http://www.cc.org.cn/wencui/010102200/0101022000.htm.
14. Anonymous, "Key Summaries of India" (cited August 15, 2003), available at http://www.creaders.org/articleReader.php?idx=45803.
15. Zhi Fu, "Witness India: Travel Log in Bombay" (cited August 8, 2003), available at http://www.cc.org.cn/wencui/010102200/0101022009.htm; Anonymous, "Business Trip in India" (cited August 8, 2003), available at http://www.cc.org.cn/wencui/010102200/0101022010.htm. Actually, water pollution in China is extreme.
16. Wang Xiaotao, "India's New Economy, A Blessing In Disguise" (cited August 8, 2003), available at http://www.cc.org.cn/wencui/010102200/0101022001.htm; Anonymous, "Summaries of Economic Development in India" (cited August 19, 2003), available at http://www.creaders.org/articleReader.php?idx=45803.
17. Xu Feng, "Indian Institute of Technology: A Role Model for Asian Universities" (cited August 25, 2003), available at http://www1.bbsland.com/articleReader.php?idx=11196.
18. Zou Qiang, "Lessons from Indian Information Technology Revolution and Human Resource Management" (cited August 8, 2003), available at http://www.cc.org.cn/wencui/010102200/0101022004.htm; "Indeed Intel has signed agreements with the Ministry of Information Technology, Central Schools, and 11 state governments to ensure that this program is available in many regions of India" (cited September 11, 2003), available at http://www.intel.com/education/projects/global_tour/H_10_india/; according to email communications with Anjali Nichani (K-12 education program manager, Intel in India), the program started in February 2000. The training manual is available in six languages.
19. Megaplay, "True India" (cited August 19, 2003), available at http://www.creaders.org/articleReader.php?idx=38660.
20. Zhou Qiren, "An Alternative Indian Path" (cited August 8, 2003), available at http://www.cc.org.cn/wencui/010102200/0101022000.htm.
21. Anonymous, "India from the Sideline" (cited August 25, 2003), available at http://www1.bbsland.com/articleReader.php?idx=5888.
22. Wang Xiaotao, "Indian New Economy, a Blessing in Disguise" (cited August 8, 2003), available at http://www.cc.org.cn/wencui/010102200/ 0101022001. htm.
23. Anonymous, "Summaries of Indian Economic Development" (cited August 19, 2003), available at http://www.creaders.org/ articleReader.php?idx= 45803.
24. Anonymous, "India—Asia's Another Wakening Tiger" (cited August 22, 2003), available at http://www1.bbsland.com/articleReader.php?idx=33115.
25. Zhou Qiren, "India's Alternative Road" (cited August 8, 2003), available at http://www.cc.org.cn/wencui/010102200/0101022000.htm; analysis of the roles played by Non-Resident Indians also includes Xu Xun, "India: Late

Boomer in Information Era" (cited August 8, 2003), available at http://www.cc.org.cn/wencui/010102200/0101022003.htm; Anonymous, "How Did India Become a Software Kingdom" (cited August 26, 2003), available at http://www1.bbsland.com/articleReader.php?idx=50144.

26. Huang Yasheng and Tarun Khanna, "Can India Overstake China" (cited September 5, 2003), available at http://www.chinanowmag.com/business/business.htm, also published in *Foreign Policy*, July/August 2003.
27. *China Century*, July 2003, No. D (cited August 6, 2003), available at http://www.cc.org.cn/wencui/index0307d.htm.
28. Liu Jianzhi, "India's Literacy Movement—Self Governance of the Rural Poor" (cited August 7, 2003), available at http://www.cc.org.cn/weicui/030728200/0307282004.htm.
29. Feng Keli, "Kerala State and Grassroots Constitutional Rights" (cited August 7, 2003), available at http://www.cc.org.cn/wencui/030728200/0307282006.htm; Liu Jianzhi, "Village Libraries—The Expansion of Public Space" (cited August 7, 2003), available at http://www.cc.org.cn/wencui/030728200/0307282005.htm.
30. Anonymous, "India's Democracy" (cited August 8, 2003), available at http://www.cc.org.cn/wencui/010102200/0101022007.htm.
31. Roundtable discussion, "Lessons from Kerala—India through Chinese Intellectuals' Eyes" (cited August 6, 2003), available at http://www.cc.org.cn/wencui/030728200/0307282000.htm. Roundtable participants include: Huang Ping, China Social Science Academy, Sociology Institute; Wen Tiejun, China *Reform* Magazine; Dai Jinhua, Comparative Literature, Beijing University; Sun Ge, Literature Institute, China Social Science Academy; Wu Xiaoli, Modern Literature Institute; Xu Zhaolin, China Social Service and Development Research Center; Liu Jianzhi, Linnan Cultural Research Institute.
32. All quotes from the roundtable discussion are from "Roundtable Discussion: Kerala Experience" (cited August 7, 2003), available at http://www.cc.org.cn/wencui/030728200/0307282000.htm.
33. Wen Tiejun at the KSSP roundtable discussion suggested that "between one third and one fourth of labor is exported to the Middle East" (cited August 7, 2003), available at http://www.cc.org.cn/wencui/030728200/0307282000.htm.
34. Lu Aiguo, "Social Development before Economic Development:Lessons from Indian Kerala State" (cited August 7, 2003), available at http://www.cc.org.cn/wencui/030728200/0307282007.htm.
35. Zhao Menghu, "Travel Across Southern India" (cited August 7, 2003), available at http://www.cc.org.cn/wencui/030728200/0307282009.htm.
36. Zhao Menghu, "Travel Across Southern India" (cited August 7, 2003), available at http://www.cc.org.cn/wencui/030728200/0307282009.htm.
37. Feng Keli, "Kerala and Societal Constitutional Rights" (cited August 7, 2003), available at http://www.cc.org.cn/wencui/030728200/ 0307282006.htm.
38. Zhou Qiren, "India's Alternative Path" (cited August 8, 2003), available at http://www.cc.org.cn/010102200/0101022000.htm.

References

Bhatnagar, Subhash and Robert Schware (eds.), (2000). *Information and Communication Technology in Development Cases from India*. New Delhi: Sage Publications.

Christensen, Thomas J. (1999). "Pride, Pressure, and Politics: The Roots of China's Worldview," in Deng Yong and Wang Fei-Ling (eds.), *In the Eyes of the Dragon*. Lanham, MD: Rowan and Littlefield Publishing.

Dreze, Jean and Amartya Sen (2002). *India Development and Participation*. Oxford: Oxford University Press.

Franda, Marcus (2002). *China and India Online Information Technology Politics and Diplomacy in the World's Two Largest Nations*. London: Roman and Littlefield.

Pan, Philip P. (2003). "U. N. Official Criticizes Education in China." *Washington Post*, September 19, 2003, p. A20.

Sen, Amartya (1999). *Development as Freedom*. Boston: Anchor.

Wang Fei-Ling (1999). "Self-Image and Strategic Intentions: National Confidence and Political Insecurity," in Deng Yong and Wang Fei-Ling (eds.), *In the Eyes of the Dragon: China Views the World*. Lanham, MD: Rowan and Littlefield Publishers.

Warner, Melanie (2000). "The Indians of Silicon Valley." *Fortune* 141 (10), May 15, 2000, pp. 356–366.

Wong, John and Nah Seok Ling (2001). *China's Emerging New Economy: The Internet and E-Commerce*. Singapore: Singapore University Press/World Scientific.

12

Development and Choice

Tony Saich

The chapters in this volume question many of the glib assertions made about the development trajectories of China and India. They reject the commonly expressed view of strong Chinese success and relative Indian failure and propose a more complex view of the relative success of both polities while showing that they have grappled with similar problems with more mixed results than much previous literature has suggested. Of itself this is no mean achievement and the questions raised in the various chapters should stimulate further research. One suspects that the old clichés will not slip away quickly but let us hope that we will see more nuanced research in the future. Such research is significant given that we are talking about the world's two most populous countries and lessons about what has worked and what has failed may provide important learning experiences for other lesser-developed countries striving to get out of poverty through shifting to more sustainable economic growth.

In this afterword we shall look at how the two countries compare in terms of providing their citizens with an improved quality of life and enhanced freedoms. The focus is on the quality of development rather than on the quantity of growth. Given the limitations of space, we shall concentrate on health care, equality, and governance. We find that while China has outperformed India on health improvements, the fairness and equity of its health system has been worse while income equality and governance in India have been generally better. Choosing among these depends on making moral judgments about the relative importance of these items.

Growth, Welfare, and Equality

The gap in economic growth rates is clear for all to see. From 1980 India has enjoyed per capita GDP growth of around 3.8 percent compared to that of China's roughly 8 percent. This has led to significant rises in per capita GDP and a widening gap between China and India. Whereas in the early 1980s, China's per capita GDP stood at $275 just below India's $280, by 2003 China's per capita GDP had risen to $1086, twice that of India at $545 (Morgan Stanley 2004, 1). A number of writers have sought to explain the difference in terms of the later start of reforms in India in 1991 than in China in 1978. Indeed, some of the authors in this volume follow the general consensus that reform in India only began in 1991 following liberalization after the financial crisis. However, as Rodrik and Subramanian (2004, 2–3) show, the upturn in India's economic growth predates this timing by a full decade. They argue that the impetus for economic growth in India came from an attitudinal shift in 1980 by the national government to favor private business through the adoption of pro-business policies that favored incumbents in the formal industrial and commercial sectors. This means that even in terms of economic reforms, the period for comparison is more closely aligned than a number of authors suggest. Using this time scale, China has clearly outperformed India in pure economic terms. It should be pointed out, however, that China has also invested about twice as much as India to attain this growth and there are questions about the quality of the growth.[1]

The more important questions though concern the benefits that this economic growth has brought for citizens in the two countries and to what extent quality of life has improved. From 1990 the United Nations' Development Program (UNDP) began publishing its annual human development report with the clear message that GDP growth rates alone were not satisfactory measures of development. Improved GDP rates do not necessarily translate into improved quality of life for all in society. Economic development needs to be paired with equity and the enlargement of people's choices. As the political scientist, David Apter (1987, 16) argued some years ago, "choice refers to the range of articulated alternatives available to individuals and collectivities. Increasing choice was and remains the central development 'project,' " This view has become most closely associated with the economist Amartya Sen's notion of development as a "process of expanding the real freedoms that people enjoy" (1999, 3). In Sen's view freedom is the primary end and the principal means of development. Thus, successful development should provide people with the resources necessary not only to avoid serious life threatening deprivation but also to accumulate the resources to participate effectively in society.

As David Bloom and his colleagues note (2001, 2) there is thus more to the quality of life than income alone, we need to think about "health, education, political freedom, participation in civil society and the status of women." The agenda of international organizations has shifted to dealing with this broader, more complex and interrelated set of issues. Thus, we see the development of alternative indicators such as the Human Development Index (HDI) and the Human Poverty Index (HPI) used by the UNDP.

Across the board, China enjoys higher levels of welfare than India. On average the Chinese live 10 years longer, they have an infant mortality rate that is half that of India's and enjoy a higher literacy rate. However, both have shown steady improvement since economic growth took off. A major part of the explanation for the difference, of course, derives from China's faster pace of economic growth. The major exception is in terms of equity in development where India has performed better than China. This combined with the more durable governing structures in India will affect the future trajectories of growth, an issue we shall return to later.

In neither country has the state's capacity to provide welfare kept pace with economic growth. In both cases, the gap between their global rankings in HDI terms and GNP per capita terms shrank in the 1990s. India actually made significant progress from 1975 to 1990 in the period that most people see as being pre-economic reform. In China, the HDI improvement was very strong throughout the 1990s but less so from 1975 to 1990.

It is also important to note the considerable regional variation in terms of the development level. China's overall HDI ranking is comparable to a high/middle level of human development while that of India is middle/low but this covers significant regional variation. Five of China's western provinces had an HDI ranging from 0.650 to 0.5921 putting them in the middle development category and even Tibet with the lowest ranking (0.5921) is above the cutoff for low development (0.5). By contrast three of the major municipalities (Beijing, Shanghai, and Tianjin) have an HDI over 0.800 placing them in the high level of development (Hu Angang 2004, 8 and UNDP 2004, 3). It is interesting to note that regional disparity in the HDI index is lower than that for per capita income, also attesting to relatively good social development. For India the highest rank for HDI is for Kerala and is 0.638 putting it on a par with China's western provinces and the lowest ranked is Bihar at 0.367 well below Tibet and putting it in the category of low human development. It would rank with the Democratic Republic of the Congo; 168 in terms of nation-states. Nine of India's fourteen states rate a low human development level (Singh et al. 2002, 6).

China enjoys lower levels of poverty than India as measured by the HPI,[2] however China's official figures (using $0.66 per day) underestimate the real level of rural poverty.[3] Both countries have made significant strides in reducing poverty, but there remain serious problems. In particular, a significant group of rural poor have not responded to policy measures, market openings, and the benefits of "trickle down" that have been part and parcel of economic reform in the two countries. Additionally, a very large group is vulnerable to economic downturn and liable to recidivism.

While we are used to thinking of urban poverty in terms of India, this has been an emerging problem for China and the increasing numbers are a direct product of the economic reform measures. The official Chinese statistics do not cover urban China and until very recently no systematic study had been carried out. The number of urban poor is estimated to have risen to 20 million in 2002 (Hong 2003), while the number of urban residents who received the minimum subsistence support was 21 million in 2003. Li (2003) suggests that there are 30 million in urban China with a monthly income of 150 to 300 *yuan* (83 cents to $1.20 per day). Such figures clearly underestimate urban poverty and do not include the migrant population. A 1999 survey by the State Statistical Bureau revealed a 15.2 percent immigrant poverty rate, some 50 percent higher than the local communities they lived in.

India has performed better than China in keeping the levels of inequality lower. A significant rise in inequality has occurred in China and the main reason is the urban–rural gap (see Chang 2002, 336). This is not a new problem. The urban–rural income gap of China, which was 2.6:1 when reforms began was, according the International Labor Organization, the highest in the world—a reminder that Maoist China was not the egalitarian utopia it has been taken to be. In India in the mid-1970s the gap was 1.4:1. Initial pro-rural reforms in China caused a drop in the early 1980s before it rose again to 2.8:1 by 2002.

Perhaps of most concern is not inequality itself but the fact that it has been rising under the reforms. When economic reforms began, the

Gini coefficient for the two countries was roughly comparable; China's was 0.33, while that for India was 0.32. By 2001, that for China had risen to 0.45 (UNDP 2004, 189) but some studies suggest that it may be as high as 0.49. By 2001, the Gini index for India had remained basically unchanged at 0.33. Not surprisingly we see a skewing in the distribution of income and consumption.[4] For China especially, a country that still describes itself as socialist, these trends are difficult to justify.

Health Care

The challenges faced by the two countries in the health sector are comparable. Public spending is low, there is a great difference in access to care between the rich and the poor and between urban and rural dwellers, and preventive health spending is lower than curative care, the latter being highly favorable to the richer sections of the population in distribution, and very few in the population have access to health care insurance. Both countries would benefit from allocating more resources to public health but this alone would not be enough. In particular, they both need a more efficient and equitable health financing system. A World Bank report (Peters 2002, p. 15) commenting on India (but its comments are equally applicable to China) noted that it needed a "financing system that has compulsory membership, a socially acceptable and affordable package of benefits, pre-payment, and risk-pooling for people with different incomes and health status."

China enjoys higher overall levels of health, partly because of faster economic growth (WHO 2001, 152–153) (see table 12.2). However, the two countries have both advanced significantly since 1980 while India has outperformed China in the overall fairness and efficiency of its health system (see table 12.1).

Table 12.1 China–India: health system rankings (1997)

	China	*India*
Fairness in financial contribution	188	42
Overall goal attainment	132	121
Health expenditure per capita	139	133
Levels of Health attainment	61	118
Overall health system performance	144	112

Source: WHO, 2001.

Table 12.2 China–India: health indicators (2002)

	Life expectancy at birth	*Under-5 infant mortality (per 1,000 born)*	*Maternal mortality rate (per 100,000 live births)*	*Tuberculosis (per 100,000)*	*Births attended by skilled personnel (%)*
China	71	37	56	250	89
India	61	96	540	431	42

Source: The figures for 1980 are taken from Eberstadt, 1988, pp. 131 and 136. All other figures are from WHO, 2004, pp. 136–137 and 150–151.

Table 12.3 China–India: health spending (2001)

	Expenditure on health as % of GDP	*Government expenditure on health as % of health expenditure*	*Government expenditure on health as % of total government expenditure*	*Out of pocket expenses as % of private expenditure on health*
China	5.5	37.2	10.2	95.4
India	5.1	17.9	3.1	100

Source: WHO, 2004, p. 137.

In the coming years, both systems will face considerable challenges to improve spending, to expand insurance coverage, and to deal with the looming crisis of HIV/AIDS. At present, both countries spend far less on health care than most lower-income countries (table 12.3).[5]

Increasingly, in both countries access to health care is tied to ability to pay and to point-of-service payment. This is inefficient and leaves the poor highly vulnerable (Peters et al. 2002, 4). These high levels of personal spending are combined with low rates of insurance coverage. This change has been particularly dramatic in China with the collapse of the collective structures in the countryside and the abandonment of many social responsibilities by urban state-owned enterprises. Coverage through the rural collective medical system dropped from almost 80 percent in 1979 to only 7 percent in 1997 (*Zhongguo nongcun* 2000, 21). A survey we conducted in fall 2003 (Horizon 2003) found that 75 percent of individuals surveyed did not have any medical insurance. In India, 90 percent of the population has no form of insurance (Peters et al. 2002, 4). As a result, we see more people not seeking medical help when they need it. This is compounded by the fact that unit costs are increasing.

The consequences of these trends are becoming increasingly visible. When combined with the increasing income and regional inequality we see a very varied picture of access to and quality of health provision. Public spending clearly is important. Health outcomes are much better in Indian states such as Kerala, Punjab, and Tamil Nadu where per capita health spending is double of that of Bihar and Madhya Pradesh (Peters et al. 2002, 3). The same holds true in China. In relatively wealthy Zhejiang province infant mortality per 1,000 live births was around 20 whereas in poor Guizhou it was 60. Both infant mortality and maternal mortality are closely correlated with the use of prenatal care and attended safe delivery, two preventive services that have been adversely affected by the privatization of health care in rural areas in China (Saich and Kaufman 2005).

These weaknesses in the health systems, especially in the rural areas, are worrying as both countries face a significant challenge from the spread of HIV/AIDS. How the two countries with their different political systems deal with this threat will be very instructive. The Chinese program is state-led, does not allow for free media publication about HIV/AIDS, and restricts the kind of civil society interventions that have been successful in countries such as Thailand. In India, the state welcomes intervention by civil society and allows greater active organization and political lobbying by people living with HIV/AIDS.

The absolute number of HIV infections in India is 5.1 million (UNAIDS 2004, 37), while the figure for China ranges from the official estimate of 1 million to unofficial estimates of 6 million (Wolf et al. 2003, 56). In both countries, the disease has spread to all regions and beyond discrete sections of the population such as commercial sex workers or intravenous drug users. However, given the multitude of other social and economic problems that each country faces, while there has been much rhetoric devoted to the problem less has been done in practice and it has not been at the forefront of decision-makers' minds. Yet, the future spread of the disease could undo much of the recent social advances.

Problematically, China and India have a number of features that are conducive to the spread of HIV/AIDS. The population is increasingly mobile and will become more urbanized over the next decade.

Importantly, both populations have low levels of awareness about the disease and how it is spread and a rising Commercial Sex Worker Community with an attendant rise in sexually transmitted diseases (STDs) and low rate of condom use. In addition, both countries have increasing numbers of intravenous drug users who are not only becoming infected through joint needle use but are also passing the infection to other sections of the population, either through commercial sex work or through their partners. In China, HIV prevalence among drug injectors ranged from 18 to 56 percent in six cities in Guangdong and Guangxi in 2002, while in 2003 in Yunnan the figure was 21 percent (UNAIDS 2004, 36). In the southern city of Chennai in India, when a sentinel site was established in 2000, 26 percent of drug injectors were HIV positive but this had risen to 64 percent by 2003 (UNAIDS 2004, 36). What is important to realize is that in all at risk groups, the infection rates are increasing rapidly with the strong potential for further spread into the general population and in the future, heterosexual contact is likely to become the major transmission channel for HIV/AIDS in both countries.

In the past, China has been very successful in dealing with communicable and epidemic diseases, they accounted for only 5 percent of fatalities in 1998 compared with 23 percent in India (Wolf et al. 2003, 45). But the health sector in China has not fared well under reforms as incentives have changed and the rural health system has begun to focus more on expensive, curative care rather than inexpensive preventive medical care. It now shares many of the problems common to the Indian health system.

Governance

One area where India has a significant advantage over China that may influence future development is good governance. It is clear that China's authoritarian political system is not durable over the long term and the way in which it transitions will have a significant impact on social and economic development. India may be behind China in terms of the development of physical and social infrastructure but it has strengthened its public institutions and developed a sounder framework for effective governance. It is difficult to calculate what the effect of this will be on future development but it is clear that China will have to negotiate a difficult transition.

Most indicators show a much stronger performance in governance by India. Kaufmann and his colleagues (2003) look at six key indicators that are important for governance (see the chart in the chapter by Gilley). India performs better than China on four of the indicators only trailing in terms of political stability and government effectiveness. As noted earlier, however, long term political stability for China is debatable. While it is true that in terms of short-term indicators, an authoritarian China might appear more stable than a raucous, democratic India, over the long term the Chinese polity will have to negotiate a very difficult transition from authoritarian rule that will be unpredictable to say the least. The social indicators and the pace of economic growth attest to the better government effectiveness in China but here one caveat should be noted. The authoritarian political system allows China's leaders to focus on particular issues for a limited period of time and to mobilize resources to meet the goals. This can be highly effective but it can also have disastrous outcomes as shown when the CCP launched the Great Leap Forward in 1958 or when it has chosen to crack down on the quasi-religious group, *Falungong*, or any political opposition such as the China Democratic Party.

The World Economic Forum has compiled five indicators that compare different aspects of governance (see table 12.4). India clearly outperforms China in the three areas of press freedom, judicial independence, and protection of property rights but interestingly does not do as well with trust of politicians and favoritism in decisions.

The better performance of China on these two indicators might be related to the difficulty of expressing dissatisfaction in an authoritarian political system. In a survey we conducted in fall 2003, while there was relative satisfaction with the national level of government, there was considerable dissatisfaction with local government and the

Table 12.4 China–India: governance rankings (2004)

	China	*India*
Freedom of the press	99	26
Judicial independence	62	25
Property rights	64	43
Public trust of politicians	20	82
Favoritism in decisions of officials	43	57

Note: The ranking is among 102 countries.

Source: World Economic Forum reproduced in Morgan Stanley 2004, 6.

general perception was that when implementing policy, local officials favored the wealthy and the well connected.

Citizen satisfaction in China with government declines the lower one moves down the institutional hierarchy (see table 12.5). This is important as it is distinct from many developed economies, where satisfaction levels tend to rise as government gets closer to the people (see, e.g., Pew Research Center, March 1998), indicating that people feel that they have greater control over the decisions of local government and may be able to influence local policy and resource allocation. In China, local governments provide almost all public services and the fact that satisfaction levels decline as one gets closer to the people is a worrying sign. Those who reported that they were "very satisfied" with government service and performance comprised 86 percent for the national government but only 44 percent for the township level. A majority of Chinese citizens surveyed see local officials' attitude when implementing policy as more receptive to the views of their superiors and closer to those with money than to ordinary people.[6]

It is certain that the Chinese system will have to undergo a major transformation. When this will happen, how and with what outcome is, of course, open to major speculation. In this volume and elsewhere Gilley (2004) is relatively optimistic about the political transition in China although he does acknowledge that it might be turbulent. Yet a democratic outcome is only one possibility and not necessarily the most likely.

It should not be forgotten that the primary purpose of the CCP is to remain in power for as long as possible and its leaders are not going

Table 12.5 Chinese citizen satisfaction with government service and performance, 2003 (comparison by government level)

	Central government	*Provincial government*	*County government*	*Township government*
Percentage of residents reporting a high level of satisfaction	86.1%	75.0%	52.0%	43.6%
Satisfaction index	3.16	2.89	2.54	2.32

Note: The "high level of satisfaction" category includes both those who responded with "very satisfied" and "somewhat satisfied." The satisfaction index was measured according to the following scale: an answer of "very satisfied" received a rating of 4, "somewhat satisfied" a rating of 3, "not very satisfied" a rating of 2, and "very unsatisfied" a rating of 1.

Source: Horizon 2003.

to introduce any changes that might threaten their position and foment instability. Despite long-term benefits that would come from significant political reform in terms of ameliorating corruption and the non-transparent political system, there are strong countervailing pressures. First, China's leaders interpret democratic reforms as essentially destabilizing, undermining both social stability and economic growth. Second, the party's monopoly of power allows it to dispense patronage fueling the corruption that is a feature of contemporary political culture. Partial reform has brought significant economic benefits but has allowed the party to co-opt new elites into the power structure thus reducing external pressure for political change. Third, the Chinese system is extremely decentralized and it is often difficult for Beijing to control activities of local officials even if they should wish to. The theft of state assets, the corruption, and the use of official position to pursue private wealth are all most marked at the local levels of government. Thus local governments have little incentive to make their activities more transparent or accountable to the public at large. Fourth, with rapid economic growth continuing the new urban elites appear to have little interest in more democratic reform. Not surprisingly, as they have fared well under the existing system they see no compelling reason to change it. There is no strong constituency that favors political change. Private entrepreneurs benefit from beneficial connections to the party, or may be former party officials themselves. The laid-off workers are politically marginalized and while there has been an upsurge in farmer protest there is no evidence that the protests have gone beyond the local. Indeed, most evidence supports the view that they retain trust in the national leaders and see the problems as purely local aberrations rather than systemic flaws.

Last but not least, while there are examples of peaceful transitions from authoritarian rule, there are few, if any, examples of such a transition from communist rule. The norm has been the collapse of the ancient regime. Systemic breakdown might not lead to a democratic breakthrough but to a system dominated by the new economic elites backed by the military in the name of preserving social stability and national sovereignty. By consistently cracking down on alternatives and restricting the growth of a vibrant civil society that could form the basis for a new system, the CCP has created the possibility that the "uncivil society" might take power. Under this scenario the inequalities would continue to rise with the party becoming the preserve of new socioeconomic elites and with their power backed up by the military. The lack of political reform would produce a permanent underclass in both urban and rural China that would be portrayed as a threat to stability and continued economic progress.

To a large extent the long-term success of China's development trajectory will be decided by how well it deals with its future political transition. At some point, a new relationship will have to be built between the state and society and a greater consensus will have to be found about societal values than the simple pursuit of economic growth. A flawed transition could undo much of the good work that has been done in terms of improving the quality of life.

Notes

1. For example, the World Bank (1997, p. 2) suggests that the damage caused from air and water pollution has been estimated at $54 billion a year, amounting to a staggering 8 percent of GDP in 1995. Of this, the largest amount comes from urban air pollution at $33 billion and water pollution comprising at least $4 billion.
2. The HPI reflects the distribution of progress and measures the backlog of deprivations that still exist. It focuses on three dimensions: longevity measured by the probability of not living to 40 years of age from birth; adult literacy rates that attest to knowledge; and general economic provisioning as measured by the percentage of citizens who are not using improved water sources, those without sustainable access to improved water sources and children under weight for their age.
3. The Asian Development Bank using the norm of $1 per day in purchasing power parity and using the preferred consumption norm suggests that China would have about 230 million poor residents, some 18.5 percent of the population (Asian Development Bank 2000, 8–9). The UNDP suggests 16.1 percent of China's population fall into this category (UNDP 2003, 198). If one applies a norm of $2 per day, this would cover 53.7 percent of total population. This puts China considerably better off than India (34.7 percent and 79.9 percent respectively) (World Bank 2003, 59). Other evidence suggests higher poverty levels for China than the official estimates. For example, one Chinese scholar has calculated that 17 percent of the rural population consumed less than 2,100 kcal per day in 1995, while two others note stunting rates of 22 percent in 1998 with even higher figures in poor counties (quoted in UNDP and ILO 2002, 15).
4. The top 20 percent of the population in China, which had 36 percent of total income at the start of reforms, had 51.4 percent by the late-1990s. By contrast, the bottom 20 percent had 8 percent at the start of the reforms and 4.06 percent by the late-1990s (Lu Xueyi 2001, 93–94). The UNDP gives figures of 33.1 percent and 4.7 percent for 2001 (UNDP 2004, 189). In India, the poorest 20 percent have 8.9 percent of the income, while the richest 20 percent enjoy 41.6 percent (UNDP 2004, 190). Again this has remained essentially unchanged (Singh et al. 2002, 2).

5. Government budgetary expenditure in China stood at 15.5 percent in 2001 down from 25 percent in 1990 (SSB 2003 and Gu 2004, 1–2). However, the formal budgetary allocation alone underestimates government spending as a percentage of total health care expenditure. Chinese statistics include the category "social spending" that contains a large component of State-Owned Enterprise contributions to health insurance and related health spending. This amounts to a further 20–25 percent depending on how one calculates it. Thus, the World Bank calculates government expenditure on health at 36.6 percent (1997–2000) of total health expenditure. This is much higher than India (17.8 percent) but is generally lower in international terms. The Malaysian government allocates 58.8 percent and the Philippines 45.7 percent, while the average for lower middle-income countries is 49.4 percent (World Bank 2003, 92–94).
6. In major cities the situation is somewhat better where 41.9 percent say that while implementing policy, officials are arrogant while 42.4 percent feel that when implementing policy they think they are helping ordinary citizens. These percentages are 51 and 26.8 respectively for respondents living in villages. In major cities, 41.4 percent felt that policy execution favored those with money while only 39.9 percent thought that it took care of individuals in difficulty. By contrast in the villages these percentages were 54.7 and 23.6 respectively. A majority also felt that when implementing policy, officials sought to move close to higher leaders rather than thinking about the needs of ordinary people. In the major cities the percentages were 45.6 and 35.8 respectively with 58.6 and 20 respectively in the villages.

References

Apter, D. (1987). *Rethinking Development. Modernization, Dependency and Post-Modern Politics*. London: Sage.

Asian Development Bank. *Country Economic Review: People's Republic of China* CER-PRC 2000–09 available at www.adb.org/Documents/CER/PRC/2000/prc0106.asp (2000).

Bloom, D. et al. (2001). *The Quality of Life in Rural Asia*. Oxford: Oxford University Press.

Chang, G. H. (2002). "The Cause and Cure of China's Widening Income Disparity," *China Economic Review* 13(4) (Greenwich, CT).

Eberstadt, N. (1988). *The Poverty of Communism*. New Brunswick: Transaction Books.

Gilley, B. (2004). *China's Democratic Future. How it Will Happen and Where it Will Lead*. New York: Columbia University Press.

Gu, E. (2004). "China's Ailing Public Health System," East Asian Institute, National University of Singapore, Background Brief, No. 179.

Hong, Dayong (2003). "Gaige yilai Zhongguo chengshi fupin gongzuo de fazhan lichen" (The Development Process of the Alleviation of Poverty in Urban China since Reforms), *Shehuixue yanjiu* (Sociology Research), No. 1.

Horizon (2003). *Zhongguo jumin pingjia zhengfu ji zhengfu gonggong fuwu yanjiu baogao* (Research Report on Citizens' Attitudes to Government and

Government Provision of Public Goods) (Beijing: Horizon). This was a national survey completed with Asia Programs, Kennedy School of Government.

Hu, A. (2004). "From Unevenness Towards Coordination for China's Regional Development (1978–2004)," *China: Towards a Balanced Development. Background Papers*. Beijing: China Development Forum.

Human Development Report. Oxford: Oxford University Press.

Kaufmann et al. (2003). *Governance Matters III: Governance Indicators for 1996–2002*. Available at www.Info.worldbank.org/governance/kkz2002/sc.chart.asp.

Li, Peilin (2003). "Quanmin jianshe xiaokang shehui de sige guanjian wenti" (Four Key Issues in Completely Establishing a Comfortable Society), *Lingdao canyue* (Leadership Consultations), No. 10, April.

Lu, Xueyi (ed.) (2001). *Dangdai Zhongguo shehui jieceng yanjiu baogao* (Research Report on China's Social Strata). Beijing: Social Sciences Documentation Press.

Morgan Stanley (2004). *India and China: A Special Economic Analysis*. Equity Research, Asia/Pacific.

Peters, D. H. (2002). *Better Health Systems for India's Poor: Findings, Analysis, and Options*. Washington, D.C.: The World Bank.

Pew Research Center (1998). "How Americans View Government," March 10, 1998.

Rodrik, D. and Subramanian, A. (2004). "From 'Hindu Growth' to Productivity Surge: The Mystery of the Indian Growth Transition." Unpublished draft.

Saich, T and Kaufman, J. (2005). "Financial Reform, Poverty, and the Impact on Reproductive Health Provision: Evidence from Three Rural Townships," in Y. Huang, T. Saich, and E. Steinfeld (eds.), *Financial Sector Reform in China*. Cambridge, MA: Harvard University Press.

Sen, A. (1999). *Development as Freedom*. New York: Alfred A. Knopf.

Singh, N. et al. (2002). "Regional Inequality in India: A Fresh Look." Unpublished paper.

State Statistical Bureau (2003). *Zhongguo tongji nianjian* (China Statistical Yearbook). Beijing: China Statistics Press.

UNAIDS, (2004). *AIDS Epidemic Update 2004*. Available at www.unaids.org/wad2004/report.html.

UNDP, various years, *Human Development Report*. New York: Oxford University Press.

UNDP (2004). *Millennium Development Goals. China's Progress 2003*. Beijing: Office of UN Resident Coordinator in China.

UNDP in collaboration with the ILO (2002). *An Integrated Approach to Reducing Poverty in China*. N.p.: N.p.

Wolf, C. Jr. et al. (2003). *Fault Lines in China's Economic Terrain*. Santa Monica, CA: Rand.

World Bank (1997). *Clear Water, Blue Skies: China's Environment in the New Century*. Washington, D.C.: World Bank.

World Bank (2003). *03 World Development Indicators*. Washington, D.C.: World Bank.

World Health Organization (2001). *World Health Report: Report of the Director-General 2000.* Geneva: World Health Organization.
World Health Organization (2004). *World Health Report 2004: Changing History.* Geneva: World Health Organization.
Zhongguo nongcun weisheng gaige yu fazhan Beijing ziliao (2000). (Background Materials on Rural Health Reform and Development) in Economics Research Department.

13

Conclusion

Bruce Gilley

The purpose of this volume has been to think anew about the comparative performance of India and China, whether economic, political, social, or moral. In different ways and degrees, challenging the old cliché about a miracle in China and a failure in India has emerged as the overarching theme of the assembled chapters. But any paired comparison of countries is bound to bring out other sorts of insights as well and it is worthwhile to ponder these first. After all, our purpose here is not to tell a one-sided story but for the first time to tell a complete story. In particular, we perceive similarities between the two countries not hitherto appreciated; we gain new insights into each country as individual case studies; and finally we understand better the ways in which China really has outperformed India.

Any comparison of two cases as large as China and India is bound to stretch the homogeneity assumption of comparative research. The notion of these two countries as single entities is itself problematic, much less the assumption that those two entities are comparable. The median population of China's 33 provincial-level units is 38 million, and the median population of India's 31 state-level units is 21 million. That compares to a median population of just 7 million for the 176 countries included in the United Nations Development Programme's development indicators. Put another way, if their subnational units were countries, China and India would account for 24 of the 50 most populous states in the world. It is a bracing reminder that behind the generalizations about China and India lies considerable heterogeneity.

The essays here offer additional reasons to avoid facile comparisons. Manor as well as Huang and Khanna note the periodization difference arising from China's 13-year head start in economic reforms (1978 vs. 1991). Mukherji and Gilley note that China's particular political failures pre-reform led to the strength of its economic reform era, while India's comparative political success meant a slower pace of reform. The impact of their different regime-types is also pervasive, as noted by several authors, whether it be on foreign investment, labor regulation, population control, or minority affairs.

Nonetheless, as large, populous, and developing Asian countries with a history of cultural interchange, China and India can be fruitfully compared as long as these complexities are borne in mind.

One key insight from these chapters is the many similarities in their developmental performance. Indeed, this volume would be judged a success if it merely succeeded in showing that the oppositional nature of the contrast has obscured many similarities. For a start, it is important to keep in mind that we are dealing here with two relative success stories. China and India accounted for 4 of the 7 percentage point decline to 21 percent in the incidence of global poverty from 1990 to 2001. The United Nations goal of reaching 14 percent by 2015 is within reach largely because of these two countries. Global companies as diverse as insurance providers, car-makers, and airlines are staking their expansion on these two countries in the coming decades. Swamy notes that both countries enjoy sound external and macroeconomic positions even if their domestic financial systems are in trouble. As Gilley shows, legitimacy levels in both states are higher than what would be predicted from their income levels. Both he and Huang Jinxin suggest that the super-patriotism of China may be more fragile or constrained than appearances suggest. But it is clear that both Chinese and Indians feel good about their countries and the directions they are heading. These are two of the world's greatest civilizations that are at last building on those legacies to improve the lives of their average citizens. Gloomy paradigms about vicious cycles and ageless plights, as Albert Hirschmann and Edward Said both famously reminded us in their own ways, are a hindrance to understanding the developing world in general, and would be veritable roadblocks to insight in the cases of China and India.

Similar challenges also exist in both. Several writers note the searing environmental degradation, looming AIDS pandemics, and fiscal indigence that haunt the future generations of both countries. The plights of rural dwellers are also shown to be equally dire, whether it be in education, healthcare, or access to credit. The focus on their different regime-types obscures the fact that China and India are both weak states, at least in rural areas, unable to command the obedience of local elites.

Regime-type matters a lot in other respects, however, nowhere better seen than in the sorry plight of workers in both countries. Swamy notes that both countries suffer from extremism in the regulation of labor. India's overregulated labor market, a result of special-interest lobbying in its democracy, constrains development, reducing jobs and incomes for workers as well as forcing many poor into the informal sector. China's under-regulated labor market, the result of a one-party state's ban on worker organization, leaves workers vulnerable to Dickensian-like depredations.

There are however exceptions to the rural and labor problems in both countries, subnational units that have succeeded in improving conditions through effective economic and social policies. The successes of Kerala and Zhejiang may differ in many ways, but they remind us that "mean-spirited analysis" (using national averages that mask wide variation) in countries with more than a billion people each is bound to obscure significant regional variation. More important, they remind us that decentralization has opened possibilities for effective local political leadership in both countries.

The centrality of politics to economic reforms in both countries is brought out clearly in several chapters, an insight only possible with hindsight and comparative analysis. Mukherji shows how the political consensus of the post–Cultural Revolution generation of leaders in China, not shifting trends in global comparative advantage, was the critical factor in allowing reforms to begin there. Likewise, Manor notes that India's reforms depended less on the alleged impact of the 1991 balance-of-payments crisis than on the political vision, courage, and adroitness of a few key leaders. Reforms in China and India are not a result of "global capital" or "the IMF," nor yet of economic structures that deny human agency. They are a result of political leadership and at least some degree of social support in both countries. Sinha shows how political linkages (not fiscal incentives) explain the success of market-friendly decentralization in both countries.

Turning to the contrasts between the two, we gain two types of insights. One is absolute—deepening our understanding of each country itself—and the other relative—comparing their performances in domestic development.

While China's economic reforms have been widely hailed as "gradual" in nature, the comparison with India gives lie to that claim. Manor, Gilley, and Friedman all show how China's economic reforms have been shock therapy by any other name. The comparison with India's genuine gradualism in rural reforms, state enterprise privatization, and labor market liberalization is stark. Mukerji notes that China's sudden disposal of urban housing may be the biggest single public asset sale in world history. Meanwhile, Huang Jinxin shows that using India as a mirror, Chinese netizens have gained other new insights into their country. Among these have been the discovery that the "privileges" afforded to ethnic minorities in China may lack the most important privilege of freedom, and that postindustrial success may require very different sorts of political and economic organization than those currently in place in China.

India too appears in a new light. In particular, the unrelenting and self-wounding anticolonialism of Indian elites is marked when the comparison with China is made. Friedman notes that the anti-Western bugaboos of Indian intellectuals schooled in "critical studies" (much of it emergent from the West itself) combined with a blinkered parochialism in the villages to shut off India from the early days of economic globalization just as China was opening to it. Huang Jinxin notes the irony of Chinese netizens discovering the virtues of India's colonial heritage—its English capabilities, its dispersion of political power, and its effortless mixing with things and people foreign—even as many Indian intellectuals continue to fulminate over the atrocities of the Raj. (China continues to suffer from a similar self-wounding rage with respect to Japan.) The contrast with China also tempers the widespread perception that India is somehow terribly governed for a country of its size and income level. As Gilley, Huang and Khanna, Saich, and Sinha show, Indian governance measures up quite well when the comparison with China is invoked. The truth of the matter, as Manor and Friedman suggest, is that India's warts are simply in plain view, while China's are not.

The notion of China's comparative success over India comes in for much scrutiny here, but in several respects we find it to be true. Friedman warns against romanticizing India's experience and we turn up many sobering reasons. While rural services appear equally bad, Mukherji argues that as a whole, subnational units in China perform better in delivering services than their counterparts in India. Along with Swamy he also notes that China has clearly outperformed India in the provision of public infrastructure, particularly roads and power. Saich points to the better gender and health outcomes in China. China's faster economic growth is both a cause and consequence of its superior performance on these fronts.

Huang and Khanna offer a bittersweet account of the comparative reaction to their now-famous claim in 2003 that India may catch up to China. The sober and detailed analysis of the Chinese, contrasted favorably with the delirious and hackneyed responses in India. As this volume was being prepared, news appeared of Chinese manufactured Hindu idols beginning to gain market share in India, while the Chinese rugby team trounced India 50–15 in inter-Asian play. These are not mere amusements. They reflect a China that in the reform period has displayed a remarkable agility and organizational capability in the face of international competitive pressures, one deeply redolent of Japan's nineteenth-century Meiji reform era.

Even without the new insights this volume provides about India's superior or equal performance to China, the insights above would seem a worthy contribution. But if reversing deep-seated but inaccurate and harmful paradigms is rated a greater contribution, then I have indeed saved the best until last. And that is quite simply to restate how the essays here have recast the ages-old comparison between Asia's giants as a successful China and a failed India.

In the realm of economic development, India by no means pales in comparison to China. As Gilley and Swamy show, India's developmental gains have been nearly as good as China's since 1975, even though China's reforms began more than a decade earlier. India performed worse in the three decades until 1975, but since then the story has changed. Today, as several authors point out, India has many clear economic advantages over China—more efficient energy use, less income inequality, less state involvement in the economy, a successful software industry, far superior equity markets, and better economic and environmental governance.

Several writers point to China's attraction of larger amounts of foreign direct investment than India. Yet the difference shrinks on closer examination. Part of China's "success," as Huang and Khanna show, owes to the stifling of domestic private enterprise, and another reason, as Swamy notes, is its fortuitous location surrounded by fast-growing or rich countries (Japan, South Korea, and Taiwan) compared to India's poor periphery (Pakistan, Bangladesh, and Burma). Part of India's "failure," as Gilley and Friedman both note, is that its democratic polity constrains the nonconsensual use of state power for "the investment climate" and the corrupt sale of public assets to foreign investors. In any case, as both Sinha and Swamy note, the investment gap is much smaller if accurate statistics, comparable definitions, and the sizes of the economies are taken into account. Here as elsewhere, the notion of China as a success and India a failure proves false. As one widens the evaluative horizons, India's foreign direct investment performance appears as good if not better than China's.

Indeed, inaccurate statistics from China are another refrain that makes many writers hesitant to endorse even the best-known "evidence" of superior Chinese performance. Saich questions China's poverty and AIDS figures, Swamy and Huang and Khanna its FDI figures, Mukherji its fiscal figures, and Gilley its regime-support figures.

Moving beyond strictly economic concerns, the notion of China as a success and India as a failure becomes even less plausible. In the realms of political and social justice, there has arguably been an "Indian miracle" compared to China. Friedman provides the most detailed process tracing of the pre-reform era and notes that China's performance then came at huge cost that only the most callous utilitarianism could justify. Gilley also notes that pre-reform period was one of one-off disasters in China and endemic failures in India, but normative comparison suggests the former was much worse from a moral standpoint. India's people have never endured state-imposed famines and pogroms of the scale and persistence seen in China.

In initiating economic reforms, several writers note the gradual and consensual nature of India's approach compared to China's, a fact with both inherent and instrumental advantages. That approach resulted from a constitutional democracy in India in which both constitution and democracy are taken seriously. China's constitution and its claims to democracy are hollow. Mukherji notes how India's institutionalized federalism provides a cushion against central government instability that is lacking in China. That is all the more damaging in China's case because central government instability there is less constrained by the norms of democratic politics. The periods of stability in Beijing have depended on a unique consensus on policy matters, or the influence of powerful party elders, neither of which provides a long-term solution to political difference. As Manor notes, reform shifts in India have reflected genuine policy differences, whereas reform shifts in China have reflected factional battles. Saich's evidence of disparate burdens in China's health system compared to India reminds us that outcomes must be discounted if achieved at the cost of fairness.

Using objective governance indicators covering things like the control of corruption, the rule of law, regulatory effectiveness, and economic and environmental management, India performs better than China. This matters not just for the business environment but also for the realization of freedoms that are valued as ends unto themselves. The notion that freedom depends upon the nonconsensual imposition of order proves to be false. Democracy, then, is not the main ill of

India but its greatest virtue, as Friedman notes. The American scholar Barrington Moore, Jr. turns out to have been wrong about the necessity of massive coercion in rural reforms to achieve social justice: India's rural poor have successfully organized and gained modest benefits as well as dignity, while China's rural poor remain *by official policy* dispersed, immobilized, and sub-human.

In the years to come, as MacFarquhar's discussion of succession and Sinha's discussion of the durability of decentralization both show, the stalled political development of China may prove to be its greatest weakness. Basic questions that need to be resolved by any political system such as the transfer of power, the rules of the game, and relationship of the state to citizens remain up for grabs in the Chinese system. As Chinese society becomes more empowered and more diverse as a result of economic reforms, the possibility of those uncertainties leading to political crisis will grow. India by contrast has already achieved the difficult "soft infrastructure" of press freedoms, the rule of law, regulatory effectiveness, and constitutional stability. This may turn out to be of tremendous long-term advantage to India as China contemplates the costs of this transition.

The contrasting paths of China and India should be a ripe field for the development of new theoretical perspectives on political development, just as events in postcommunist Europe have spawned a rich literature. Until now, the lack of serious comparative work on the two giants has precluded such a literature. The essays in this collection offer glimpses into the sorts of perspectives that could emerge. For one, the contrasting styles of "state-building" in China and India suggest that there are in fact two distinctive methods available to state-builders. The approach of "domination" over society taken by China is countered by one of "accommodation" to society by India. Coercion, central power, and economic capture are not the only routes to a modern state. Citizenship, federalism, and fairness appear to be just as effective. The same lessons apply to the centrifugal forces unleashed by rapid economic development. China's conventional response of boosting central taxation and bolstering political organization contrasts to India's equally successful response of giving voice to those affected and controlling inequalities. Second, the relationship between economic development and democracy appears to warp in light of these two "outlier" cases, India with a democracy long before its time and China with no democracy long past its due. Conventional wisdom in the social sciences says that economic development both brings and consolidates democracy. That may be true as a correlative statement, but the mechanisms by which it does may vary widely. India's democracy has deepened *because of* the intensity of debates on the growing economic pie, not in spite of them. China's new middle class and private sector, meanwhile, are staunchly antidemocratic, but the inequalities created by rapid growth have spawned demands for inclusion from the poor.

Ultimately, we are forced by this volume to consider "the ends of government," the main question of political philosophy and one that cannot be ignored any longer by social scientists, journalists, activists, and policy-makers. The notion of crude economic indicators like GDP/capita or exports, or of crude political indicators like the stability of policies or administrations cannot suffice. Religious belief, democratic participation, cultural tradition, communal integrity, social voluntarism, and emotional freedom seem to be valued more highly—to be the main sources of human happiness in *all* countries. These crude indicators may to some extent be necessary, but they are by no means sufficient. Scholars who study India and China have overlooked the complex ends of government to study the simple ends, and wrongly hailed China as a success and India as a failure. Rethinking the comparative experiences of China and India is thus the beginning of a more difficult but ultimately necessary rethink of how we study, help, and interact with societies whose choices may elude easy indicators.

What may be most interesting is that the lessons of this book seem to be seen already by those in China and India. It may be that the wagging tails of domestic discourse are more indicative than the snarling teeth of security analysts and international observers. The two countries are waking up to the fruitfulness of learning from each other, interacting more with each other, and acting more in concert in the cause of global justice. If the two great unfulfilled bilateral relationships of the world are China–Japan and China–India then at least one of these shows prospects for resolution. More important, for the first time in their modern phases, the elites of China and India are recognizing their shared features and proposing a much closer relationship for the twenty-first century. Reaching this point of mutual respect will require a continued rethink of the old paradigms about the comparative success of China and India. We hope this volume has made a worthy contribution to that effort.

Index

Printed in the United States
64951LVS00001B/103-288